Nest Egg Investing

NEST EGG INVESTING

THE LIFELONG PROGRAM FOR FINANCIAL INDEPENDENCE

Brian J. Sheen

Certified Financial Planner

G. P. PUTNAM'S SONS   NEW YORK

Thank you for all the help and support from Adrienne Ingrum at G. P. Putnam's Sons and from my agent, Peter Miller, who made it all possible. My thanks also to Karen Cozzolino, Lynn Helm and Barbara Ludt. To my daughter Springsong Tawna and my son Ariel Voyager: let this be my gift to ensure your future success.

G. P. Putnam's Sons
Publishers Since 1838
200 Madison Avenue
New York, NY 10016

Copyright © 1987 by Brian J. Sheen
All rights reserved. This book, or parts thereof,
may not be reproduced in any form without permission.
Published simultaneously in Canada by
General Publishing Co. Limited, Toronto

Library of Congress Cataloging-in-Publication Data

Sheen, Brian J., date.
Nest egg investing.

1. Finance, Personal—United States. I. Title.
HG179.S455   1987   332.6'78   87-2268
ISBN 0-399-13185-X

Typeset by Fisher Composition, Inc.

Printed in the United States of America
1 2 3 4 5 6 7 8 9 10

Contents

Foreword 7

Introduction 8

PART I
1. Starting With Zero Dollars 13
2. Making Ends Meet 28
3. Why Are You Working Every Day? 36
4. Dreams or Reality 45
5. Your Personal Blueprint 49
6. Building a Million-Dollar Portfolio for Under Six Dollars a Day 57
7. The Price of Wealth 78
8. Beware of the Booby Trap 82
9. Failing Your Way to the Top 89
10. Going for the Gold—The Golden Years 93
11. Keeping Your Personal and Estate Affairs in Order 101

PART II
12. Banks Aren't as Safe as You Think They Are 127
13. Myths About Insurance 147
14. Why Mutual Funds Never Perform the Way You Expect 161
15. Why Trading Stocks Will Lose You Money—But Make Your Broker Rich 173

16. Why Bonds Can Be Charity 187
17. Why Direct-Placement Investment Trusts and Limited Partnerships May Be Your Best Bet 198
18. Government Subsidies Can Make You Rich 212
19. The World Before You 220

Glossary 222

Foreword

Nineteen eighty-seven begins a new era in America. With the new tax laws in place, new opportunities and challenges await every investor as our investment marketplaces realign to the new rules of the game. Never before in US history has such sweeping change in our tax laws occurred, and the effects will be felt throughout America and the world for many years to come. Although the apparent result for many is a tax decrease, for many others it will be the opposite. It is important not to be put off guard by the political propaganda of lower rates: in fact, for many these lower rates are imposed on a much larger income base. *Nest Egg Investing* will show you how to properly apply successful money and career management techniques in accordance with the latest tax changes so as to ensure your financial security and prosperity.

Brian J. Sheen is available for personal consultation or speaking engagements. For more information please write Sheen Investment Management Group, 1515 North Federal Highway, Suite 406, Boca Raton, FL 33432.

Introduction

Who among us can deny that at one time or another we have dreamed of enjoying all the luxuries our world has to offer? For some of us these fantasies have included yachts, homes on the ocean, Rolls-Royces, or perhaps a summer place in the south of France; for others, leisure or social prominence.

This book will take you on a journey that will turn your dreams into reality. Warning: Wealth will not likely be acquired by buying a lottery ticket, winning the quiniella, marrying into a rich family, or receiving an inheritance from your millionaire uncle. But it can be yours if you implement the basic, workable principles contained in this book. Not only will you build a handsome nest egg that will ensure your financial independence, but you will derive the profound satisfaction of having achieved the goals you have set for yourself. Add to this a lifelong adventure of traveling the road to success, meeting one challenge after another head-on, and you'll begin to understand what living life to the fullest means.

Square One

One of the first discoveries you'll encounter when embarking on your new venture is determining how much you really want to make your dreams become reality. It is vital to ask yourself this question.

Many people fantasize easily enough, but possess no deep and burning desire to work toward a dream. Unless you devote full, unswerving attention to reaching your goals, your chance of success is one in a million. Be honest with yourself right now and make a knowing decision with 100% commitment to achieving success.

If you have made that decision, write the following on the lines below: *I want to be financially successful and I am willing to put in all the hard work necessary to accomplish this goal.* Then sign and date it.

_____
_____
_____

Signature: _____ Date: _____

For what shall it profit a man who inherits the earth, yet loses his soul.

MATTHEW **16**:**26**

PART I

1. Starting With Zero Dollars

John and Ellen live in a two-bedroom apartment in a big city and have a combined annual income of $40,000. After paying for rent, food, utilities, child care, clothing, and entertainment, they seem to barely make it through each month. They have a four-year-old daughter, Judy, and want another baby, but can't see how they can afford a second child, particularly since they also hope to move to a better neighborhood. They want to take an out-of-state vacation next year. John works for a utility company, has been doing quite well, and is expecting a substantial raise within the year. Ellen, who has worked full time for the last six months, doesn't find her job fulfilling. She would like to pursue something else but is not sure what. They have discussed in detail their goals and dreams, but never have sat down to formalize or figure out just exactly how they are going to achieve them. Neither John nor Ellen is extravagant, but although they use their credit cards sparingly, one card is already near its limit.

John and Ellen are an average couple looking for more of the good life, wanting to get ahead.

First, they should draft a complete list of family resources: salary, commissions, bonuses, dividends, interest, and miscellaneous income. Next they should list their assets and write up a budget pinpointing exactly where their money is spent. From this they can see spending habits and locate areas of extravagance or neglect. By quantifying and giving it a comparative value toward other spending areas or desires, John and Ellen can begin to build a nest egg.

This is where most people fail. They are too lazy to compile all of last year's checks along with charge card receipts to analyze where their money goes. Money is the energy, the exchange that helps us afford those items that are necessary to meet our goals. Only by assessing their assets, income, and outgo can John and Ellen see the basic flows of energy available.

Next John and Ellen should get out their personal blueprint and begin to examine their priorities. They must determine which, if any, financial sources are available toward helping reach their goal. John feels comfortable with the progress he is making at work but realizes he needs to establish better contacts at the managerial level. Meanwhile, Ellen wants to expand her horizons and become a realtor.

These two are very common goals. You may need further education to enhance your knowledge and abilities as well as to network in the community with other leaders and successful people. Freely giving of yourself to your community is essential in any plan for success. If you aren't willing to study or pursue these other endeavors, you may be working in a field where you have no burning desire to succeed.

Time became a major factor for John and Ellen. It was discovered that Ellen could attend a specially designed college course for two hours on Saturdays as well as an evening adult-education course during the week. Within six months to a year she could complete schooling to become licensed in her field. John, on the other hand, explored the path his corporate senior executives had traveled. After checking around, he discovered the most dynamic and respected groups in his area were the Jaycees and the Chamber of Commerce. John's corporation would be happy to pay his dues, so cost was no object. Scheduling time to participate, however, would be difficult. John and Ellen both immediately agreed that Sunday would remain a family day. There would be at least two weekday evening during which the family would always be together. Since they needed Ellen to work, she would attend an adult-education class twice a week and take three credits a semester until John's raise came through. Then she could cut back work hours and study more.

Additionally, after reviewing their budget, they agreed to cut electricity and heat usage to lower their utility bills by up to 25%. Quick showers and running short loads of wash became a way of life. They cashed in their whole-life insurance policy, replacing it with term insurance, cut out extravagances such as expensive dinners, car-pooled, and began clipping grocery coupons. Buying clothes on sale and discovering generic brands at the supermarket helped them "find" more than $300 per month—nearly $4000 a year. They decided to earmark this $4000 to begin their investment portfolio with Individual Retirement Accounts (IRAs). This pivotal move generated $1500 in tax savings, established their nest egg, and substantially increased their cash flow.

With their priorities set, John and Ellen found it easier to develop their financial strategies. Soon they began supplementing these moves with a reading and concept-learning program. Each vowed to read one book a month, alternating on motivation and their personal area of business interest, whether it was management, economics, or marketing. They borrowed special motivational cassette programs from libraries for listening to in the car while commuting. By using thirty minutes a day for learning through listening and thirty minutes a day for reading, they logged approximately 365 hours of study a year, or the equivalent of almost nine 40-hour weeks of study.

There were of course some major casualties with all this planning, and the biggest was television. They agreed not to allow the tube to interfere with personal or business relationships. Television was purely entertainment for relaxation when all their work was done. Reading while in the john or relaxing in the tub, listening to cassette tapes while eating breakfast or traveling to and from work, gave them a constant source of inspiration and fortitude.

John's goal for the first year was to become sufficiently active in the clubs and projects he had joined to be known as a good, dependable worker. He considered taking a minor leadership position in some capacity the following year. He developed a strategy for making connections to move up the ladder during the next five years and to obtain the prominence as well as social and political clout that were necessary. John and Ellen also agreed to supply each other with at least half of Saturday for personal indulgences, whether extra sleep, creative writing, thinking, or outdoor activity.

This ensured a regeneration to charge their jets and let each other privately ponder all of the goals and activities in progress, to modify or add to as necessary. John and Ellen were amazed at how successful they were at scheduling themselves. They felt they had more time on their hands than ever before. The more they worked on activities within their schedules, the more they seemed to accomplish. This generated more hours for relaxation, reflection, and enjoyment of their achievements. They worked hard together, *with* each other, and *for* each other. Five years later John was a junior vice president with his utility company, earning $45,000 a year. Ellen had become a million-dollar producer with one of the area's major real estate firms. She had involved herself with the Chamber of Commerce and other organizations around town and had gained an excellent reputation as a dynamic sales representative and community activist. She raised lots of money for charity and demonstrated a strong commitment toward helping others. Now, with their increased income, she had the freedom to work only part-time and devote herself to a special cause she had always dreamed about. Their income during that five-year period had doubled, enabling them to buy a house in the suburbs. Interest paid on their mortgage helped shelter their taxable income while they built equity in the property.

This case is but one of numerous transformations I have observed. Many couples take many more aggressive steps to improve their circumstances, wheeling and dealing in "no-money-down" real estate or perhaps investing in highly speculative commodity strategies. Without doubt these are ways for people to make things happen. Yet, the risks, stress, and frequent lack of predictability in these ventures can create many more woes. I've always been upset over how the proliferation of no-money-down real estate seminars geared to generate financial wealth neglect to emphasize how many investors end up failing miserably. Rarely do seminar leaders mention the instances of bankruptcy and divorce. Mind you, I feel real estate and high-risk speculation are valid strategies for creating wealth. Yet I want investors to realize that only a small percentage of speculators will make millions through these aggressive techniques, just as only a few "investors" will ever score in the New York Lottery or the Irish Sweepstakes.

Allan Goldberg was a lawyer. Employed in a southern town with an overabundance of attorneys, Allan found his pay less than satisfactory. He was tired of working for $22,000 a year and being the schlep for one of the senior partners. He had always dreamed of his own practice. Yet, being new to the profession and having little money, he felt trapped. He would be forced to wait for seniority at the firm to get the bigger cases and, thus, a larger income.

During his few years of practice he had developed a liking for banking law. Allan had opportunity to work on a few cases and rapidly established good relationships. He was complimented on his work. One evening he sat down for a heart-to-heart talk with himself. He was miserable over going nowhere. He considered leaving the legal profession. Allan felt that unless he could establish his own firm and substantially increase his income, he should enter a more lucrative field. He wasn't sure which to pursue, although he knew his father would probably be able to help. Wanting to maintain his independence, though, made Allan recognize that it was time to go for it. He sat down to list his assets and all the financial responsibility he carried. He then wrote up, in detail, the cost of opening his own practice. Putting in phones, paying rent, and someone to type his briefs were included.

His conclusion was that if he combined all his assets, liquidated everything, and was willing to risk being broke within six months, he could set up his own office. Cutting his salary to half what he had been earning, he would be able to survive. Allan was excited by the prospect but also frightened. He knew pursuing the plan was the only smart thing to do. He'd rather risk losing it all to find out exactly how he stood than work unhappily for someone else. His major problem was how to secure clients. With only three years of experience, unable to take clients away from his existing firm, it wouldn't be easy. Hence Allan's dilemma. If he took the risk, how should he go about bringing in business?

The next morning Allan picked up the newspaper and ran across some interesting statistics. He rediscovered something he had known all along. The banking industry was experiencing a record number of failures, not to mention other problems. The FDIC and FSLIC were creating many bank mergers and conducting investigations into a number of banks throughout his state and elsewhere. All of a sudden a bell in Allan's head rang. "Imagine," he thought, "my area of specialty is having a tremendously increasing demand. With my experience and the low prices I can charge, I'm a natural for being able to get some of this legal work delegated to me."

He began to study how the FDIC and FSLIC worked and made a fantastic discovery. Each organization had a small, overworked staff. He immediately got on the phone, put together résumés, and began to make appropriate contacts with both agencies, letting each know that he was available to help and that his fee was 50% lower than major firms in the area. Would they give him a try? Results were phenomenal. Before he knew it, Allan was off and running with five cases working. Within six months he was able to pay his bills and still take as much salary as he was getting working for someone else. Shortly Allan found himself with a hefty 35% increase in pay and a backlog of cases! He had taken the risk, found the opportunity, reached for it, and grabbed hold.

His client roster grew, as did his reputation for doing a competent job at a reasonable price. Slowly Allan increased his fees and hired more help. Shared offices and a shared typist were discarded in return for private offices and a personal staff. Anyone meeting Allan today would find it hard to imagine the meekness and fear that contained him for so many years. Some people even claim

Allan's self-confidence and cockiness can be a bit much. But with his newfound financial independence and achievement of goals, his supporters say he has the right. Starting with almost nothing, Allan Goldberg took the risk and gave his all to a dream. He went for the rainbow and found a pot of gold at the end.

Like so many Floridians, Diane and Jack were from out of town. Married for two years and without children, they had tired of the cold weather and poor job potential up north, deciding to make a new start. Each had sat down to develop plans for what they wanted in their future, both separately and together. Borrowing a few dollars from their parents to make the move, they had decided to tackle Florida. Neither one had much going, since their work experience was minimal and the pay scales being offered in their job areas were low. Nevertheless, they were determined to move into their respective fields: for Diane, financial planning, and for Jack, the hotel business.

Since their funds were severely limited, they decided Jack would accept an estate maintenance job while learning the assistant manager's position at a hotel. This provided them with a roof over their heads. Diane updated her résumé and presented it to every financial planning firm in the entire region. She was willing to start at low pay in any position so long as she would be given growth opportunity. Financially, they just made it through each month. Finally, two months after pursuing interview after interview, a small yet growing financial planning firm hired Diane. Because of an oversupply of qualified personnel in this field, and because Diane lacked many qualifications, she had taken a job dependent on her ability to upgrade office production. She would receive only a percentage of the increase in sales realized through her work. In return she would be fully trained in each area of financial planning in accordance with her ability and initiative. Diane wasted no time, diving into her work, learning and putting in six days a week. During her first two months she earned only $400. But she gained tremendous experience and was permitted to start her licensing training.

Jack, on the other hand, continued studying hard at his managerial training and—despite having to get lots of mileage out of his one blue suit—attending seminars at corporate headquarters. During this time they both supported each other, deciding that weekends would be used for studying and possibly working. They would take at least two evenings a week to spend time together, and vowed not to lose sight of their bond in marriage. Six months went by quickly and Jack's assistant manager training ended. A position would be opening in the hotel within the next few months.

Meanwhile, Diane made great professional strides, preparing for her license examination. Her income—a grand total of $400 during the first two months—reached $6000 for the next four months. Already she was beginning to see daylight. Diane projected that within the next six months her income would reach $12,000 to $14,000. She listened and she learned, read book after book on financial-selling techniques, and assimilated every scrap of information the people she worked with would provide. Her boss was impressed with her performance, diligence, and the speed with which she learned. At the end of her first year he informed Diane that because of her track record he would consider taking her in as a junior partner within the next couple of years. For a twenty-four-year-old, new to the business, this was indeed exciting news. Her commitment to work seemed to go into overdrive. The next twelve months were truly fantastic. Since she was being personally trained by the company's owner, Diane was permitted to tackle even more difficult training. Obviously her work had paid off. In that time her salary more than tripled, reaching more than $50,000 during her second full year. Jack and Diane bought a house and a car.

Meanwhile Jack had excelled as an assistant manager. He found a more prestigious job at a neighboring hotel in which he accepted a 30% pay raise. A mere two years later, this struggling couple from out of town now earned $80,000 to $100,000 a year combined income and had two stock purchase plans toward gaining ownership in a business.

Diane and Jack are still turning dreams into realities, fulfilling plans that they had written down when first coming to Florida. In fact, their first baby is due shortly. Being in the financial position they've established, the idea of getting private in-house help whereby both Diane and Jack continue their careers was agreed upon long ago. Diane's job has been arranged so she can handle a number of responsibilities from home shortly after the baby's birth. Starting with nothing but a desire to succeed and the willingness to work hard, this couple created their opportunities for financial wealth and independence.

One of the great advantages we have in our country is the tradition of an entrepreneurial system by which ambitious people don't have to get caught up in a treadmill. In America workers need not spend twenty or thirty years moving up, but can go into small businesses and make a big mark quickly. The reward of owning your own business or being part of a small and growing business is immense. Sure, the risk of folding and being out of a job is higher than when working for a government agency or a Fortune 500 company. Yet the rewards are so much greater and the experiences so much more enriching. The chance of using your own initiative and making a noticeable impact is much greater in your own organization than in one with thousands upon thousands of employees.

As long as you have the ability and willingness to work, don't be caught up in the prevailing bad habits of much of our society: those who demand immediate gratification are nearsighted and will prevent you from seeing the long-term perspective.

Training, knowledge, experience, and building one's résumé can be more important than accepting a job that pays 50% to 100% more. To reach financial independence, you need to constantly take on new challenges in areas that present opportunities for growth. *Don't be seduced by the false feeling of safety provided by a regular paycheck.* You must be willing to sacrifice time and energy as well as some immediate pleasures to make this type of investment in your future. Examine all options, whether it involves cutting out television, starting an hour a day of reading and cassette learning, or finding an apprenticeship-type position to gain experience and knowledge. The structure of our society for hundreds of years involved a grueling apprenticeship in the trades at very low wages, but this is, for the most part, no longer true. An entry-level job no longer means starvation, merely a cut in pay.

Who do you suppose has the better chance of succeeding, the person who has a written plan that he is implementing uniformly, taking 10% of his salary and investing it to get good rates of return and tax benefits systematically for thirty years or the person who thinks about it occasionally, talks about it occasionally, but has never done anything definite? The great talker finds himself or herself living from month to month, barely able to pay off charge cards or installment and mortgage payments. Talkers sacrifice future prosperity for momentary pleasure, wasting money on fads and self-indulgence.

Avoiding Unnecessary Taxes and Wasting Money

The following are three major ways people waste money and pay unnecessary taxes:

(1) Failing to understand or utilize tax laws to minimize taxes, (2) failing to understand the array of alternative-investment vehicles that give higher returns, and (3) being too lazy to implement career planning and use available techniques of financial planning. These errors lose many investors, over a lifetime, in excess of $1 million dollars that could have been in their pockets.

IRAs

Unbelievable as it seems, only three Americans in ten currently utilize individual retirement accounts, which we will examine in detail later. Yet this could save up to $1000 or more per year, on taxes, which, compounded over thirty years, can easily come to half a million dollars. How can you afford not to open an IRA? I will have more to say on this topic.

Life Insurance

I continually shake my head over how many singles and newly marrieds buy life insurance plans. They often end up commiting between $500 and $2000 a year toward an area that offers them no tax deduction for having made the investment and normally provides mediocre rates of returns. Why so many single individuals carry life insurance is also a puzzle. Who will suffer if they die? The life insurance sales representative?

You may be able to save between $500 and $1000 a year just by knowing what type of insurance to purchase. Your best bet is to buy the lowest-priced term insurance that permits frequent reentries into the program. This permits the insured to pay the lowest possible rates. Many people do not need insurance at all, for there will be no financial hardships created at death. This is true for many older people who made payments on a policy while their children were growing up. They have failed to realize that the policies are no longer needed once their offspring have fled the nest.

To continually pay premiums, unless coverage is needed, virtually never makes sense. Of course the picture changes if the policy is earning dividends and the cash value can be borrowed at low rates while accruing tax benefits. Also, if your health is poor it might be foolish to cancel. Nevertheless, by cutting back on life insurance you could average $500 a year savings over what it normally costs during a forty-year period. This can add up to more than a quarter of a million dollars.

Car Purchasing

I don't understand why people buy brand-new cars. My policy always has been to buy at least a two-year-old one. It never has made sense that the moment a car leaves the showroom floor it loses up to 25% of its value. To me that's a large markup. If there was a stock that cost $40 a share, and you knew that the next day you could sell it for only $30, I don't think you would buy. Why not get an already depreciated car in excellent running condition? Some dealers and states even guarantee a used vehicle's roadworthiness. At the same time you can save $1000 to $2000 a year from lower payments. There's always the risk of inheriting a lemon, yet I've seen many lemons plucked fresh right off the tree!

Homeowner's Insurance

By increasing the safety and protection of your house, homeowners often can decrease the cost of home coverage by 20% or more. Installing smoke alarms, security systems, and other protection measures may pay you back in a multitude of ways.

As you see, the long-term viewpoint is what's important. The first control you have of your cash flow and of your savings ability is to use all the necessary strategies to spend your money wisely. When the dollar is very strong, buy a used foreign car, for when the dollar weakens, the value of your foreign car could increase. Why does Germany's Mercedes-Benz decrease only slightly in value upon purchase whereas America's luxury Cadillacs lose value immediately and almost never come back? Through proper maintenance of your car, and by being an especially safe driver, you can take all this one step further to shop around for cheaper car insurance. How often have you shopped around to find the best values? In some instances that might mean a savings of $50; in others, $200. Yet, over a lifetime, these numbers can grow significantly. Do you qualify for a safe driver's discount or do you live close enough to your work to receive an additional discount? But always make sure you have proper coverage for liability, medical, and other areas. An error on your part or a lawsuit on the part of another could eat into your nest egg unless you carry adequate automobile insurance.

Understanding car loans can also save you thousands. Buyers today often secure four- to five-year financing. Usually car loans have you pay most of the interest cost for the entire five years in the first two to three years. This means that in the fourth and fifth years a car buyer pays little interest and mainly principal. If you were to sell you car after three years, you would have little equity in it and have to start paying interest again on a new loan. Always try to pay off your car before buying a new one to get some equity buildup and not pay extensive interest costs. If unable to get special low-interest dealer financing, consider a personal loan versus an auto loan since rates may be lower.

Divorced Parents

Probably one of the most difficult positions to be in when starting a nest egg today—and one which rates growing concern—is that of heading a single-parent family. Mothers or fathers who have sole custody of their children and have no spouse to help generate income can have trouble finding the time and money to develop a nest egg. Obviously, receiving child support or alimony can make creating a nest egg substantially easier. But today, sole custody is no longer unusual and needs some special thinking.

Creating a special pool of single-parent families that will alternate weeks or months of helping each other out in the evening while each parent advances an education or career could be useful. Or share your apartment or home with another family of similar means to pool resources à la television's *Kate and Allie*. Do not immediately rule out these alternatives because they infringe on your privacy or invade your space. Look at the longer-term, bigger picture: your space may *never* be your own until you have the financial ability to create independence. Too often fixed ideas such as these interfere with flexible, workable solutions. *Starting with zero dollars is nothing when compared with zero ideas or zero willingness to work hard.* Think positively and plan accordingly. Fortunately our minds do not have meters on them and we are not charged for their use. Let your mind become fertilized. Creative use of support groups, neighbors, friends, and families will help you establish a variety of alternatives to needing extensive seed money for building your nest egg.

The Overview

With application of simple tax- and dollar-saving techniques you can come upon new sources of money for your future use and prosperity. Consider all the savings possible and you can spend your way into financial independence.

One of the most profitable means I have found for people to find sources of lost money is to write up an item-by-item statement of every dollar spent during a three-month period. This includes miscellaneous expenses when shopping or going out, and can be done by looking over checks and credit card statements and keeping cash receipts. It is always fascinating to see what type of budget an individual keeps. You will find a number of frivolous items that taken by themselves may look like nothing, yet when added together with other purchases they can have major economic impact.

I remember sitting down with one couple and, after seeing where their money was spent, we were able to gain an additional $350 a month. How? By having them both make and take lunches to work instead of eating out, by shifting their spending habits to buy in less expensive stores—always looking to purchase clothes off-season to get the best prices—as well as by having them shop around and obtain cheaper automobile and health insurance. Combining errands helped them put less wear and tear on the car, and they learned to shop at the less fancy supermarkets. Each step can go a long way toward finding those necessary dollars when you seem to have none to begin your investment program. Such reappropriated dollars can help you educate yourself, increase your worth, or begin an investment plan through an IRA or other investment vehicle.

I always recommend that you spend a minimum of 10% of whatever income you generate on an investment account to train yourself into the investment habit. It may also be necessary to cut up those charge cards if you find yourself perpetually paying large interest costs when you overspend. How many credit cards do you really need? I've seen families work two, three, or even four months for nothing but paying off interest on all the consumer items they "just had to have."

Capitalizing on Your Talents

Besides finding ways to reduce your spending, there may be simple methods to capitalize on your talents. Often, when working in one profession, you will find there are ramifications which present other opportunities that may permit you either to moonlight or perform a similar job with better pay. Police officers frequently moonlight as security staff, and may find themselves receiving lucrative contracts at increased pay to take the risks of going into business for themselves. Many workers employed by major computer companies act as consultants to businesses and individuals needing programming, operational assistance, and training. Musicians often double as music teachers, while actors awaiting their big break earn money as voice instructors or drama coaches.

Finding ways to expand within your field by taking on additional jobs may at times be necessary to generate those extra dollars for investing.

Investing in Education

It is often said that merely graduating from Harvard automatically tacks on an additional $10,000 a year to your salary. Even if the advantage were half of that, over a lifetime that edge can work out to hundreds of thousands of dollars. Education and training in whatever field you choose often play a crucial role. *Rarely is raw talent so exceptional as not to be influenced in the work world by educational background.*

For some, education might consist of evening courses at a local college to get another degree to qualify for a raise. For others, it comes in the form of listening to cassettes, doing specialized study, and researching everything possible in the field to become a self-proclaimed expert. Francis Bacon once said that knowledge is power. The more knowledge you consume within your profession, the more powerful you will become. By listening to a cassette or reading a book for thirty minutes a day, you are making an investment in yourself. Your ability to consume lots of information and evaluate it, using creative thought and innovation, will set you apart from others. Knowledge of your profession and changes in your field are vital and can be enhanced with little or no dollars. Many businesses will pay for work-related courses, and these opportunities should be pursued.

Investing in Health

One of the greatest returns you can get that needs zero money is your health. Your productivity and longevity depend on the degree to which your body is tuned up, functioning, and healthy, and upon whether your mind is clear and positive. The consequences are obvious when you let your health deteriorate. Filling your body with poisons can cloud your mind. Increased medical costs for doctors and hospitals, medication, and therapy, as well as lost time on the job can drain your financial resources as well as your vitality.

Maintaining your health costs very little. Yet such care can bring many dividends as you become a more dependable, effective, and positive-thinking individual. Daily exercise, proper nutrition, and necessary relaxation play an important role in building your attitude and self-reliance. As you learn to discipline your body, you begin to understand the necessary factors in becoming a disciplined investor. Don't you think employers notice when you are absent often, a bit foggy, or look unhealthy? How can you expect someone who takes little responsibility for his or her own well-being to assume responsibility for fellow workers and subordinates? The way in which you take care of yourself speaks worlds of your actions in other areas.

Brainstorming

Brainstorming is that creative process whereby you set your mind free to consider every angle and possibility in attacking a problem or achieving a desired result. Once your goals have been set, visualized, and your resources determined and evaluated, you can sit back with all this information (both on paper and within you) and let your imagination run wild. The sequences of events before your eyes will begin to unfold as you see some goals dependent upon other goals. It may necessitate creating sub or preliminary goals before reaching your final destination. At times you may want to seek opinions from friends or other successful associates. Reading autobiographies by those who've already achieved success can be valuable. It is important when brainstorming to have uninterrupted time with no distractions. By focusing on your desired destination, you can see a world of opportunities unfold before you.

Your Final Look

Looking at what you have written down, you can see that your life is filled with many exciting challenges, for the joy and reward of achieving financial and personal independence are what make our country great.

I have discovered an interesting procedure that perhaps ties it all up. It involves trying to postulate what will be said about you upon your death. Imagine that you have lived your life to a ripe old age. You've just died and your survivors are writing your obituary. What would you want them to say? Which accomplishments would be recognized and how would the rest of the world view the way you have lived your life? Would you want to be known for having reached your goals and being a loving, family-oriented person? Or would you like to be remembered as a wild adventurer who never had roots, never cared about anything or anyone, and so rode the high seas? I find that this approach offers an opportunity for adjustments that you might want to make when looking over your blueprint. Make the refinements to ensure that what you want at the end of your life has in fact been achieved during your life. The purposes and goals, the plans and projects, and the guidelines you have developed for yourself will create your ideal life.

They also will affect the way in which you will come to measure it. It is vital that your activities be properly aligned with the plans and dreams that you have written down.

Just as a two-ton automobile can be knocked out of alignment by a small pothole, so must refinements be continually made in aligning your present and future plans with your overall lifetime goals. Successful people normally love telling others how they became winners. And they almost always are willing to talk about actions that worked or failed. You may want to talk with others who have traveled paths similar to your projected plan. Understand that your overall life-plans will be broken down into smaller, individualized segments. Do not expect someone else's winning plan to serve every aspect of your life. Based on your needs and desires, you will set priorities on which avenues to follow first. As you build strength and gather support from others, you'll be surprised at how many plans you can have operating at once. And each plan can turn a dream into a reality through use of your personal blueprint.

2. Making Ends Meet

Money represents an exchange of energy; it is a simple way to transfer energy between two parties. Can you imagine the inconvenience of a farmer wanting to barter for a new pickup truck having to haul a thousand chickens to the dealership? Yet, by bringing a check for $15,000, which represents the farmer's sale of those same chickens plus their eggs, business can be transacted. Paper and metallic money facilitate an exchange of energy. And, as we have seen, a large amount of money to initiate your plans is not essential.

Sure, all of us would like to be able to stop working and dedicate ourselves 100% toward the necessary education, training, and launching of a new career or business. Yet rarely is this practical. Therefore it becomes vital to, as we did in Chapter 1, match your available economic assets with your personal goals. This may mean looking beyond your personal resources and those of your (presumably) supportive family.

Utilizing the full resources of the family seems to have fallen from favor today as most young men and women in America leave home early to strike out for independence. Nevertheless, not too many decades ago many families lived together harmoniously for a good portion of their combined lifetimes to share expenses and better combine their resources for mutual goals—financial and otherwise. Too often pride or poor communication stand in the way of the most efficient solution that a young family might utilize in reaching its goals. Having been out of the house for five or ten years, the idea of moving back in with your parents—or even grandparents—might seem uncomfortable, even humiliating. Yet if such a move can buy you the time to reduce your overhead and focus more energy toward building your new life, do not write off that possibility. Temporarily sacrificing your privacy and having to operate under somebody else's household rules might save you years of struggle. Archie Bunker's daughter and son-in-law utilized these methods to complete their schooling and get a foothold on new careers. Your family may not be as colorful as the Bunkers' but with proper discussions this possibility could be explored.

The ability to align financial needs to begin your program may take on other aspects as well. Special grants, scholarships, or work-study programs, as well as offering your services cheaply in return for an apprenticeship, must all be considered. A couple might agree to have one person work to support the household while the other obtains training or schooling. Many young married couples have put each other through college and internships using this technique. This of course might involve a difficult sacrifice for the spouse who is held back from immediate achievement of his or her goals while the mate moves ahead. But such delays can be tolerable as long as a couple agrees on its goals.

Family Synergism

Probably one of the greatest sources of success or failure is the way in which the goals shared by a husband and wife mesh. Although working alone may at times seem to accomplish a great deal, the incredible effect of a couple working together toward the goals increases the chance of success threefold. Why threefold? The answer is simple: not only is there an additional party to contribute, but a "third party," that of combined efforts, is created.

There are countless examples of how lack of cooperation and coordination of marital goals leads to undue stress, emotional upsets, business and career failure, divorce, and poverty. A family unit is a team that should be working toward mutual goals as well as the individual goals of the team members.

Philip and Carol were deeply in love. They met while in college and soon were married. Philip had always wanted to become a partner in a local engineering firm. Carol, in addition to wanting children, planned a career in dental hygiene. They often discussed their goals and had gone over in detail the different commitments necessary for success. For Philip, it would mean many hours working on company projects to build a name and reputation within his company. It meant being active in the community in various organizations, to build name recognition and bring in new projects to his firm. He knew that there would be up to ten years of this hard, dedicated work before he could be considered for partnership. But he was ready, willing, and able to make this commitment. Philip knew that he would be well rewarded financially and would have a great sense of personal accomplishment.

For Carol, special technical training would be mandatory. She would have the flexibility to be able to work part-time while raising a family and then later move back to full-time employment. She also knew, as they had discussed in detail, that she would be called upon many times to work with her husband on community projects, attend social functions, and would, in addition, have to hold down the fort while he burned the midnight oil at the office. Before marriage they had talked about this in great detail, and both of them had their eyes wide open on what the future held. The goals they had established were set in motion. The day after Philip's graduation, he took a position with the engineering firm. Three months later they were married. Carol went on to finish her training. She had received some financial help from her parents. Together Philip and Carol helped set up their small apartment and began on the road to success. As the years went by, Philip invested many hours at his job. He got involved with several community-minded groups. Carol was always beside him with a smile at any banquet or event, demonstrating their unity to his associates.

They earned respect from every person they met. Their dedication to each other and to their goals was obvious. Over the years, as their two children grew up and they maintained a simple, comfortable life-style, they continued to implement their plans and enjoy a certain degree of comfort. Sure, there were times of stress. When emergencies occurred at work, Philip was barely seen around home for weeks on end. There were times of loneliness and doubt when Carol thought it all wasn't worth it. Maybe they should consider another way to live. . . . But their tenacious desire to succeed pulled them over each hurdle. It was not surprising to discover that upon completing his ninth year with the firm, Philip was made a partner. Now, with their additional income, Carol, who had been getting a bit itchy to do something different, found herself in a position to move.

Having accomplished their primary goals—Philip was a partner and the children were in school—they now turned their attention to the purchase of a new house and a new career for Carol: nursing. Philip was all in favor of Carol's new career goals and they discussed them in detail. They planned for her to first go to school part-time to get the necessary credits. They would hire domestic help to handle some of the household burden while she studied. As Philip was now well connected in the community, he inquired about the best open nursing positions. Having helped build two of the local hospitals, he found it easy to talk to the heads of these two institutions and set up a job interview for his wife upon completion of her training.

Philip and Carol were a strong unit. Sensibly, each took the necessary time to go off occasionally alone and let loose. Philip went hunting or fishing. Carol sewed, golfed, or visited her family. Never did they lose sight of their dreams or how they would help each other toward fulfillment personally and as a couple. Success was theirs.

Ron and Jennifer also were deeply in love. They met at a nightclub and soon found it difficult to be apart. During their courtship they traveled and partied while falling increasingly in love. Ron was an accountant and Jennifer was a receptionist at a law firm. Ron had always dreamed of owning an accounting firm. Jennifer had always wanted to see the world and have a family. Ron, in an off-season period, wined and dined his newfound love in exotic places including the Caribbean. It wasn't long before they were married. Jennifer agreed to continue working at her receptionist's job and they moved into a nice new apartment that Jennifer was excited about decorating. January rolled around and tax season fell upon them. The candlelight dinners and long weekend adventures were set aside as Ron was forced to work six and a half days a week, ten, twelve, and fourteen hours per day. Jennifer found herself feeling lonely; suffering from the solitary nights and empty weekends. She demanded more attention and time. Ron tried to explain that until the tax season was over they couldn't spend much time together: during the next few months he would earn 75% of his yearly income—and that's what paid for the travel and the apartment.

Jennifer's dissatisfaction showed up at home and on her job. The tension in the household was obvious, particularly as April came around. Ron seemed to be home only long enough to sleep, shower, and shave. Jennifer started going out at night looking for diversions. Finally the tax season was over, and the April 15th party at work brought new hope into Ron's life that now they would be able to have time alone together.

At first things seemed back on track. But there was a vague feeling that something had changed. Ron tried to recapture old times by taking Jennifer to Acapulco. They had a good time and everything seemed to be rolling again. But Jennifer still seemed distant. She did not want to return to her receptionist job, she told Ron; she'd rather just stay home for a while. This would mean tight finances, but Ron, feeling guilty about all the time he had spent away, agreed.

Jennifer now had lots of time on her hands. She found herself staying in bed late and not keeping the house very tidy. She watched soap operas all day and reluctantly prepared dinner each night. She wanted something more in her life but didn't know what. Although she saw more of Ron, there still were times when for weeks on end he would be distracted by a large audit. She became even unhappier. This affected Ron's work as well. No longer was he relaxed and refreshed. He always seemed to be on edge and worried about something. His work began to deteriorate, as his supervisor pointed out on more than one occasion. Ron's mind was no longer immersed in his work: he had the proverbial "problems at home." Ron thought it would be a good idea if they saw a marriage counselor to discover why their relationship wasn't working out. After all, they had been married only fourteen months. Unfortunately Jennifer disagreed, so they didn't go. Life went on. Finally one of Jennifer's girlfriends told her about a new secretarial opening at a small clothing manufacturer. Jennifer, bored and wanting to get out of the house, jumped at it. She found the work challenging and the people she worked with stimulating. Things seemed to get better at home now that she had a purpose. But now Jennifer had some late hours to work herself, and there were times when Ron would come home to an empty house and a TV dinner.

Once again the tax season arrived, and Ron was buried in accounting cases. He saw Jennifer only briefly at breakfast and to kiss her goodnight. Jennifer, meanwhile, had immersed herself in the new job and found there were excellent opportunities in an assistant buyer's position that would soon be open. She started befriending her supervisors and the "powers that be." This turned into long workdays and many nights out discussing business over dinner. Ron and Jennifer now appeared to inhabit two separate worlds; the distance between them widened each day. Jennifer seemed increasingly uninterested in ensuring that the house was cleaned, food was stocked, and meals prepared. Once again Ron's work performance took a nosedive as his worries at home began to create internal conflicts. He found himself drinking more. He said it didn't affect him, but his close friends knew he was trying to ease the pain coming from the pressures at work and the pressures at home.

When Jennifer was finally made assistant buyer, it was a proud day. Ron prepared a candlelight dinner. As they celebrated her new job, Jennifer informed Ron that she would have to go on buying trips during June, July, and August. Ron was shattered.

Now not only was his job going to keep them apart from January to April, but hers would separate them from June through August!

Their next year "together" seemed to consist of only occasional breakfasts. The less they saw of each other, the more Ron drank. From the lines that came onto his face during the next year, you would have thought a decade had passed. His work deteriorated further. With his marriage crumbling and his drinking interfering with his job, two younger accountants were promoted over him. Then his annual raise didn't come through. His supervisor had repeatedly been forced to reprimand him. Ron's enthusiasm vanished and his work became drudgery.

Meanwhile Jennifer missed her freedom. Discontent began building up as the excitement from her new position wore off. The combined dissatisfaction of both Jennifer and Ron mounted. Tempers flared more often. It was no surprise a year later when Jennifer filed for divorce, left her job, and became a secretary at a local construction firm. Ron, in the meantime, was badly shaken. His work seemed to deteriorate proportionately to the amount of alcohol he consumed. In three and a half years, this love affair had fallen apart and severely affected both Ron and Jennifer. Ron now went about his business in a totally depressed state, barely functioning. It took him three years to pull himself together and renew his enthusiasm for his goals. Jennifer continued stumbling along at various jobs, trying to find herself. She had never determined what she wanted out of life, much less what she wanted to do. Today she still drifts from one job to another quitting when she is bored.

Ron and Jennifer are an example of a couple that failed to set goals for themselves individually and for their marriage. *Taking things as they come is nothing but a matter of letting other people control you.* The tension, grief, and emotional aggravation were considerably greater than in the first case history. This is not because Ron and Jennifer were any less in love; and not because they were any less capable in their professions. Failure to set specific goals denied this couple a future to work toward.

The confusions generated from conflicting desires were enough to destroy whatever future they tried to create. Improper direction will work against any activities or goals you are trying to achieve. If Ron and Jennifer had more thoroughly discussed what those difficult four months around tax time would be like, she could have been better prepared. She could, for example, have helped establish community relationships and thus find potential clients for Ron's practice. Or she could perhaps have been a secretary and receptionist and played an important role in their business. But the lack of a defined direction created continual counterintentions and pitfalls in the other's plans.

Precision teamwork is a key element in financial success and emotional fulfillment.

Maybe you've been married for five or ten years now, or even longer. Perhaps you're going about your various tasks in a way that doesn't necessarily interfere with your spouse's goals, but doesn't contribute either. Maybe you've never discussed or even considered discussing how you could help each other achieve personal goals. Most couples have never put down on paper what their family goals are, other than perhaps raising healthy children. Yet it is never too late to create a plan, and new sources of power will come to those who do so. Despite years of living together, you may be amazed to learn the dreams that have been latent in your mate's heart and mind. Once you have established a personal plan of action, you should compare it with your mate's to work out any areas of conflict. Align your goals toward helping each other achieve mutual goals.

A family plan of action can be created in the same way as the individual plans, except that the husband and wife now must sit down together, review their personal plans, and then come to agreement on a family plan. This might include deciding how large a nest egg you want to create and how much income you want. It might entail what traveling you want to do or where you both would like to retire and when. It might entail a joint venture of creating a family business and ensuring that parents and grandparents are taken care of to fulfill your family obligations.

If your children are old enough, they too might be brought into this discussion. Their feedback can be important since these decisions will affect them. Failing to define intentions on both an individual and group basis can only create unintentional conflicts and difficulties for the future. Such family conferences might seem like a waste of time. Yet how efficient was it for Ron and Jennifer to waste three and a half years together and be worse off at the end than when they started? Many marriages that have dissolved for lack of a coherent, specific plan have led to broken homes in which each divorced partner lives near the poverty level, loaded with more responsibilities and emotional disharmonies than ever before. Creating a nest egg takes a combined effort. Nest eggs can be like eggs themselves. Eggs are fragile and when mishandled crack. When improperly cooked they are inedible. It's only by establishing how you want your eggs prepared that you can gain satisfaction.

When was the last time you sat down with your spouse and discussed in detail (1) how you feel you are doing now, (2) how you feel about all that has happened up until now, and (3) where you want to be going together in the future? Have you ever put this in writing for a proper evaluation? If you were running a business, wouldn't you periodically review the prior year, current operations, and establish a strategy for the next twelve-month, three-year, and five-year periods? Running a life is not much different from running a business: your success or failure will depend upon your strategies and your skill in implementing them. Take time *now* to write and review you and your spouse's personal plans, and create a joint plan. This will launch a synergism that will increase your cash flow and give you proper utilization of your finances so that each of you does not go off in opposite directions spending money needlessly. Once your goals are established, you can work toward understanding the larger economic world and how it can be used to create wealth.

3. Why Are You Working Every Day?

Congratulations! Now that you've firmly made up your mind that financial success is a desirable achievement, you can begin to study the varied techniques for attaining riches. Keep a pen or pencil handy so that as ideas are stimulated from your reading, you can write them down.

Obtaining Wealth

Through my seminars, radio shows, and television appearances, I have met countless people who have attained various levels of financial independence. I have discovered only two workable methods of achieving wealth:

- Through highly disciplined savings
- Through the operation and growth of some type of business venture.

Method One

Of those creating wealth out of savings, the majority have accomplished this over a thirty- to forty-year period. They've made continual sacrifices throughout their lives scrimping and saving, doing without and tempering their desires in order to create enough wealth for retirement.

Unfortunately this also means they have lived 80% of their lives not enjoying the very luxuries for which they were saving! For many, this potential for happiness vanished forever through loss of health or declining mental capacity during retirement. Others have established a set pattern of living at a level well below their dreams, so that even when their nest egg generates financial freedom, they are unable to enjoy the luxuries for which they had so diligently planned.

I have clients with more than a million dollars' net worth and annual income above $100,000 who have so restricted themselves that they save most of their income and live almost entirely off Social Security. I'm startled when working with these couples to learn how often the wife is totally unaware of the wealth they've created or the generous income they receive.

They have become so accustomed to driving an eight-year-old car, going to early-bird specials, and inconveniencing themselves on other super savers that they don't dare make use of their riches.

Although stringent saving is a valid and important method of obtaining riches, it is definitely not my favorite. My personal philosophy is to live each day as if it were my last, in the fullest way possible.

Too often I have seen young friends and associates drop dead of heart attacks or die in car accidents. And I've watched their bodies become ravaged with cancer. Planning for the future is necessary, but living *only* for the future is not. Save for that rainy day, but learn how to enjoy the sunshine while it is bestowing its warmest rays upon you.

The purpose of saving should *not* be to gradually and continually amass funds for use during retirement: it should be to establish successful investment strategies to build a nest egg. Put aside money each week as seed money to establish a business that was formerly a love or hobby, or to invest in joint venture or partnership arrangements with others who possess special skills, talents, or products.

In later chapters on budgeting I will explain how to turn expenses into assets and how to properly spend your money to create future wealth. I am not adverse to saving money, but I advise against hoarding it for savings sake, as an end in itself.

Saving is a discipline that should begin in childhood. Kids should deposit a portion of their allowance in a piggy bank. (There is a big difference between a piggy bank and a hog bank—pigs get fat and hogs get slaughtered.) Saving should continue throughout life. For example, everyone should set aside a portion of his or her income for an IRA and maintain a small emergency fund. But future capital-formation can be accomplished only be creating additional opportunities to utilize savings and to protect the value of your money from inflation/deflation and taxes.

Method Two

Building and/or creating a business can be an excellent approach to acquiring wealth. For those who are less industrious or do not want the aggravations and long hours of running a business, the purchase of rental properties and management of these investments can create wealth. For others, partnerships and joint ventures can achieve the same purpose.

"It's a Hard-Knock Life"

You heard about the rat race while growing up, yet it wasn't real to you. Now you examine your life and perhaps find disappointment. Activities, attitudes, and behavior you despised and shunned during adolescence are an integral part of your life today. Hippies have turned into yuppies; collegiate rebels have become execs.

Life may have gotten you so "caught up trying to keep up" that you never get a chance to get ahead. Instead of allowing one problem after another, one disappointment and another, pile on top of you, hindering any true progress toward achieving your goals, you must add *predictability* and *control*. This can be done only be learning how to properly manage your life and your resources. To do so, it is extremely valuable to visualize the ideal method of achieving that goal. When you can fully *define* and *picture* everything you want to achieve in its most perfect state, *and* the best way of reaching it, you have a measuring stick to judge your progress.

Find a quiet place where you can think without distractions. This could be a room in your house, or you might have to drive to a deserted park or beach. Now, sit back comfortably, close your eyes, and imagine in as much detail as possible exactly what would be the ideal accomplishment concerning your job, your material wealth, your family, and yourself. Picture it as real, so that you can see not only the beautiful house and car but also visualize your net worth statement and see the bottom line. Read your money-market-fund account statement and picture the taxes you are paying on the wealth you have accumulated. The more you detail it, the more you crystallize your thinking, the better chance you have for accomplishment. Do not hold yourself back here. Make sure these are *your goals* and *your personal desires* and not what others have set for you. You are the final judge of whether you are a success in life. Now, make concrete these images in a *goal book* in which you actually paste in pictures of the house and car, a desired award, or whatever. This will give you a magnetic pull that will exert its invisible forces to draw you closer and closer to these goals in your life.

Your Beginning

Obviously the best start one can ask for in life is to have been born into a family that has planned for your birth and was well prepared to undertake the financial and emotional responsibility necessary to ensure your future. Unfortunately, few of us were anticipated to such an extent. Mainly our parents tried to get by as they raised us, trying to stretch their funds to take care of our immediate needs or to put aside some money for our education. Many, perhaps most, parents do not achieve the level of financial success that they have dreamed of. But this is no reason why by uniting your efforts and working together with your parents, they couldn't help you and your children achieve financial success. During a child's first stage of life, the most important asset management occurs with development of his or her personality and future goals. The more love and nurturing given by the parents, the more understanding and education, the better off the child. Utilizing tax-saving methods also becomes important, since you can use your child's zero tax bracket to shift taxable investment income to accumulate for his or her future. Teenagers who realize that no money has been set aside for their higher education may need to get a part-time job to save for their future and take responsibility for themselves.

A child who is allowed to help out at an early age gains a vital edge on life—knowledge of how to go out into the world to make his or her own way. Even toddlers can handle small tasks, and these successes can be rewarded. Throughout childhood, learning the value and importance of exchanging services or goods is vital in creating a successful participant in the game of life. Mowing lawns, shoveling snow, running errands—all can help enhance your children's future as they learn the need and value of work. Teaching children to take responsibility for their own situation establishes a strong foundation for successful attitudes and habits as adults. It's never too early to learn that we get out of life only what we invest.

As we move further along in the information era, the ability to assimilate and process vast quantities of data will become essential in everyday living. As man is forced to compete with computers on every front, it will be his ability to think and implement his creative plans that will be a key to survival. *There is no cost too high or sacrifice too great when it comes to the proper education of your children and yourself*. But you must go beyond those educational services that are given to you free and seek every possibility in which your child will be in a stimulating, challenging, and nurturing environment. Your children must work hard in "slow" areas just as you should create new challenges and stimulations in areas where they excel.

Education must be taken beyond the mere passing of exams. It must concentrate on the application of concepts. Whenever possible, hands-on experience should be encouraged, and work-study programs, apprenticeships, and internships in chosen career areas should be pursued. Part-time afterschool work and summer jobs in your child's chosen field will go a long way toward distinguishing between glamour and harsh reality. Having opportunities to be involved with different businesses and related fields may also prove fruitful in helping paint the big picture. Choosing the right high school (if choices are available) and, even more important, the right college, becomes vital since it is through experiences and associations established at these levels that your child will create a strong network of friends, associates, and colleagues for building a future. Don't underestimate the power of this type of interaction. You will discover that the motivated, hardworking students will be the individuals you will run into later in your life: running the banks, construction companies, manufacturing firms, and computer outlets. Your own growth can hinge upon such contacts. Build your bridges carefully and ensure that they lead to destinations you have set in your mind. It is through those last few years of high school and the beginning of college that one should begin to crystallize and implement a lifetime plan of action.

Career Planning

Hopefully, as you had the opportunity to experience many different areas of work during childhood, you are now in a position when leaving school to set out on your career. Regardless of your occupation, you now must ensure that you get the synergy of the best and most powerful businesses in your chosen field. You will be able to learn from the most successful execs and receive millions of dollars in valuable training as you look, listen, and study exactly how they work to achieve success. The level at which you enter the company is of little importance. *But do not accept jobs in areas that pay more but do not lead toward your personal destination.* Whether it is sweeping floors, answering phones, or being a gofer, do whatever you can to get involved with the most successful company in your field. Then, by doing your job well, you likely will be discovered and promoted through the organization, receiving invaluable training for your career and life. As Gilbert and Sullivan said in *HMS Pinafore*, ". . . and he polished up the handle so carefully that now he was the admiral of the Queen's Navy."

Warning: Do not be swayed or influenced by friends, family, or financial considerations when accepting your first job out of college. Just make sure you have chosen a leader in your community or elsewhere (you must often be willing to relocate) that is pivotal to your advancement in the field. You cannot learn how to be a great snow skier in Florida.

Financing

Establish every line of credit you possibly can, with credit cards, equity lines, and loans. If you are employed at a good salary, this won't be difficult. If you plan to go into business for yourself, lines of credit will be hard to come by, so do it now. Try to increase the credit limits on all your charge cards; in an emergency you might need to depend on them.

Trading Up

Another trap to avoid once you have made your first step toward training is overlooking the importance of moving to another organization in your field since you have obtained most of the knowledge and training you need or intended to get. It is always good to gain perspective from assorted leaders in an industry. Since different companies have a variety of managerial philosophies, it is vital to learn not only what the top competitors in your field are doing, but also the strengths and weaknesses of these different approaches. Ways to help finance any business venture are limited only by your own imagination. Getting your family to help back you may or may not be the best means, since blood may run deep but money runs even deeper, and you may find yourself with some very loud silent backers. Having your family or even a friend sign for you on a note may give you the opportunity to access into other people's accumulated wealth to help you create some, but once again this ties you down to the cosigner's constant surveillance to make sure you will be able to pay off the debt.

The key to any financing you must do at this stage lies in your marketing ability. You must be able to enthusiastically present and sell a written business plan for exactly what you are looking to accomplish, what it will cost, and what benefits will be received.

More than anything else, your attitude and professionalism are what count. When dealing with bankers it often is not so much your business ideas that matter, but how well you get along with and can motivate the loan officer in handling your request. Being friendly with a number of bankers by establishing different accounts and making an effort to let them know who you are can be vital. Meeting bankers in Chamber of Commerce meetings and other civic activities gives you the opportunity to use this community network to your advantage. There is no better way to win recognition from your banker than to become involved with his or her civic club, take on a major project, and run it successfully. Here, without any money of your own, you establish yourself as a leader and a success before your peers. What an excellent opportunity to add value to yourself!

You may also want to investigate local venture-capitalist groups, since these financiers are more apt to invest in start-up operations. Unfortunately, they also look for much higher rates of return and you may have to give up a percentage of your enterprise for the time being. Other possibilities lie in partnerships with friends who believe in you, where all contribute a small sum of money to help you get started. Or you may find existing business owners looking to retire. You can walk in with no money down and buy out the business, taking it over and just paying them a percentage of the revenues. Organizing other individuals who also may want to strike out on their own may give you the opportunity to bring in a number of self-motivated, already-productive individuals in your field to create a synergy that could be managed and run by you. Just putting ads in local newspapers and venture-capital newsletters also may help you solicit support for your ideas.

Whatever approach you decide on, remember that you must be creative, enthusiastic, and have goals so well visualized in your mind that you can easily transfer this concept to others to stimulate and excite their imagination and profit potential.

Attitude Is the Key

If you are reading this and still ho-humming to yourself or still find yourself without any motivation toward action, I suggest you do the following:

- Make a list of the successes—no matter how small—in your life. Write down each time you've set a goal and achieved it.
- Next to these write down who or what helped you do so.

You should be feeling much better now—and if not, you need to repeat steps 1 and 2, going back further or looking into different areas of your life.

If after doing this you do not feel revitalized—review each time you tried and failed as above and then *redo* your list of successes. Sometimes we get stuck, dwelling on failures.

End this process as soon as you find yourself feeling very good or have some new awareness of life and yourself that inspires you to undertake action or changes. This process for rekindling lost energy and spirit works very effectively.

Attitude

Many people fail not because they don't try but because they booby-trap themselves. You see this all the time when people undertake tasks and say, "Oh, I'll never win," or, "I can't win at this," or, "I can't . . .".

Thought precedes action. Don't direct yourself toward losing. Your actions are determined by your thoughts, whether they be pre-programmed or current. Your attitude is the inner representation of what your emotions and actions will be on the outside. What you think is what you are.

What do you think of yourself and of your chances for succeeding? What self-image do you have of your own abilities?

Your attitude determines how much space *you* give *yourself*. Space to think and space to act. Don't let bad attitudes close you out.

If you try to succeed, to become financially independent, what is the worse possible thing that can happen if you fail? Now think of something worse than your response to this last question. Chances are you could handle even the worst. But remember: the worst is not likely to happen if you create a viable plan to turn your dreams into reality.

Get excited about life. Go out and try. Each time you fall down or fail, laugh it off. Set out on the exploration of your life. Be willing to meet its challenges and accept the results that you create by your own continued persistence and unending motivation.

Major Points to Reconsider

1. Your commitment to success
2. Saving versus investing
3. Visualizing your ideal life from start to finish

4. Family planning:
   a. Childhood
   b. Schooling/education
   c. Career activation
5. Attitude is the key
6. Learning to find the tiny success that lies within every failure

4. Dreams or Reality

How do you measure your progress? By a bigger house, a nicer car? Do you compare yourself with everybody else around you and decide you're doing okay? There is no one else to compare yourself with but *yourself* and *your* own standards.

Only by *writing down* your goals and specifically defining them can you measure the success you are actually achieving. In the last chapter I explained how you should begin to visualize your lifetime goals—both long-term and short-term. But these images will always be mere dreams if you do not write them down. Putting them on paper will help you turn your dreams into action plans. By being forced to look at your goals, and read them every so often, you can determine your batting average. Think about it! Can you imagine athletes never keeping track of statistics? How would players negotiate salaries if nobody knew what their abilities were? Maybe some can talk themselves up better than others, yet be batting substantially lower.

By assessing your list of goals, first on a one-year, then a five-year, and then on a ten-year basis you can see whether you have had a profitable plan. Show your list to your family. Each member should have an important role in helping you reach your goals. Meanwhile you can reciprocate by helping your family members attain their goals. By announcing these goals and telling people what you are aiming for and how, you can create a synergy. During the past ten years, working with the Jaycees, I have personally trained thousands of young men and women throughout the country. Of those I have surveyed, 90% have never established, defined, and written down their goals. Those who are successful, whether as real estate developers, insurance representatives, engineers, doctors, or whatever, have more often written down their goals with full definition. I cannot stress enough how much better you will do if you put your goals in writing and place them in an often-viewed location.

Your engines were started with visualization, so take out a few pages of paper or get a notebook and write down all your lifetime goals.

Now review your list, adding to it whenever you think of a new goal. (If you don't like to write, dictate into a cassette recorder.)

Look over your list carefully or replay your cassette. Eliminate those "goals" that can be labeled wild fantasies, such as making love to all the most beautiful men or women in the world, or being shipwrecked on a desert island for twenty years with the actor or actress of your choice. Retain each goal you would like to accomplish in the next five, ten, or twenty years for which you would be willing to work hard. As out of sight as some of the dreams might appear ("to be the most successful and wealthiest member of my graduating class") it is in stating these *overall goals* that you can create *subgoals* that are more easily attained. To earn $50,000 a year could then become $100,000, $200,000, and finally a million dollars a year, working in the proper sequence.

Of course there are always those who continually shoot for the pie-in-the-sky and the three-million-dollar jackpot. But of course the higher the stakes, the higher the odds are against you. This does not mean you shouldn't shoot for the stars. But if you follow a nest egg approach, success occurs on a gradient scale and is realized in a predictable manner.

Anticipation is one of the most important elements in our life. In fact, life is 99½ percent anticipation and one-half percent realization. The moment of realization—whether it is election to office, a best-selling record, or a major career achievement—has as its pinnacle one very short moment that never again can be fully grasped. Too often, once goals are reached, new ones are not established. Yet continually setting new goals is the only way to keep your life interesting and happy.

Prioritize

Prioritize your goals. You must know which ones have the most immediate importance and which are longer-term and can be concentrated on later. You cannot work toward every goal at once. (However, working toward one goal will help you achieve goals in other areas as well.) You must set a challenging task to keep your interest piqued, but at the same time not be overwhelmed by trying to accomplish too much, too quickly. Determine which goals you would first like to achieve within the next year in accordance with a long-term goal.

For example, your goal is to be made vice president within five years. Subgoals—Year One: to be the most outstanding teller at the bank. Year Two: to be promoted to assistant loan officer. Year Three: to be rated as top assistant loan officer. Year Four: to be promoted to loan officer. Year Five: to be promoted to a vice presidency. First we look at the overall goal, and each year we take another step toward that. Different goals necessitate different steps. Sometimes you can leapfrog over various steps, other times you add steps to make smaller intervals. There is a progressive nature inherent in goals. Just as one note cannot make a song, the progression of notes played together form a melody and create the impact and beauty of music.

Rating from 1 (lowest) to 10 (highest), establish the immediacy of each of your goals.

Burning Desire

Wanting, needing, longing for, dreaming about, or just talking about your objectives will help little to reach your goal unless you have this vital ingredient: burning desire. That is something you want with all your heart, something you are willing to commit your life to, and work hard for it. Burning desire is what cements the link between dreams and reality.

Everyone has a desire to be financially secure and independent, so this, too, needs to be properly defined and targeted. I find many people feel financially independent with an income of $20,000 a year, since their desires and needs are low. Others find it difficult to live on $200,000 a year. They like travel, personal indulgences, and reaping all the pleasures this wonderful world has to offer. What dollar amount do you need for financial security and independence? Unless you can define that in today's terms, your ability to plan for the future is greatly reduced.

Ask yourself: How much income in today's dollars would I need to truly enjoy myself and have all the food, clothing, shelter, travel, entertainment, and other activities that I so desire? You may want to work up a proposed budget first to better visualize this and see how it feels. Don't just take a dollar amount out of the air. Write that number down. This is an important number because it gives you the target income necessary to achieve financial security for your future. The question now is: What do you do to ensure that this occurs? This process will be examined throughout this book to help you learn the different steps you must take to achieve that dream.

Review:
1. Never underestimate the importance of writing down *your* goals.
2. Create synergies.
3. Set priorities.

5. Your Personal Blueprint

Can you imagine what would have happened when the first nationwide railroad from California to New York was being built, had there not been a set plan? Construction workers would have crossed some winding waterways numerous times. They might have wandered through mountains, creating unnecessary expense and lengthening travel time. Instead, the first step was to survey the land, to draw a map marking the most efficient path. As in building a house, if you do not have blueprints you may end up with plumbing for a toilet in your bedroom and a shower in your closet.

A personal blueprint is therefore necessary to understand what you want from your life and to set into motion the powerful unconscious strength in your mind.

The primary step is to make a complete list of everything you have ever dreamed or wanted to be, do, have, travel to, or attain. This list should be created and added to as other things come into mind and could be three, five, ten, or more pages long, depending on your goals. Such a list allows you the opportunity to rearrange goals, working toward accomplishing the most important ones first. You may be amazed at how many goals can be worked on simultaneously to accomplish two, three, or more dreams at once.

Without viewing the relationships between those deep-down goals for your life, you cannot begin to create the mandatory blueprint for building your future. Each of the following six areas should be looked at from this viewpoint: self; family; professional, social, fraternal groups; mankind as a whole; plants, animals, and the physical universe; spiritual fulfillment.

Priorities

Trying to achieve everything at once is almost as foolish as doing nothing and expecting something to happen. Too often we find ourselves caught up in pursuing those things that are the easiest and not those that are the most productive. Priorities must be based on the most important goal at that moment. Time can independently change priorities, so you must set them, based on your short-term and long-term needs, trying to project into the future.

Long-Term Goals

Of course, some goals which you have stated will be the culmination of having achieved lesser goals. Therefore creating the proper sequence and channeling the proper energies into accomplishing each step in its proper turn becomes critical. Although there may be times when subgoals are skipped over, it is only because of having stepped to a point beyond, eliminating a need for the lower goal. You should set your priorities in each of the six categories mentioned above. This action alone will begin to bring great stability to your life. Instead of bobbing around in so many directions and going nowhere, you can now see the forest through the trees.

Further Visualization

Next, as you set your priorities, sit back and visualize how you would feel, how you would behave, what you would look like and how your life would be upon achievement of each of those goals. Letting your mind wander, looking at all aspects of the goal and putting yourself there as if the achievement had already occurred, you begin to connect the present with the future.

Here, visual aids are of key importance, and the creation of the "dream book" I discussed earlier becomes worthwhile: using a photo album and cutting out pictures of the car and house that you want; drawing copies of sample tax returns and net worth statements, putting a future date on it; drawing pictures showing yourself receiving awards and actually going out to get a copy of the award, putting your name on it so you can look at it every day. It works.

I vividly remember setting a goal to be on the cover of a major magazine, particularly *Success* magazine, by the age of thirty-five. While touring Universal Studios in California, I saw magazine covers where film experts would take your photograph and place it behind a mock copy of any magazine on file. I've kept this framed mock copy in my house to look at constantly. When friends and neighbors see it and congratulate me, I reveal that the "magazine" is a mockup, but is in fact what I expect to have happen by 1987. Invariably they smile, wishing me luck. This is one of the great uses of a dream book. Not only will it help you to visualize clearly, but it also can help communicate your goals and dreams to others so that they too can assist you.

Resources

Now list all of your personal resources. Every person has qualities, talents, and abilities that can be utilized in exchange for a valuable service or commodity. You may have tremendous patience, or find it easy to make friends. You may know how to throw a great party or write a moving letter. Each personal skill or ability has many different applications that, when put into the business world, have a lasting value. Your personal resources are those valuable traits that make you unique. You must capitalize on them. Working with your resources of energy will be a primary force in helping you accomplish your goals. To achieve certain goals means that you normally must develop levels of skill. Also consider your weak points. Unless you accurately assess both your strengths and weaknesses, you can never ensure that you have gained increased abilities to accomplish a goal. List both your good points (attributes) and weak points. Important areas to examine include ability to communicate; persistence; ability to get along with others; study habits; talents; special problems, fears, and attitudes in different areas; ability to start, change, and stop; and to delegate responsibility. How do other people relate to you? What are your reading abilities? How much do you read and what?

Remember, unless you are adding value to your life through more personal discipline and training (whether that means being nicer to people or more promptly answering phone calls and mail, or whether it means taking evening courses in typing or learning how to run a computer, or whether it simply means more enthusiastic action and self-motivation), you will not have the energy to carry yourself past the competition. Nor will you be able to overcome other barriers encountered throughout life.

Creating a personal plan is much like creating a financial plan. You set your goals, you list your resources, and you set about a sequence of actions for investing your energy (money) in properly allocated and timed actions to reach a desired financial end.

Now that you have listed your goals and your personal resources, you can begin to combine these to work toward your goals. If financial independence is one of them, you would (1) calculate and write down the amount necessary in today's dollars to have financial independence (a) in terms of income and (b) in terms of net worth. (2) You now must look at a target date when you expect to accomplish this. Is your goal within fifteen, twenty, or thirty years? This provides you with an average to determine how much must be accomplished each year, possibly in terms of getting progressively higher to reach this goal. That is, you may want to accumulate a million dollars over twenty years. However, since you are barely able to save a thousand dollars a year now, you first would work up a plan whereby in the earlier years you would make smaller contributions. In later years you would make larger deposits toward the ultimate goal. In setting goals, remember the bite of inflation. A million dollars in today's terms, at a mere 5% inflation rate, will have the purchasing power of under $250,000 in thirty years.

Next you must demonstrate how you are going to obtain these funds. It now becomes imperative that you target your goals realistically in small steps to provide yourself with the encouragement of small wins at every level. You cannot reach the top of Mt. Everest from its base without having taken thousands of steps in between. You cannot reach any destination you are aiming for unless you are willing to traverse a long and sometimes rocky road.

Navigation

Can you imagine going on a journey in a ship with no rudder and no set destination? Your goals act as your rudder, and your personal plan of action sets your destination. It takes time, energy, thought, and communication to create a personal plan. Yet, not to take the hours necessary to work out a plan while you will invest tens of thousands of hours working over forty or fifty years of your lifetime would be foolish. Creating a definite strategy and implementing it with hard and persistent work is sure to pay off many times over.

Constantly review your plan, ironing out difficult areas or modifying your course if the winds blow too long in a contrary direction. Don't let laziness or inaction get in your way. Don't let others deter you with negative thoughts or counterintentions. By openly reviewing each other's goals and intentions, you and your spouse or business partner can ensure that there will be no conflicts at later dates. Each person in your support system can find something to contribute.

With your goals set, priorities determined, and resources acknowledged, you can begin to construct your own personal blueprint for creating financial independence. Now comes the important task of transforming the words you have put on paper into a commitment to action. Your resolve must overcome any barrier necessary to accomplish each specific step *within a set time*. Without projecting a time frame in which each step of your plan should be completed, you will never be able to convert your dreams into reality. The process is known as *targeting:* setting specific deadlines in which something will be completed.

No successful professional builder would attempt to put up a home or shopping center without knowing when construction materials were scheduled to arrive. A builder could end up with lumber scattered all over the lot or wait months for cement to be delivered in order to pour the foundation. Failure to work up a timetable, a schedule for arrival of electricians, plumbers, and other specialists would lead such a careless builder to bankruptcy.

A timetable—setting targets for each step of your plan—becomes invaluable because this puts an anchor in the continuum. A timetable also gives you a measuring stick for how well you are accomplishing your goals. Targeting firmly places the sequence of actions in your mind and in the world around you. You often need to involve other people and businesses, and you will be forced to tell them of your plans to ensure that they supply the items you need within the designated time.

Review:
1. Write down plans to connect your thoughts with reality.
2. Set targets to connect action and plans.
3. Assess your personal resources.
4. Align your plan with goals for your future.

Sample Plan

GOALS

1. To own a 20-room mansion
2. To visit the Taj Mahal
3. To own my own bank
4. To become vice president at bank
5. To earn $100,000 a year
6. To be on the cover of *Time*

(continued)

7. To meet Brooke Shields
8. To have $100,000 per year income in 1987 terms at retirement

You can almost see a proper sequence of events within these goals. Obviously it would be unrealistic to expect to own a mansion without first having the income to finance one, or to own a bank until sufficiently trained to run one.

PRIORITIES
1. Become vice president at bank
2. Earn $100,000 a year (senior vice president's salary)
3. Own a bank

GOAL
Become vice president at bank

PLAN
What would have to happen for me to be made a vice president at bank? (What will I need to do?)

1. Be recognized for great work by the president
2. Bring lots of new business into the bank
3. Be well groomed and always on time
4. Be enthusiastic, cooperative, and positive
5. Be promoted to assistant vice president
6. Be made head teller
7. Finish my college degree
8. Take on extra responsibilities whenever possible
9. Receive recognition for community work
10. Always be helpful and do the best job possible

RESOURCES
With these ideas, you then relate them to your resources:

Strengths	*Weaknesses*
Always punctual	Shy
Always neat	Poor selection of clothes
Good with numbers and people	New to community and know few people
Read all necessary industry papers	Haven't finished college
Strong desire to succeed	Never managed others
Willing to work hard	Spend too much time socializing and watching TV

Your Personal Blueprint

PLANNING
Where resources and brainstorming combine to create the proper timed sequence of events.

MAJOR NEEDS
1. To become a better communicator
2. To meet lots of important community people for business contacts
3. To learn how to manage

PLAN STEPS
1. Maintain a positive mental attitude *always*—Jan. 1
2. Redo budget to minimize unnecessary expenses and begin a savings plan—Jan. 2
3. Join Toastmasters and attend meetings regularly—Target Jan. 12
4. Check with Chamber of Commerce to determine best two civic clubs to join—Jan. 14
5. Join two civic clubs and get involved—Jan. 28. A: Run small but important projects in each club—June 1
6. Get schedule of classes and curriculums from local colleges—Jan. 30
7. Select college to complete needed credits—Feb. 14
8. Enroll in college and transfer transcripts—Feb. 15
9. Begin schooling two to three nights per week and get good grades—March 1
10. Find a discount clothing outlet and purchase one new suit of reasonable quality every three months—Feb. 20 (Make known this is what is needed for your birthday)
11. Volunteer to help run bank's 4th of July Picnic—June 1
12. Volunteer for special fall projects at bank that report directly to president—Aug. 1 (Wear best suit that day!)
13. Receive award for hard work from each civic club and ensure president of bank finds out—Sept. 1
14. Volunteer to help with Christmas party—Nov. 14
15. Complete necessary credits and receive college degree—Dec. 12
16. Be promoted to head teller and get 20% raise in salary—Dec. 20
17. Invest salary raise in IRA account.
18. Continue to save 10% of salary to build for new house downpayment.

At the end of the year and during it, these steps need to be reviewed, modified, added to, and implemented. At the start of each year the plan must be extended.

6. Building a Million-Dollar Portfolio for Under Six Dollars a Day

Applied Apathy

Out of tens of millions of people currently qualifying to open IRA accounts, it is startling to learn that only 30% of them have done so. This means 70% of the population is ignoring this great government subsidy to help ensure your future nest egg at retirement. Another startling fact is that of the 30% who did open accounts, 70% put their money with a bank or savings and loan in a money market fund or CD.

Instead of using IRAs as an opportunity to learn about our economic system and invest for real rates of return, investors are seeking the "safe" route to certain financial insecurity. People seem to forget that with an average 10% inflation rate during the next thirty years—a very possible situation—a million dollars will be worth only $57,300 in today's terms. Even at 7% inflation, which has been the average over the last fifteen years or so, this would mean that the million dollars you have accumulated would have a purchasing power of only $125,000 in thirty years. It's incredible how just by increasing your rates of return from 8% to 12% makes a significant difference over this time period. Look at Figure 6-1 and see why it pays to go for extra risk. Remember that $100,000 becomes a million at 10% after approximately twenty-five years. Yet if we were to put that money into ten different investments, eight of which went to zero and two of which grew at a rate of 20% per year, we would end up with $2,560,000!

With proper diversification and dealing in quality investment areas, that number should easily be improved to succeed at least half the time, which would result in a $6.5 million instead of $1 million. Which size of nest egg would you rather have?

Figure 6-1: $2000 CONTRIBUTION ON JANUARY 1

		Values at Age 65 at		
Age	Total Deposits	7%	10%	14%
25	$80,000	$417,218	$973,704	$3,059,818
35	$60,000	$202,146	$361,886	$ 807,474
45	$40,000	$ 87,730	$126,004	$ 207,536
55	$20,000	$ 29,468	$ 35,062	$ 44,090

Figure 6-2: THE DIFFERENCES IN IRAs

	Brokerage Plans	Bank IRAs	Annuity IRAs
1. Money Insured	Possibly	Yes	Yes
2. High Current Market Rates	Yes	Yes	Yes
3. Certificate of Deposit	Yes	Yes	No
4. Money Market Funds-Daily	Yes	Yes	Yes
5. Stocks	Yes	No	Yes
6. Covered Option Writing	Yes	No	No
7. Bonds	Yes	No	Yes
8. Government Securities	Yes	No	No
9. Mutual Funds	Yes	No	Yes
10. Oil Income Partnerships	Yes	No	No
11. Real Estate Partnerships	Yes	No	No
12. Business Partnerships	Yes	No	No
13. Annual Fees	Yes	Possibly	Possibly
14. Opening Fees	Yes	Possibly	No
15. Monthly Contributions Possible	Yes	Yes	Yes
16. Re-investment Possibility	Yes	Yes	Yes
17. Costs for Changing Investments	Yes	Yes	Yes
18. Flexibility	Yes	Little	Some
19. Guaranteed Lifetime Income at Retirement	No	No	Yes
20. Switching Fees	Yes	Yes	Yes
21. Ability to Change Investment Vehicle w/o 60 Day Restriction	Yes	No	Possibly

Retirement

Probably the largest tax shelter that we have today, one of the most up-and-coming areas in the investment market, centers on retirement plans—individual retirement accounts, Keoghs, qualified pension plans, 403B plans for teachers and nonprofit organizations, profit-sharing plans, defined benefit plans, defined contribution plans, SEP plans, and the vast array of other plans. Retirement plans are thus one of the most dynamic areas of contemporary finance. It is estimated that by 1990 half of all major projects will be financed through these plans, which are growing at the rate of trillions of dollars each decade and will very likely continue at an even higher rate. The IRA program, permitting a $2000 contribution per employed person, per year, and an additional $250 for a nonworking spouse, probably can be traced to the failure of the Social Security system. IRAs represent long-term investing, which stimulates the country's growth through private enterprise. By putting aside $2000 each year, or less then $6 a day, you will enjoy many new investment opportunities. Keogh Plans are for self-employed individuals who can put $25,000, or 25% of their adjusted gross income (whichever is less), into a retirement plan, and, as in the case of IRAs, deduct this money dollar-for-dollar from gross income. This cuts taxes substantially. A person earning $100,000 can contribute and then deduct $20,000 from his or her taxable gross income and reduce taxable income to $80,000. This individual would enjoy $5600 in tax savings. In other words, the first year that he invests the $20,000, he has already saved $5600 in taxes. An immediate 28% return. If, in addition to that, he earns 15% on his money, his total reaches a 43% return in the first year. Where else can you get that kind of a return on your money? *Whether it's an IRA or a Keogh, every working person should open one of these plans.*

Another attractive feature is that you can invest retirement plan money in many places—bank certificates for different maturities, annuities for fixed or variable rates of return, a self-managed account in one of the brokerage houses for the purchase and sale of stocks and bonds, or real estate investment trusts and partnerships for long-term growth. Some people go into mutual funds to play the stock and bond markets. You can enter a money market fund or a combination of investments. IRAs are normally very inexpensive to establish. Often there is no cost involved at all.

It is important, though, to understand the flexibilities of an IRA. For that reason I include Figure 6-2.

IRAs—The New Rules

There still remains a very viable and exciting investment for all those who may still open IRA accounts. Under the new tax law, single filers with adjusted income over $35,000, and couples with adjusted gross income over $50,000, would no longer be allowed to deduct an IRA contribution *if* they participate in an employer-sponsored pension or profit-sharing plan. Single individuals with incomes between $25,000 and $35,000 and couples between $40,000 and $50,000 will see their deductions being phased out as their incomes rise, if they have other retirement plans. Workers who are *not* covered by a retirement plan are still able to have a tax-deductible contribution of $2000 per individual and an additional $250 for a nonworking spouse. Even though you may not be *vested* in your corporate retirement plan, you can not make tax-deductible IRA contributions if your income exceeds the new limits, as you are in fact covered by a pension plan. Yet an apparent penalty exists for married taxpayers filing joint returns whereby one spouse has a retirement plan and the other one doesn't. Under these circumstances if their adjusted gross income is more than $50,000, the individual not covered by a pension plan will also lose the IRA deduction! The effect of filing separate returns still needs to be clarified. For individuals above these set income levels may still make $2000 contributions to an IRA, but this will not be a tax-deductible item.

It therefore becomes inappropriate for most investors to make additional contributions, as the penalties for early withdrawal become too steep to make them attractive. Instead, to help build their retirement accounts, investors should consider variable-life programs and municipal bond funds that will give them the tax advantages and flexibility that they should maintain for their future. In the nondeductible IRA accounts an investor will be allowed to use special accounting procedures so that a portion of the money withdrawn from these accounts would be tax-free based on a ratio of the deductible IRA plan's assets compared to nondeductible IRA plan assets. If an individual wanting to withdraw $1000 had a total of $10,000 in an IRA, with $8000 from deductible IRAs and $2000 nondeductible IRAs, only 20% of the $1000 would be considered as coming from the nondeductible IRA, with taxes and penalties on the remaining 80%. Additionally, the 10% penalty for early withdrawals if made before the age of fifty-nine and a half would be waived if the money is withdrawn in equal installments over a lifetime such as through an annuity. Yet, if retirees withdraw more than $112,500 from these plans, they will pay a 15% penalty on withdrawals over that amount. This extra penalty may not apply to contributions made before August 1986.

Your Largest Tax Shelter—Retirement Plans

An interesting trend developing in the financial industry is the increasing number of investments which heretofore were unavailable for pension plans. These are now becoming viable investment vehicles for managers of IRAs, Keoghs, pension plans and profit-sharing plans.

Through the use of specially designed institutional pension-only accounts, I have seen attractive penion investments yielding 14% to 18% in conservative equity-participation mortgages and all-cash real estate. These plans give yearly evaluations, which are required by many pension plans, and enable money managers to closely monitor their performances in terms of income and gains. Many of these investments are available for those with self-directed accounts for as little as $2000. They make attractive alternatives for achieving both income and growth objectives and thus ensure your money will have a higher purchasing power in the future than it does today.

Individual pension plans for closely held corporations, professional associations, and the like can be some of the most lucrative areas of tax savings for an individual. Not only may you contribute an annual amount of up to $100,000 without taxes into a retirement plan, but you may have the flexibility to borrow $50,000 of that sum for a period of up to five years should you need it. (As tax laws are constantly in a state of flux, speak with a pension consultant for the latest tax update.) You *can* pay your plan a going interest rate and maintain the use of your money without ever paying income taxes on it, while getting a tax deduction for the interest you are saving yourself!

Facts and figures illustrating how this works must be determined on an individual basis to show the benefits. Pension experts are becoming ever so valuable in today's environment. They belong on your team with a CFP, CPA, and tax attorney.

Recently there was a major trend among many large corporations to redefine their pension plan at different interest rate assumptions. The higher the assumption, the lower the cash contribution. This created a bonanza of free cash for these companies to operate with as they withdrew their now overfunded plan (because of higher rate assumptions) to reduce debt. Not only has there been a chance to help employees build for retirement and save taxes, but the corporations have also derived many benefits. Unfortunately, if low interest rates on long-term investments continue, these plans may become underfunded! Let's face it, the strength of the corporation is what determines its value to employees. Certainly a corporation's strength affects future employee benefits. (Although there is a special government agency that provides pension benefits for failed corporations, $1760 per month is the maximum amount.) It's important to understand that anything done in the interest of keeping the corporation solvent should be considered a valid maneuvering of funds as long as pensioners don't suffer. The key in establishing a pension plan is determining how much money can be committed to the program. Next, information must be gathered on who will be covered and how contributions will be controlled. After that, a visit to a pension-plan expert is in order. These specialists should have computer programs set up in which to feed your information. They will help design a plan in close alignment with your wishes, normally at a low cost.

Many pension plans created during the last ten years need to be re-evaluated, since laws have changed markedly.

Once your pension is established, it is important to commit money in conservative, inflation-oriented investments. I say "conservative" investments since there are no tax benefits for losses within a pension plan. My preference is to go into high-yielding annuities, real estate, participating mortgages, government security funds, or well-managed mutual funds. These normally permit investments as small as $500 and allow them to be placed at intervals. Special types of business partnerships might also prove fruitful.

Don't overlook timing for your pension-plan investments. The sooner you act, the more money you will have. If you had the cash in a money fund all year and waited until December to deposit into your retirement plan, you'd have earned taxable interest all those months that could have been sheltered through your retirement plan with tax-deferred income. You can keep those dollars in the same money fund. Just make sure they are earmarked as part of your retirement plan. Example: If you contributed $2000 at the beginning of each year and earned 12% a year, you would have $540,585 after thirty years. On the other hand, by delaying your contribution until the end of each year, you would have only $482,655 after thirty years—a considerable difference. In fact, the near $58,000 difference is almost enough to total your contributions for thirty years ($60,000)!

Although IRA, Keogh, and other retirement plans are the best ways to save on taxes, there are many other easy strategies.

Ideal Investment for Retirement Plans

For pension, profit-sharing, Keogh, IRA, and IRA rollover plans, I would consider mortgage participation trusts and limited partnerships. Specialized investment banking firms throughout the country have packaged a diversified portfolio of participating mortgages into special limited partnerships strictly for retirement plan investing. Rates of return between 12% and 18% have been available, while obtaining a 25% to 50% equity participation in any increased value of the underlying property. These plans are particularly attractive to pension plans seeking high current interest rates and a hedge against inflation. Risks depends on which mortgages are within the portfolio.

William Brennan, the noted limited partnership analyst, cites varying degrees of risk with the multitude of mortgage limited partnerships currently being offered. For example, if the partnership intends to make construction loans or junior mortgages (which are subordinated to a first mortgage on the property), the economic risks are enhanced. In the case of a junior mortgage, it sits in a secondary position to the principal lender in collecting the loan balance if the property is sold. Construction loans entail their own risks. Construction may not be completed or, upon completion, the property may not be leased.

When reviewing a mortgage investment, one principal consideration is the loan-to-value ratio. If a property costs a million dollars, you don't want a partnership that lends a million dollars to the purchaser. You want some of the purchaser's money involved so that if the property drops in value the property owner's money is lost, not your mortgage principal. The more money the owner has in the property, the less risk to the mortgage holder.

Conversely, the more money an owner has invested in the property, the lower the interest he or she is willing to pay you (the lender). Most mortgage investment vehicles set a maximum loan, compared to the value of the property, of about 85%. More conservative investors should look for a loan-to-value ratio of about 75%.

Don't become overly excited with the returns promised by some aggressive partnerships. Some current sales material indicates that an annual return of 16% to 20% can be expected. But with mortgage loans running at about 10.5% to 11.5% from commercial lenders at the moment, any buyer willing to pay predictable returns at significantly higher levels either has virtually nothing invested in the property or anticipates problems.

Investors who have followed tax shelters in the past can liken the high returns promised in mortgage limited partnerships to the high write-offs promised in some real estate equity partnerships: the more enticing the promises, the more frequent the pitfalls. One further word of caution regarding mortgage partnerships: front-end loads and operating charges imposed by the general partner can vary enormously. Typically, front-end costs will run 10% to 11% of the amount you invest for sales commissions and organization expenses.

In addition, the general partner will charge the borrower fees for loan application and loan origination. Normally this charge is about 3% to 3.5%, but it can go as high as 7%. Admittedly, this is not a charge to the investor, but it will certainly enter into a borrower's decision on interest rates he is willing to pay and the risk he is transferring to the lender.

Despite the above caveats, mortgage trusts and partnerships can be very rewarding. They offer several benefits: a reasonably assured annual return in the form of interest payments on the mortgage, and inflation protection if economic conditions deteriorate. When evaluating these investments, read the offering materials closely to make sure you understand the deal. Don't take unnecessary risks. A competitive return, in the area of 9% to 11% annually, with a cushion against inflation, should be satisfactory.

Why Consider Mortgage-Backed Securities?

In the past twenty-five years, inflation has outpaced the rate of return on conventional mortgages only once. Usually, a 2% to 4% spread has existed between the two (see Figure 6-3). Essentially, by dealing with a mortgage-backed investment, you are removing the middleman (the bank) and placing your money directly where a bank would. The difference is that instead of the bank earning 9% to 12% on its mortgages and paying you 5% to 6%, you are collecting the full 9% to 12%—a 50% increase in return—which, when coupled with equity participation in the underlying property, more than justifies the increased risk.

These mortgage investments are liquid and therefore still give you access to your money in times of need, as long as you can tolerate market fluctuations. Ideally, we hope to see one day a variable-rate participating mortgage which will combine the best of both worlds.

There you sit—on top of the fence. On one side, you must have a good income to survive. On the other side, you feel it important to

Figure 6-3

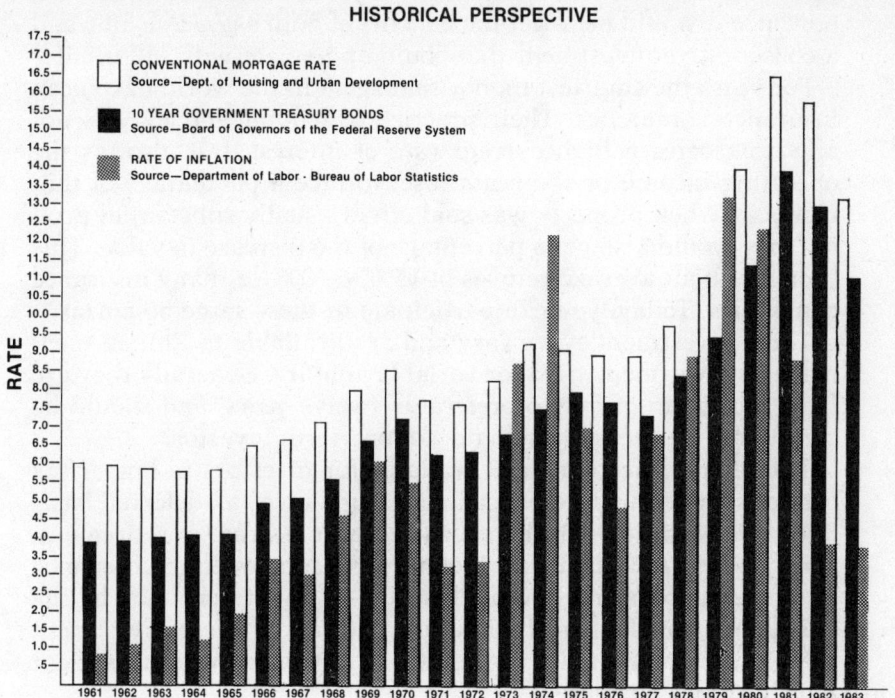

maintain the purchasing power of your principal and future income.

You've lost heavily on bonds you bought in 1970 and which still have years to go. Even if they matured today, two-thirds of their purchasing power has been lost. Unfortunately, their maturity is not for years, and because of the low-rate fixed coupons, they're selling at a 20% discount as well.

It didn't take long to realize that even an AAA insured MBIA or government-backed bond had tremendous market risks and inflation risks. If we just maintained our average inflation rate for the past ten years, a $10,000 bond maturing in ten years would have only $5000 worth of purchasing power!

You recognize that real estate has been an excellent investment as you watch your house appreciate while you deduct interest costs over the years. Still, you are leery of the lack of liquidity in investment properties. You find yourself sitting on the fence in short-term CDs and money market funds, being penalized by unnecessary taxes, loss of purchasing power on principal, and a very poor after-tax return of 4% for those of you in the 30% bracket. Oh, how nice it would be to get the benefits of both a good income and a conservative investment that could appreciate with inflation!

For years the smartest money managers in the world have been insurance companies. Their practice of lending money was not only to receive a high current rate of interest, but also, as the operating income or the rents rose, to take a percentage of that increase. When property was sold off, at usually substantial profits, they would also get a percentage of the increase in value. This brought about average returns of 15% to 20% for many insurance companies. Today, you can participate in these same bonanzas.

These investment types vary and are available in limited partnership, investment trust, or variable annuity. Generally they are for a minimum of five to preferably twelve years, and should be considered by the intermediate- to long-term investor.

Tax-deferred accounts are available for investors in higher tax brackets, and your interest can compound on a tax-deferred basis until it is withdrawn at, hopefully, a lower tax rate in retirement.

For conservative investors looking for income with maintenance of further purchasing power, this type of investment may be the answer. Although there is liquidity on most of these investment vehicles, the market risk that exists in any bond-type investment must also be considered.

As money market funds made savings accounts obsolete in the '70s, as single-pay plans such a Pacer Plus, Keyplan, and Discovery Life leapfrogged municipal bonds in the early '80s, participating mortgages are here to change the face of income-oriented bond buyers forever. (Pacer, Keyplan, and Discovery Life are all rated excellent. Pacer is issued by National Home Life Assurance; Keyplan by Keystone Provident Life, a fully owned subsidiary of Travelers Insurance; and Discovery Life by Prudential Insurance Co.

As described, a participating mortgage is usually a first mortgage on up to 80% of the value of a property. Most of the participating mortgage investments have quarterly distributions. Look for the ones with deferred interest returns which might run anywhere from 2% to 5%, paid at the time the loan is paid off.

Other characteristics you want to look for are the opportunities for increases in quarterly income as rents are adjusted for the CPI and a percentage of the gain on property value.

This is nothing more than cutting out the middlemen—the banks, and the insurance companies—and investing directly in what makes them the most money. Why should you let the bank charge 12% to lend your money for a mortgage and then pay you only 6%?

For minimums of $1000 for IRAs or $5000 for investors, you can choose from a government-guaranteed participating mortgage fund like American Insured Mortgages (AIM) or a nongovernment issue like Resources Pension Share (RPS) or Balcor Pension Investors (BPI), which generally bring a slightly higher return to compensate for the additional risk. There's even a zero coupon participating mortgage partnership to lock in your reinvestment rate (over 12% in February 1987) like Resources Accrued Mortgages (RAM). (AIM, RPS, and RAM were developed and sponsored by Integrated Resources. BPI was developed by Balcor/American Express.)

Some of these plans are specifically designed for retirement plans such as IRA, pension, and profit sharing, while others diversify their funds with one-half participating mortgages and one-half all-cash real estate to provide taxable investors with enough depreciation write-offs to shelter their income taxes. Determine your objectives and invest accordingly. Finally, you can receive a good income with an inflation hedge as well.

Figure 6-4 represents some examples I have seen through the years:

Figure 6-4

AMERICAN MORTGAGES FOR RETIREMENT PLAN (1984)

Average Cash on Cash*	Average Deferred Interest*†	Average Simple Return‡
12.48%	6.07%	18.55%
14.50%	5.78%	20.28%
14.02%	4.25%	18.27%
13.35%	4.59%	17.94%

*current cash flow (that which you receive on a quarterly basis—now)
†accrues and is not received until the fourth and up to the eighth year
‡in addition to this simple return, there is normally a 10% to 30% portion of the increased property value that investors (you) in this partnership will receive (assuming the value did increase) and you do *not* share in loss unless loan cannot be repaid.

Of course, for those more conservative-minded individuals, the government-backed participating mortgage funds would appear to be even more appropriate. Although you may expect a rate of return of 9% to 13% in today's market, it may at least give you extra peace of mind to know there is less credit risk within those funds.

An interesting combination of two types of partnerships was born recently when 50% of the money raised by the sponsoring company (Balcor/American Express) was put into equity participation mortgages and 50% into purchasing apartments for all cash. In this situation, the retirement plan investors received 33% more income than the nonpension investors. (You could purchase this for an IRA or pension or for yourself outside of any plan.) In return, the nonpension investors received 100% of the real estates' depreciation, since the pension investors could not utilize it. The final makeup of this trust had nonpension investors earning 8% income, fully tax-sheltered, along with additional excess write-offs to offset taxes on other income. This would continue to occur over the next few years. The pension investors received 10% to 12% while expecting an additional 3% to 6% from property value increases.

These plans are opportunities to hedge against inflation by owning real estate. Remember: *most wealth in the United States has been created through the real estate business.* Rarely can we be smart enough to get in on the ground floor of the next IBM; you must to some extent rely on money managers to spot the next stock trend. You must let experts in the real estate field do the same.

A special type of real estate investment emerged successfully in the late 1970s. Storage warehouse partnerships have been created to take advantage of man's desire to accumulate while smaller houses are being built. These "mini-warehouses" have caught on rapidly throughout the country. Originally they were supposed to be low-cost-per-unit buildings on a potentially attractive commercial property, generating a positive cash flow and tax benefits while awaiting the underlying real estate to appreciate. After the ten- to fifteen-year holding period, the properties would then be sold, the inexpensive mini-warehouses demolished, and the property put to better use.

Only recently have these first mini-warehouse deals begun to reach their maturities. Investors whom I placed in these programs in 1977—even though the real estate market has been poor in the '80s—are finding that their $10,000 investments on which they had been receiving an average of more than 20% cash flow for the past few years are now going through their first property sales. Now they are being returned an average of $35,000 for every

$10,000 investment made, while still maintaining an equity position in some of the properties. It would be impossible to forget how insane my clients thought I was when I first presented them with what I considered an innovative idea long before the craze developed. Now mini-warehouses have become a part of American life. Other trends in which investors can reap an even greater return remain to be identified.

Deferred Salary—The Best Thing Since Paid Vacations?

With salary reduction plans in force, employers retain and invest part of participants' salaries or bonuses. (Employees who opt to receive their full pay in cash, of course, are not participants.) The deferred pay, plus whatever it earns, goes untaxed for the employee until he or she finally receives it. This allows the funds to compound tax-free to greatly enhance the investment return.

Ordinarily, distribution is expected to occur after retirement, but the funds can be withdrawn earlier in certain cases of financial hardship. The IRS has yet to spell out just what constitutes financial hardship, but speculation is that the term will cover medical bills, purchase of a home, and education expenses. Employees can also borrow from a 401(k) account if the plan permits. The maximum an employee can have deferred is $7000 per year. Salary reduction plans do not rule out individual retirement accounts—an employee can have both. Some CPAs consider 401(k) plans superior to IRAs and suggest if only one of the two is affordable that it be 401(k). For taxpayers not permitted to have an IRA, these plans become indispensable.

The deferred salary may be invested in companies tax-qualified plans such as profit-sharing, stock bonuses, and other arrangements for the benefit of employees. There must be a formal program, however, that meets the requirements of section 401(k). One requirement is that a minimum percentage of a company's employees participate in the plan. Salary reduction could have an unfavorable effect on an employee's other benefits, such as group term insurance. Insurance coverage might be reduced if it were based on the regular paycheck. Salary reduction because of this deferral does not reduce pension benefits based on salary.

Employers, too, benefit from 401(k) plans by helping to provide for the financial security of employees at little cost to themselves—much less than they might spend on traditional retirement programs.

Your CPA can advise, of course, whether and how a 401(k) plan might be affected by state and local taxes.

Later we will discuss methods of receiving tax-free income instead of taxable dollars and how to use tax shelters and special techniques to lower your tax bites. Other possibilities exist which will be described briefly:

1. Repositioning taxable funds to a family member for future use in a lower tax bracket via tax-deferred annuities, variable-life plans, or prepaid college tuition funds.
2. Incorporating to utilize pretax dollars to pay for health, life, or disability insurance as well as other fringe benefits.
3. Converting ordinary income from dividends, interest and capital gains tax-deferred plans that allow tax-free compounding and special tax-free "borrowing" provisions.
4. Avoiding Social Security taxes by establishing a family-run Subchapter S corporation to receive dividends and not ordinary income.
5. Turning hobbies into tax benefits.

Large-Corporation Savings Plans and Stock-Purchase Plans

Today many corporations offer special retirement savings plans whereby employees can add up to 6% of their gross incomes into a tax-deferred savings plan and the employer matches (adds) up to half of your contributions. On a $30,000 salary this may be investing $1800 in a tax-deferred fund whereby your employer adds $900! A 50% first-year return! After meeting a certain vesting schedule of participation in the plan (usually being in the plan five to ten years), investors will be able to utilize these funds, though usually at retirement. Stock-purchase plans may allow employees to purchase shares of a firm's stock at up to a 15% discount on the current market price without paying any commission. This can be a particularly attractive way to accumulate corporate stock, averaging the price paid over a long tenure of peaks and valleys with a corporation. And as long as the corporation is healthy, it may prove to return very handsomely for you.

Do be careful, however, since some corporations have very strange policies as to when you are allowed to pull out of these plans. I heard of one with requirements that to withdraw your stock from the plan, you first had to prove that you had an income equal to what the value of your stock annuitized would give you on a monthly basis.

Self-Employed or Incorporated Individuals

There exists today a variety of specialized plans for those in business for themselves which begins with the Keogh Plan and may have more technical names such as Defined Benefit and Defined Contribution Plans, or Employees Stock Option Plans (ESOPs). Moreover, there are other techniques, particularly for corporation owners, to turn over the business that they've worked a lifetime for at the most advantageous tax rate possible. Remember, the importance of saving on current taxes is not always paramount. The ability to invest and diversify your monies is also a key freedom that you should have.

I remember one client who, upon selling his business, was forced into a special holding company whereby the only sensible investment was to move all these proceeds, representing over 80% of his entire net worth, into the stock market. He felt very uncomfortable. Of course in an up market, one just smiles at how good things can be. Yet to risk putting so many eggs in one basket in later life can be frightening indeed. Laws constantly change in these areas. As part of your annual study, you must bone up on major changes that may affect you. You'll want to limit investments in some areas and pour more into others, depending on these changes.

There are of course skeptics who think that IRAs, pension plans, and similar investments are undesirable. Here is an article I spotted several years ago:

Thirteen Reasons Not to Invest in IRAs

[The following is reprinted from *Information USA*, Special Report, No. 16, pp. 1–2, by Matthew Lesko.]

> *1. $1,000,000 in 30 years is worth only $15,100 today!* That's right. All the advertisements that promise to make you a millionaire in 30 years if you invest in their IRA don't tell you what $1,000,000 will be worth in 30 years. The same percentage of interest they assume to pay you over these 30 years will also work against you in inflation. Here are the facts:
>
> • At an inflation rate of 10%, it is the same amount as having $57,300 today.

- At an inflation rate of 15%, it is the same amount as having $15,100 today.
- At an inflation rate of 20%, it is the same amount as having $4,200 today.

2. *Your tax bracket will be 50% higher in 30 years.* The ads tell you to put away tax-free dollars now so that you can spend them later when you will be in a lower tax bracket. But consider these factors:

- In 30 years, do you want to be making less money than you are now? If you don't, then this sales pitch doesn't hold for you.
- If you spend $1,000,000 over 20 years of your retirement, that means your taxable income will be $50,000 per year. Is that lower than the tax bracket you are in now?
- Over the next 30 years, the average tax rate is likely to increase by 50.5 percent based on the rate at which the taxes have risen over the past three decades.

3. *A hefty 10% penalty plus taxes for early withdrawal.* If you take out any money before age 59½, you will be hit with a hefty 15% penalty. That means if you withdraw $10,000 at age 50 it will cost you $1500 plus the extra tax on $10,000 additional income.

4. *No down payment for a house, money to go to school, or funds to start a business.* You cannot use your money in an IRA as collateral for anything. If you are saving to buy a home or to someday start your own business, you're stuck. You cannot use the money for collateral against a loan, and if you take it out you pay the penalty.

5. *There are wiser investments and better tax breaks.* An IRA may not offer the best investment opportunity or tax shelter. Consider other investments such as:

- income producing property;
- an advanced degree that improves or maintains your skills;
- your own business which offers what is probably today's best tax shelter.

6. *You have no leverage on your investment money.* One of the best ways of making money on your investments is by using other people's money. For instance, mortgages in real estate or margin accounts for investing in stocks and commodities. The laws governing IRAs eliminate all investment purchases requiring debt.

7. *You will miss out on some of the biggest investment opportunities of the 1980s.* Having your money locked in an IRA precludes you from some of the biggest investment opportunities during the '80s. Besides not being able to invest in leveraged real estate or brokerage house margin accounts, you also cannot invest in the following: metals, art, stamps, rugs, gold & silver bullion, antiques, whiskey, gems, coins (under the 1986 Tax Revision Act, gold and silver coins issued by the US are allowable), collectibles.

8. *No losses may be claimed.* Unlike ordinary investments, you cannot claim losses against other gains. For example, an investor who opens a self-directed IRA with a broker may decide to take an extremely risky investment in hopes of high tax-deferred earnings, but if this fails, the investor could conceivably lose a great deal or all IRA funds and may not benefit from claiming this loss.

9. *All IRAs are not safe.* Bank IRAs are insured by various federal agencies up to $100,000 per account. Mutual funds are not insured and brokerage house IRA accounts are insured only up to the current market value of the stock and bonds in the portfolio. If your stocks take a plunge, so do you.

10. *Management fees and commissions.* IRA plans set up with mutual funds, brokerage houses or insurance companies will normally require a management fee plus any brokerage commissions involved. Management fees can run from a minimum of $50/year to one percent of your assets invested.

11. *You lose investment flexibility.* Although you can transfer your account from one IRA to another, you close off most investment options as described in Reasons #4, #5, #6, #7, #8, and #10.

12. *Who knows what the future holds?* No one can predict what will be economically viable or beneficial in the next five years, let alone what will be a wise investment 30 years from now. Remember back in the '50s how good and secure Social Security appeared to be?

These criticisms are valid. But to fully understand the purpose of an IRA, you must realize that there is absolutely no guarantee that there is ever going to be adequate purchasing power with this money. Nonetheless, you must build a nest egg for survival in retirement, and the best way to do that is through an IRA plan. An IRA permits you not only large tax benefits but a chance to see your money grow without any current income taxes being paid. Compare IRA benefits with investing in any other type of plan.

Where else can we get the flexibility to go into real estate partnerships and earn tax-deferred income, or to trade stocks and buy bonds at high, normally taxable rates and let profits compound in our account on a tax-deferred basis? From a comparative basis, no matter what the final worth of the money is, I do not believe there is any place you can do much better. Despite his arguments, Lesko also said, "Many government and economic forecasters predict that the nation's Social Security system will run out of funds. In addition, it is doubtful that Social Security alone can support an individual at retirement. This makes investment in an IRA worthwhile."

Sheen's Reasons Why It's Smart to Invest in an IRA

1. Expecting 15% inflation when we've never seen it and it's running at 2% is absurd. If our current deflation continues, your $1,000,000 may be worth more! Even if inflation continued at 5% to 10%, you would still have substantial purchasing power if your money was properly invested with nest egg investing strategies. Lesko fails to note the huge compounding effect of tax savings. That alone may add up to an additional quarter of a million dollars in benefits compounded over a lifetime.

2. Your tax bracket may be 50% lower in thirty years! With tax brackets now indexed to inflation, today's income level will produce lower taxes as time and inflation move along. The average personal income tax rate has not increased at all in the past four years.

3. The penalty may be worth it. The ability to compound without taxes is the world's eighth wonder. However, even though every IRA should be considered for a long term, things don't always work out that way. For example, consider the case of an investor in a 28% bracket who has put the maximum allowed into his or her IRA for the past five years. Since he's in the 28% bracket, he's saved $2800 in taxes on his contribution alone. And that's not counting whatever his IRA money may have earned.

Now our investor is out of work and he or she needs that IRA money. The current penalty for early withdrawal is 15%. Assume our investor's lowered earnings drop him into the 15% tax bracket. He can pay the penalty along with his 15% tax and not be any worse off had he not contributed to his IRA.

Remember that even if you are in a lower tax bracket, you can invest in an IRA and over a minimum of five years still be able to pay the penalty for early withdrawal plus tax *and* actually save money over what you would have paid in tax on income without an IRA.

Also keep in mind that even if your income remains constant, your tax bracket may drop more than 10%, again offsetting the penalty.

4. *Money you can't easily fritter away.* Not being able to use your IRA monies for routine purchases or collateral is an excellent way to enforce savings. The US, by the way, historically has one of the lowest rates of savings in the industrialized world. Tax benefits you get each year more than offset some of the disadvantages in not easily gaining access to your IRA money. I expect the US to eventually follow Canada's lead with similar programs by allowing use of these retirement funds for downpayments on homes. As this growing portion of savings becomes ever more important, I'm certain Washington will find additional ways for taxpayers to stimulate the economy through use of IRA money.

5. *Are there wiser investments and better tax breaks?* There are *no* wiser investments or better tax breaks. IRAs are an integral part of the best investment opportunities and tax shelters. Consider that within your IRA you could (1) have income-producing properties, (2) save enough in taxes to get an advanced degree for maintaining or sharpening your skills, (3) be able to invest in other businesses through investment trusts and limited partnerships, (4) invest in government securities and get a tax deduction for doing so while paying no current taxes while compounding.

6. *You have no leverage on your investment money.* Since America seems bent on using leverage, and since too much leverage in a retirement plan can produce inadvertent tax penalties, the IRA becomes an important part of your financial investment foundation. It is invested in all cash and is a conservative base that every investor should establish. Also, remember the laws governing IRAs do not eliminate all investment purchases requiring debt. Through buying different stocks, you can invest in companies that have gone into debt within their corporation for you. That won't reflect within your IRA, yet you can take advantage of the leveraged growth situation.

7. *You will* not *miss out on the biggest investment opportunities of the '80s.* Although there are a number of invest-

ments currently not permitted for IRAs, it is vital that any investor portfolio be well diversified. Those misguided people who do not invest in IRAs because they cannot invest in everything might say you should never own real estate because you can't qualify for a highly leveraged million-dollar tax check. It is easy enough to find different stocks for mutual funds which profit from the increase in prices of those prohibited investment vehicles and participate in these same markets using different investment vehicles.

8. No losses may be claimed. A true negative is not being able to deduct any losses. Yet this helps qualify the type of investments made within this portion of your nest egg to maximize safety and income rather than relying on speculative gains.

9. IRAs are a safe investment. Bank IRAs are insured, and government mutual funds are government guaranteed. Stocks usually carry no guarantee. Yet, through using special retirement plans with different insurance companies, you are guaranteed to never get back less than the funds you have deposited. Funds such as the Integrated Capital Appreciation Plan that gives investors an array of leveraged securities, stock funds, money market funds, bond funds and high-yield funds as well as others such as the Keystone 100, through a Traveler's subsidiary, all ensure that one's beneficiaries would never get back less than the amount deposited. It is not a question of whether an IRA is safe or not, but rather of how you invested your money and what degree of safety those investments carry.

10. Management fees and commissions can be tax-deductible. Most setup fees for establishing your IRAs can be paid with money that is not part of your contribution, yet you may be able to deduct these costs on your tax return depending on your income and total fees paid. When dealing with mutual funds, and particularly the variable annuities that give you a family of funds to choose from, there are many funds with no initial sales charges. In those cases, 100% of your money is put to work for you. Nothing in life is free. To get top management for your assets, you should count on spending up to 2% per year. But considering the 4% to 5% annual charge made by the banks (50% of your annual return), and their low returns, these figures are quite reasonable.

11. You do not lose investment flexibility. Through your IRA, you can contribute into stocks, bonds, real estate limited partnerships, participating mortgages, CDs, money market funds, gross mutual funds, income mutual funds, foreign mutual funds, specialized mutual funds in gold or health care or electronics or energy. Through the use of mutual funds, investment trusts, and limited partnerships, IRA holders are able to enter into such a wide array of investments as to render our opponent Matthew Lesko's objections absurd.

12. Who knows what the future holds? No one. Nonetheless, preparing for your retirement while receiving current tax benefits and building an estate for yourself and your family is vital. This government-subsidized savings program is a must for any American who does not want to depend on the willy-nilly policies of the politicians. IRAs should be an essential portion of your overall nest egg investment portfolio.

Conclusion

There is only one way to win the tax game—know and apply the rules. If you don't, you're penalized; if you do, you're rewarded. Not utilizing the expertise of your CFP, CPA, and possibly your tax attorney is foolish. Using only one of these can also be unwise, since each has particular expertise. Unless you plan to make a full-time job of keeping up on the new tax laws and alternative investments, you must put together an investment team to help protect your nest egg from the wolves.

7. The Price of Wealth

When living in Boston a number of years ago, I shared my Brookline Castle apartment with three roommates. In our upstairs suite, Scott created a beautiful environment and worked diligently at his nine-to-five job. Realizing he was getting nowhere at work and that he was not achieving his lifelong dream of becoming a lawyer, he started putting away all the money possible. Then, living frugally, he went back to school full time to fulfill his dream. He'd worked many years to save the money for law school. When he finally enrolled, Scott found it tough. He studied day and night for three years to earn his degree. Sometimes he became discouraged and considered giving up, but he saw it through. He found no difficulty in securing a job. Within five years he was a well-known, successful attorney in his community, earning almost three times what he had previously made in a job he didn't like.

My other roommate, David, was in different circumstances. Bored with college, he had gotten himself specially trained to program microcomputers, and had identified some trends in the Boston area among emerging companies that were taking over the market. He ended up specializing in microcomputers for a company that had the lion's share of the market and was earning a comfortable living by consulting and setting up programs for little companies. One day he suddenly recognized a wonderful opportunity: the need of basic computer programs for small businesses using microcomputers. There was little competition. He longed to tap this market, yet it seemed impossible to work his job and still create these programs. By chance, along came Arnold—a friend with no direction—who was looking for something to do. David proposed that they team up to create and market these software packages. His friend knew nothing about computers or programming, so how could they undertake such a task? Refusing to accept defeat, they hashed out a plan. David worked all day to support them while he trained his friend on computer programming in the evenings. They shared a room and expenses to get their new project off the ground. The quarters weren't all that comfortable, and no doubt their social life was greatly curtailed. Sometimes their inventiveness in finding girlfriends with apartments of their own rescued nights when logistics broke down. They worked diligently. David's friend caught on quickly and before long was making great progress. Months passed, and long hours into the morning were not uncommon as they began to create and assemble their software packages.

Finally the time came for marketing the programs. Soon their idea paid off. Within months things started moving so rapidly that they hired new people to expand. Within two years they moved to California to set up a nationwide distribution network and found themselves running a multimillion-dollar company. Before long they both sold their stock in the business and retired. They were now wealthy. David went off to start all over again on the East Coast, and his friend left to enjoy the fruits of his labors for which he had labored so hard. The long hours, the discouraging obstacles that they overcame, the persistent and unwavering toil, resulted in success. They took advantage of an opportunity that later might not have existed. Today the market is saturated with software programs, since entrepreneurs throughout the country have jumped on the bandwagon.

Julian, on the other hand, paid his dues a different way. Criticized and ridiculed for his apparently bizarre style in painting, he was insecure and lacking in direction. Finally, after many vicissitudes, he immersed himself in the SoHo art scene in Manhattan. He lived in shabby quarters and surrounded himself with some of the greatest young artists the world has yet to recognize, painting and establishing contacts in the art world.

Year after year he labored in poverty. Eventually he was recognized and was featured in *The New York Times Magazine*. His works were praised as masterpieces throughout the world, and every exhibition was pre-sold.

I could go on endlessly relating success stories that I've observed over the years and with which I have had the good fortune to be associated. Possibly some of your own of friends have moved out of the old neighborhood to the classier side of town or have attained financial success. These people were without exception dedicated and hardworking. They worked not by the clock or under the standards of anyone else but their own. Each was self-driven toward the completion of a task that was his or her life's commitment. It seemed that they always were busy making something happen, whether setting trends in their field or reading of previous successes, whether studying their competition to find strong points whereby they learned or examining weak points to capitalize on, or staying with a project for fourteen or sixteen hours a day, for a month, a year, or longer, to realize their visualization of achievement. Success must be paid for.

It is interesting to note how so many men and women who have become rich soon realize the lack of fulfillment money brings. Pleasure from mere material objects can be fleeting. Sooner or later many successful people look inward and understand that the only three meaningful and lasting facets of life are faith, hope, and love.

As you pursue your road to success, remember that the price of wealth will be too high if you have to sacrifice your beliefs and values. But neither should you fall for the myth that there is an inherent dignity in poverty or failure.

As you seek wealth, keep in mind the following practical pointers:

Credit Cards Can Be a Deadly Habit

The misuse of credit cards can place an unnecessary burden on an ambitious young man or woman. True, there are occasions on which it is important to maintain a prosperous image, or reward yourself for an achievement by dining out or buying something you've always wanted. However, overuse of credit cards can saddle you with intolerable monthly payments and put a strain on your budget—a strain that can shake or destroy a marriage. Living below your means while saving to go into a new enterprise will pay off in the long run.

The Only-One Syndrome

As I review my own career and life, I recall that it was often difficult to share my experiences, particularly when I was considering going far out on a limb—taking major risks while looking for major rewards. There seemed to be no one on a comparable level who was heading in a similar direction. Unfortunately, those who would have been best to communicate with at this point were competitors!

Talking things over with yourself and others you respect is vital. Seek out colleagues—even competitors, if trust can be established—to share your thoughts with. Friendships are essential; isolation is too high a price for success.

I found communicating with God to be even more important in coping with this "only-one" feeling. While I'm not attempting to proselytize, I would recommend knowing God to anyone. You will find it easy to open up and discuss your problems and projects for the future.

Danger Signals

Major changes in your sleeping, eating, or sexual habits could signal stress overtaking you. Be sure to give yourself the leisure and the time to create intimate relationships. Don't always be on the run. Granted, there may be times when that isn't possible. But if your life is merely boredom, with no interest in your job, friends, or family, it might be time to prioritize your different life-style possibilities and evaluate what is contributing to and what is detracting from your life. Consider which other areas you need to work into to stimulate and motivate yourself. Being overly angry with the world may be just an indication that you are beginning to be pushed downward; perhaps you're trying to swim against too strong a tide. Although fantasizing is desirable in helping you develop new dreams and projects, overindulgence in the desire to run away can be harmful. So can resenting your work or feeling indispensable at it. All may indicate that you need to reset your job priorities and realign expectations of yourself and your career. There are apt to be times when you are tired, overworked or exhausted: reluctant to reassess your life. But if you keep planning your schedule, you eventually will have time for a housecleaning of expectations and building of your future. You may have to move on to other areas. Through proper delegation of job responsibilities, you can recharge your batteries by moving into a less stressful area that you enjoy.

The price of wealth may be great and can cause many personal and family stresses and strains. Yet when properly understood and dealt with, these can all be used to help strengthen an individual and a family. Review earlier chapters where we discussed goal setting and communication to ensure that a good support group is built up for you.

8. Beware of the Booby Trap

Elephants are among the most powerful creatures on earth. But have you ever noticed how they are kept docile by a chain around their leg that is attached to a stake? Surely you don't believe that this huge animal, capable of ripping down circus tents, cannot pull away from a mere chain and stake. Well, of course, he could. Yet he doesn't even try. Why not? Because, as a baby elephant, before he became so strong, trainers chained his leg to a stake. When he wanted to run off and play (as do all children), he would keep trying to pull away, cutting his leg and causing pain. Eventually he realized that attempts to run away meant pain and failure. So he stopped trying.

The same concept applies to fleas at a flea circus. First being put beneath a glass cage, they hit the cage and hurt themselves when trying to fly away. Quickly they learn their limitations for safe flying. Soon the glass container can be removed and the fleas will not try to escape.

Are you like an elephant or a flea? Do you find yourself caught up waiting to collect your retirement benefits in ten, fifteen, or twenty years so that *then* you can go about enjoying yourself? Do you want to be in full control of your deepest destiny, making key decisions instead of following those made by others? Don't you want to set your own directions and manage your own success? Looking for job security and financial contentment may bring emotional insecurity, and living in a nice house and driving a nice car surely won't compensate for that.

A trainee can start out in an entry position at between $20,000 and $40,000 per year, and over time he or she could double or triple that. The years go by, income goes up, and he or she starts moving toward higher ground. Life seems to be going well. Ten years later the $25,000 annual salary is $60,000, and he or she is due to move up with the company. Within three years he's promoted, even though this means moving to a new location that he doesn't particularly like. Still, he's been promised that if he does well there, he'll probably be able to return with a promotion to the home office. Sure enough, twenty-two years have gone by now and he or she has done well. Salary is up to $110,000 and he's brought back to the home office at a raise to $130,000. He's now a vice president and life seems fine.

Sound like a nice story? Nevertheless, had this career employee undertaken more risk instead of being a "renter" within a corporation, or had he more wisely negotiated his abilities, he could have done far better.

If you take a job at $25,000 and twenty-two years later earn $150,000, a 7% average rate of inflation for only the last ten years would mean that the $150,000 you're receiving twenty-two years from now would have a purchasing power in today's terms of only $37,500. Over twenty-two years your income will have increased only 50%! Is that amount worth fighting in the trenches most of your life?

And, when you retire, unless you have used some of your money toward purchasing company stock, the results of your hard work will be enjoyed by other people. Fortunately, many stock-purchase plans are available. Yet you might ask if three or four hundred thousand dollars' worth of stock represents your value to that company over twenty-two years? If, instead, you had purchased a good piece of income property, your money might have increased ten times over during that same period.

Avoiding the Pitfalls

Don't work for others unless the job permits you to grow and to demonstrate initiative. Your work should allow you to take on new challenges while moving laterally or upward as opportunities arise or as you create them. Begin with a top corporation in whatever field you plan to succeed in. The training you'll receive will be important to help develop good work habits and to learn how the biggest in the industry operate. This will enable you to develop future strategies once you understand your top competitor's strengths and weaknesses. This is a great advantage. Corporations such as IBM, Xerox, and General Motors have excellent reputations for special training programs. As a result they have spawned many of their own competitors. After receiving an inside look into the industry leaders, you are better equipped to compete. Quickly determine the area that you want to concentrate on and learn all you can. Do not disperse your attention too widely since that can add many years toward the realization of your goals.

Once you've been trained and have mastered the basics of the corporation (and this could be anywhere from one to five years), look to trade up your position. Major competitors in the industry that could utilize your experience and training are your ace in the hole. If you have performed well and have special training your competitors need and are aware of, they will be interested in using your talents (without the cost of training) *and* get an inside look at their competitor. You usually are able to increase your salary by 25% to 50%, which is the minimum to make a worthwhile switch. Further, you want the chance for a 50% to 100% increase within one to three years to bother with such a move. If you can build up your credentials and track record, your training and expertise in your field after two or three switches of this nature, you will have the inside track on 50% to 60% of the competitors controlling the market in which you want to operate. By developing either the reputation necessary to raise money, or having put aside enough money yourself, go into business for yourself. You can compete aggressively, knowing your competitors' soft spots and where your strong areas are, and can take advantage of their weaknesses.

Just as a free agent makes best use of his or her limited time in the big leagues to negotiate better salaries and contracts, so should you try to become a top hitter and utility player, which creates proven worth and value to a team's efforts to win a pennant and get to the series. Consistency, experience, and training speak very loudly in the marketplace, particularly when companies are experiencing problems and need to look elsewhere for solutions. I am reminded of a neighbor who recently left a top post at IBM to move to a large computer company which had experienced major losses over the past few years, jeopardizing its future. When asked why he would leave such a long and secure tenure at IBM to undertake a risky venture with an ailing corporation, his response couldn't have been more in line with my own personal thinking. He said he could imagine the possibility of becoming the Lee Iacocca of the computer industry. He knew the reward could be great—personally and financially.

I know my suggestions fly right into the jaws of the recently praised Japanese corporate philosophy. But my Western aggressiveness and impatience demand that I believe man should reach out, create, and fulfill the limits of his own personality and abilities. Only by being willing to step away from the crowd and take the heat on your own can you truly test your strength and convictions. Also, unless you keep pace with the changes around you, business trends can turn negative in your field. Many long-term employees, for example, in steel, farm equipment, and automobile manufacturing are out of jobs. The only true safety and security in life is that of knowing how to reap the benefits of your capabilities. The emergence of the service and information eras will transform into Edsels many old faithfuls who sought security in size.

YOU as an Investment

You are an investment. Investing in yourself includes continuing education, specialized training, and reading, listening, and watching trends. Learning is the key to gaining knowledge and power: learning to choose your friends, your work, and the efforts you expend. Each adds value to you. Corporate executives reading this book, if not already angered to the point of throwing it down, should recognize that more new jobs are created and more impetus given to our economy by small businesses than by large ones.

Incorporating

Incorporating is a legal procedure whereby you officialize a business venture by forming a corporation (that is, by creating a set of bylaws, board of directors, and shareholders—all of which can be yourself). After paying a small registration fee to your state, and possibly to your city and county, you may go into business within this corporate entity. It is no longer you, John (or Joan) Smith, operating the business, it is John (or Joan) Smith, Inc. Why go to this expense and trouble? Well, very simply, for this reason: (1) If John (or Joan) Smith, Inc., acquires large amounts of debt and defaults on it, your personal property is protected from creditors; (2) John (or Joan) Smith, Inc., may now sell portions of his or her business to other investors. This allows you to raise money without borrowing. It can also be beneficial to attract and help keep good employees. As the corporation grows, you can offer a stock-purchase plan. This permits you to sell your interest in the company to your hardworking, committed employees. Special ESOP plans allow this to be done with pretax money. You can receive medical insurance and $50,000 of life insurance in *pretax* dollars. The corporation purchases it, saving you $500 to $1000 a year. You create equity buildup within your corporation: the goodwill, the accounts, the furniture, the various company assets that can now be sold on a corporate basis. You can even sell some or most of the stock and still maintain a position in the company, offering a guiding hand even though not caught up in day-to-day operations.

This can lead to lucrative consulting contracts as part of your retirement. You can still collect a portion of the profits for some time into the future. As a corporate owner, you are now able to set up your own retirement plan and get whatever is most advantageous for *you* and not for the company. You can charge many business events to your expense account, since you answer only to yourself. To cover special schooling, you can set up educational reimbursement trusts to help pay for education with pretax dollars. The same goes for medical reimbursement trusts to be sure there are no out-of-pocket costs for your medical bills or medical insurance. You can employ family members, thereby spreading the income and allowing your spouse and children to utilize IRA accounts and be taxed at lower brackets. You create a separate entity to build credit and have two sources of borrowing; one personally and another through the business. This can be valuable if you undertake other ventures in the future.

Having been a management consultant for years, working with many small corporations as well as midsized and large ones, I can testify that it is no easy task to run your own business. You must assume many different responsibilities. The buck now stops with you: you take the rap for any misjudgments you make in the marketplace. But if you enjoy making things happen, watching a business grow, and are willing to accept full responsibility for success or failure, you can reap immense pleasures and attain financial security as well.

Not only will the tax benefits accrue along with the buildup of personal equity in your business, but you will be able to transfer this wealth created within your business to your children or your children's children. The two greatest sources of wealth that I have observed have stemmed from building a business or buying income real estate. Properly financed, and with hard work and imaginative marketing, the opportunity afforded by being in business for yourself is astounding.

I recall a television interview in which we talked about finance, investing, and motivation. Afterward I learned that the local television hostess was a bit envious of me. Although she had been in TV for only a few years, she had already established a good reputation. But she still was not earning the income she desired. She longed to expand into other fields but just didn't see how. My view of her situation was completely different: I saw nothing but possibilities on her horizon. She could help train people for media appearances, do special marketing, or become a television consultant. She could produce for public relation firms, utilizing her familiarity with media techniques. Other possibilities for her staggered my imagination at the time. Yet, with her negative attitude and fear of risk, three years later she remains in the same job at the local television station and has no plans for immediate advancement.

Leapfrogging

Your training and work experience are valuable and need to be properly marketed. Many retirees have turned into part-time consultants, demanding and getting large hourly fees. Never forget the long-term perspective; if you keep at it, you can make major changes in your life-style.

Be careful of the "golden handcuffs" of pension and profit-sharing plans. These long-term traps laid by corporations are to discourage you from bailing out. If you have been with one of these firms for a while, you may already be vested in a number of their plans, and you should be able to take your money and move it to an IRA rollover account or transfer it into a new pension plan. Or you may want the money to help go into business for yourself. See your financial planner and a management consultant familiar with these procedures.

I am reminded of one client who, having worked with a major computer concern for many years, had an opportunity to join a new firm started by former employees of IBM. It was a small group, and in order to bring in his expertise, he was granted special stock options and an immediate stake in the company. Showing true pioneer spirit, he took this bold step and went into business. Things went well at first, but within a few years there was a turnaround. The pioneers were on the brink of bankruptcy. Fortunately the expertise and respect they had built up in that short period of time, and the potential tax benefits of being purchased with a loss carry-forward, made it attractive to another regional computer company. Although the firm was disbanded, it was bought, and the transaction involved over a million dollars. A nice reward for having failed. Even failure can lead to success.

True security does not consist in falling in line with the rest of the crowd to join the ranks of the corporate-ladder climbers. Corporate life may give you the security of knowing that there will always be food on your plate, but you may find your dreams fading fast. Leapfrogging or forming your own corporation are two ways to derive as much wealth as possible from your work experience, talents, and training. With the right blueprint, persistent implementation, and a burning desire, you can avoid the comfortable trap of nine-to-five and turn your ambitions into piles of gold.

9. Failing Your Way to the Top

We often take life too much for granted. Your biggest risk of failure stems from being one of the forty-nine out of fifty persons who will retire without an adequate nest egg.

Failure is part and parcel of living. We are almost constantly confronted by our own and the failures of others. Failures drain your vitality the way overuse deadens a battery. Each one lowers your energy and siphons your oomph. Success, however, recharges batteries and can actually increase your power. Fortunately it seems to take only one success to offset every three to five failures. If you run into a succession of failures when beginning a new project or job, you may be tempted to give up and never try again. Here one must begin to understand the importance of what "average" means. It is a word that should give you encouragement to go on and on, failing repeatedly before ever deciding to quit. In order to build an average, it is vital to make as many attempts as possible. Think of it this way: In baseball, every team member starts with a zero batting average. No at bats, no hits. Every day players step up to the batter's box, attempting to get their first, second, and third hits. Whether you get to bat and miss twenty times in a row or never get up to the box at all, you are still batting zero. Yet if after twenty attempts you get your first hit, you substantially increase your batting average. Even better, you've established a pattern of success to build upon.

This statistical reality extends far from the baseball diamond into the heart of American business and industry. Consider the epitaph on the milk-can-shaped tombstone of Gail Borden, the eccentric, persistent founder of Borden, Inc. It reads: "I tried and failed. I tried again and again and succeeded."

Don't give up on your dreams. Keep trying again and again. It is he or she who has persistence and dogged determination who will succeed. Remember, too, that each time you fail, you should get coaching or advice on what went wrong in order to strengthen yourself and not predispose yourself to fail that way again.

Remember, a baseball player who bats .350 is saying that 65% of the time when he comes to the plate, he will strike out, ground out, or fly out. Yet, for being right just 35% of the time, he can command a fabulous salary. So can you.

Meanwhile, remember that an individual who is right 25% of the time, thus batting .250, is categorized as marginal. The player needs to capitalize on how he or she got that 25% to increase it to 35% and thus become a high-salaried player.

Watch children learning how to walk. All the effort they keep putting in on standing and falling, standing and falling, eventually pays off.

Failure is a necessary element in living since it turns on the energy and lets it flow between the two terminals of negative and positive. One without the other is worthless, and we become powerless if there is no interplay. Much like the yin and yang of Eastern philosophy, and the apparent attraction between opposites. Unless you charge yourself between the positives of success and the negatives of failure, you can never have the energy to build your nest egg. You must maintain a positive attitude of humility and self-criticism to be able to understand your responsibilities for failure and learn how to improve your handling of similar situations the next time.

Consider the practice of any skill, whether it be playing the piano or computer programming. Making a mistake does not reinforce making another, but instead helps guide us toward making better moves. This brings us into today's wonderful world of technology, where we can scrutinize our every move, our every word. With a videotape recorder, a camera, or even a cassette player, we can make records of our performances—in sales, the performing arts, public speaking, sports, or whatever. After recording, we can critique our own work or bring in professional coaches to help us polish our efforts. Schools and advisory services abound throughout the country. There you can seek professional expertise in developing the finer points that can lead to success. Yet, doing things correctly *does* reinforce you to continue that pattern. If you repeatedly play a piece on a piano incorrectly, you would be able to identify the error and rework the passage, but once having played it properly you would find it easier to achieve success a second, third, and fourth time. Eventually it would be hard to envision how that passage ever caused you problems. This illustrates the importance of failure. Without ever reading the music and trying to play, you can never enjoy its benefits.

Failing Your Way to the Top

Without ever investing in yourself or the different markets, you will never understand how the game is played. You'll be penalized from being able to play at all. Remember, even though you may run into a string of bad investments, it is deadly to say, "Well, gee, I invested in a real estate deal once and lost money so I will never do it again."

The key here is to invest money in smaller amounts in several deals so that even if a couple go belly-up, your profits from the others should more than compensate. You will have gained not only experience from both success *and* failure, but a good overall rate of return on your investments. One of the big mistakes many investors make is to get so excited about one opportunity that they fail to diversify.

Using the concept of averaging in investing, you should almost take a failure with a bit of pleased excitement since each one shows you are a little closer to success.

Let your profits run long to enjoy the success, and cut your losses when you see the trend moving away from your original expectations.

I like how the Chinese use the same symbol for crisis and opportunity. Crisis obviously signals a potential for failure. But that in itself becomes a great opportunity to learn, readjust, rethink, re-plan, and try again. Once you overcome the initial emotional reaction to a failure (real or prospective), snap to it. Concentrate, think positively, and keep dreaming about those winning investments while learning from those that go bad. Once you stop getting into the batter's box to swing, your average will be zero. In short, failing to try is trying to fail, just like failing to plan is planning to fail. *Don't ever be guilty of not trying.*

I have established a tradition of repeating to myself whenever my hopes are temporarily shattered or I encounter a setback, "The harder they hit me down, the higher up I bounce!" Develop your own favorite philosophical energizer.

Just because you've previously lost money in one investment area, doesn't mean *now* is not the time to reinvest in that same area. At a lower price, it might be wise for you to use the nest egg investment strategy for dollar cost-averaging. Let's say you've taken a hit after investing $10,000 in 100 units of a limited partnership. Your $10,000 is now worth $2000, representing an 80% loss in value. Dollar cost-averaging at this point would have you once again invest: $10,000 to buy 500 units (priced at $20 each) of the same partnership.

All told, you'd have 600 units at an average cost of $33 per unit. Your stock is depressed. By having bought 500 units so cheaply, you can show a profit if each unit rises to only $35 per share. Had you avoided acquiring more of that stock, taking your lumps with an 80% drop in valuation, you would have had to wait until the stock returned to $100 per share to merely break even. Now you see how dollar cost-averaging works.

Do this when your initial failure centers on poor timing rather than on other weaknesses in the investment. Remember, cars eventually had a major impact on the horse and buggy trade.

Once again: failing to try is trying to fail. If you think every job you land will work out and satisfy all your desires, or if you think every investment you make will turn into a bonanza, you are in for a rude awakening. Once you've experienced some hard knocks, don't shy away from re-entering the investment arena. Use your upgraded knowledge and personal experience with certain investment areas to chalk up some winners.

The key element to succeeding is: *After careful study, give it a go!* Try to see what it's like to score, and always have an alternate plan of attack should things not work out. Be willing to fail repeatedly, as long as you can edge closer to your goal. Over a lifetime, hitting just two out of ten puts you way ahead of those who never took a swing at all.

10. Going for the Gold—
The Golden Years

Let's examine the major steps you'll be taking to build your nest egg for personal financial independence.

At Age Twenty Begin To—

Fully assess the potential of your chosen profession and tailor your college studies accordingly. Check government and business studies on what supply and demand factors will be within the next decade or two. Then focus on specific areas and geographic locations where the most expansion can be expected.

Seek summer jobs in career areas in which you intend to specialize. Also, seek part-time work-study programs to gain practical experience that will complement your academic achievements. Such programs often help you get your foot in the door of the nation's top corporations.

List your goals and ambitions to ensure the above steps are in alignment. Start making lists of important connections you can make while still in school. (The parents of some of your classmates may hold key positions with various corporations.) Set up a network file for the future. Establish a correspondence list to keep your contacts informed of your educational progress and current goals. You can never have too much support.

Pursue all your coursework with practical applications in mind, and put particular emphasis on study areas that will be germane to your chosen field. Aim for at least 95% comprehension.

Earmark 10% of any spare dollars earned from work-study and summer jobs to invest. It's never too soon to focus on the workings of Main Street or Wall Street. Put your remaining available dollars in money market funds to help pay for your schooling and possible relocation after graduation.

Establish a résumé of school activities that may be directly related to some of your future responsibilities. (Being head of the law review would be a big plus when joining a legal firm; winning a science fair prize could spur an engineering or science career.)

Consider where you want to be in ten years and visualize the scene. Write this goal down and check to see if your plans based on these steps would help you achieve success. If not, re-evaluate and realign your plans until they more realistically point toward your ten-year goal.

Checklist for nest egg investors at age twenty:

- Coordinate your educational goals with career objectives. (For example, if projections show certain areas of engineering will be overcrowded within a decade, specialize in a less popular realm. Back up your major with a solid minor or advanced study in another field, say a masters in business administration.)
- Seek relevant job experience, no matter how lowly.
- Map out your goals.
- Identify key people who can help you achieve those goals.
- Begin your nest egg with an IRA, even if you can't contribute the full amount.
- Gaze beyond those halls of ivy to the business community at large to see how your civic and charitable endeavors can expand your network of contacts.
- Visualize your entire life, focusing on achievements you hope to have made at ten-year intervals.
- Above all, maintain your flexibility. (Attempting to carve your life in stone at age twenty can cause a lot of wheel spinning. Map out your destinations first and then figure out how to get there.)

If you feel stuck, or unable to progress, or feel that you can't move on, or have lost your desire to succeed, review the assessment chart to identify what was done wrong, what's missing, and what's really bothering you. See if reworking that portion of the overall plan will bring new life to your game plan for personal and financial success.

Goal-Debugging Assessment Chart

Attitude:
- Desire: Is the goal you are working toward really yours?
- Do the rewards justify the risks?
- Do you think that someone keeps blocking you, putting you down, or working against you?
- Do you think that you have failed too many times and that you will fail again?
- Do you think that you haven't networked with other successful people in your field?
- Do you find it difficult to keep up with career-related information? (Try speedreading.)
- Have you tried to improve by taking courses in communications skills?
- Have you made a total commitment?
- Do you think that you have other priorities, and this particular activity or goal can be postponed?
- Are you unable to set priorities and find yourself wasting time on less important matters?
- Are you unable to manage your time and feel out of control?
- Do you feel it is too late or that you are too old to succeed? (W. C. Fields didn't get started in films until his sixties, and George Burns reached his peak in his eighties.)

After working through the Assessment Chart to remove the barriers, proceed to the Development Evaluation Chart to get you back on course.

Development Evaluation

- Goals accomplished to date
- Goals not accomplished to date
- Priorities of goals set
- Target dates for completion
- Personal change and enhancement to date
- Personal change and enhancement needed in order to help increase abilities to reach set goals
- Obstacles currently in the way
- Solutions to overcome obstacles with set target date for accomplishment
- Rewards achieved to date

- Rewards not achieved but still desired (i.e., what rewards will you have by continuing to attain your goals)
- Resources used or resources used but not fully tapped

Use this checklist to help you begin a brainstorming session for establishing your action plan.

At Age Thirty Begin To—

Take a hard look at whether you enjoy your work and if it is helping you advance in your career. If not, what would you prefer to be doing? (If you must make a major career change, go back to Chapters 4 and 5 on creating a plan and revise or develop a new plan of attack.)

Assess the following areas:

(Note: to answer these questions, try to set aside a full day in an undisturbed location with no pressures. Relax, have your favorite meal, sip a quality wine if you like, and *think* about the questions.)

1. Write down major goals that you have reached thus far and feel good about. Which goals have not been reached?
2. Which personal resources have you utilized? Which have you underutilized? (list these).
3. What do you see as the next step for your career? Which obstacles stand in your way? Do you have a plan for overcoming them?

By thirty you should have enough work experience under your belt to know whether you've taken the right career path. Assuming you are on target, you now should be in a position to begin creating some type of equity within your business. Whether this be through stock options, profit-sharing, or other types of partnership agreements, you should have made your mark as an aggressive, trustworthy, and make-happen person. If your participation is not sufficient to achieve tangible ownership, you need to evaluate whether you are with the right company. Will it permit you to expand and eventually (if this is your goal) assume a leadership position? If leadership is not your aim, are there nest-egg-building opportunities based on your ability to excel at your present level?

You should have made ten contributions to an IRA account since age twenty, which should be worth between $30,000 and $50,000, depending on how you managed your investment. By thirty, you should also have positioned yourself geographically to both enhance your career and take advantage of property ownership. Your nest egg should be developing as you gain equity in your home and enjoy the tax benefits. By now you should have some advanced professional training and also a vast network of community contacts through civic or charitable endeavors for building your future.

If married, as your family matures, be sure that you have access to proper school facilities and the right kind of people to help enhance your children's education.

Checklist for nest egg investors at age thirty:

- Evaluate whether you've chosen the right career path, or for that matter the right career. (If not, regroup and create a new life plan.)
- Jot down goals you've reached.
- List personal resources you've utilized.
- Assess resources you've failed to fully plumb.
- Develop additional key steps to further your career.
- Evaluate obstacles and look for detours.
- Tally up your equity in the business: stock options, etc.
- Assess your equity in other nest egg investments such as a home.
- Determine whether your locale is suitable for career, lifestyle, and education of your children. (If not, look for greener pastures.)
- Remember that at thirty, you can capitalize on both the *successes* and the *failures* of the past decade to boldly move ahead toward personal reward and financial independence.

At Age Forty You Must—

Once again reassess your position and examine whether you are maximizing your opportunities. By this time you should have built substantial home equity, and your IRA account should be worth approximately $100,000. You now should have an additional $200,000 of equity built up in your firm through stock-purchase and corporate savings plans. You should be enjoying the status of a proven professional. Younger workers should be approaching you as a reliable source of advice. If germane, you should have garnered advanced degrees within your profession. You should have considered moving to the forefront with your opinions and expertise either through being accessible to the press or publishing your own works. (That old adage, publish or perish, can be applicable to more than academicians.) By now you should have developed your verbal skills to effectively act as a spokesman for your business, showcasing your expertise in your field. You should be familiar and comfortable with related professions.

Checklist for nest egg investors at age forty:

- Evaluate your progress over the past decade, reexamining key points in the previous checklist.
- Once again, tally up your equity in business, on the home front, and in your IRA, along with other investments. (Make adjustments or consult a financial planner if you feel your opportunities can be maximized even further.)
- On the business front, start reaping the benefits of being an expert in your field. (Capitalize on your two decades of experience, turning even mistakes to advantage by helping others who look up to you avoid them. Make yourself available to the press or publish articles yourself on subjects close to your heart.)
- If more education is desirable, go for it now. (You still have over two decades left in the marketplace for utilizing those credentials.)

By Age Fifty You Should—

Be reaching the zenith of your earning career. With $300,000 in your IRA account, $300,000 in your corporate pension and stock-participation plan, plus equity buildup, your nest egg should be developing quite nicely. You should begin looking toward retirement, developing an idea of exactly when to look for long-term consulting contracts to pursue after you "retire." Once again, you need to assess your goals to ensure that you are maximizing your resources and meeting your expectations. At the same time, you must determine whether you are achieving sufficient personal satisfaction. If you aren't happy with your life at fifty, get cracking on revising your game plan while you still can. With the children out of school, you are enjoying new freedom. Your personal savings are developing along with those enforced savings of your IRA, pension, and equity buildup. Chances are your house is paid for or mortgage-burning time is imminent. You may want to remortgage it and invest the proceeds to maximize your interest and deductions in these presumably peak earning years when your deductions have declined now that your children have left the nest. As responsibility and financial burdens for your children ease, you should be looking toward more personal fulfillment. Expand your horizons with travel and leisure activity.

Checklist for nest egg investors at age fifty:

- Increasingly monitor your nest egg development during these peak earning years.
- Look for new ways to shelter your income as you lose tax deductions for your children when they strike out on their own.
- If your mortgage has been satisfied, consider refinancing to gain both the tax advantage and additional capital for other investments.
- Now perhaps more than ever is a pivotal time to seek professional guidance for your investments and future security.
- Weigh your personal happiness quotient against your career success. (Put more emphasis on developing leisure interests that could prove rewarding down the road when career pressures ease.)

By Age Sixty It's Time—

To consider whether you want full or partial retirement. Can you utilize your expertise on a consultant basis to ease your demanding schedule and seize more opportunity for personal activities? Your IRA, which now has a million dollars, and your pension plan, which also has a million dollars, can easily provide a comfortable income. Depending on your tax bracket, prevailing tax laws and interest rates, you soon will decide whether to pay off your mortgage or continually refinance.

Checklist for nest egg investors at age sixty:

- Focus your thoughts on adopting a strategy for retirement, whether you plan on doing so at sixty-two, sixty-five, or eighty-five.
- Determine the viability of a partial retirement by which you keep a vested interest in your firm while turning over day-to-day operational responsibilities.
- Consider advantages to cutting the cord with your firm while establishing a new business as a consultant.
- Continue to scrutinize your nest egg investments for additional golden opportunities.

- Reexamine your entire estate and, considering tax liabilities, determine which steps you can take to ease the burden on your heirs.
- Finally, develop a plan for enjoying life and feeling like a winner after you no longer must put forty, sixty, eighty or more hours a week in on the job.

You're now on the verge of reaping the untold benefits of financial independence, thanks to the sound philosophies of nest egg investing.

11. Keeping Your Personal and Estate Affairs in Order

Maintain a place—whether it be a safe deposit box, a home safe, a desk drawer, or a shoebox in your closet—where your survivors can easily find copies of your will, any trusts you might have written up, and insurance policies on your life, your health, your home, and your car. Also include a list of your creditors, any debts or notes that you've signed or written, along with a safe deposit box key and the name and address of your attorney, CPA, and CFP. Consider writing a letter of last request to distribute your personal belongings such as the gold watch you wanted to hand down to your son, the ring intended for your daughter, or the painting above the mantel promised to your best friend. Preferably these documents are in a safe, fireproof place, possibly with a copy in another location should a mishap occur. Assembling these papers and important information is vital in handling your estate efficiently.

I'm amazed by how many people spend a lifetime with important papers stashed in drawers, closets, jacket pockets, and stuffed under beds; in dressers or behind drawers; stuck in cubbyholes. I have a friend who, when administering his parents' estate, kept finding stock certificates as well as unpaid bills in different rooms, tucked in books, and under piles of junk. The time he spent during those two years assembling information was costly from an emotional standpoint, since he was trying to deal with grief, and from a financial standpoint, since he had to keep the estate open longer. Once your valuable documents are accounted for and properly organized, examine the more important ones that actually pass on the wealth you have accumulated to those persons you designate.

Passing Your Nest Egg to Your Heirs

One of the most upsetting financial-planning experiences I've ever witnessed occurred with two clients who procrastinated in straightening out their estates. They wanted to ensure that their money would go to specifically named beneficiaries. Unfortunately, before taking the necessary steps, both were killed in a car accident. Because of these deaths (and it was ruled that the husband died first), the wife's estate received all the assets they held in joint names. It was her second marriage, so the money now in her estate would go to her children from her first marriage. The intention of her husband was that half of it would go to his present wife and half to the children of his first marriage. But because they delayed, his lifelong work and his intentions to help his children were nullified.

When glancing at the disposition of estates of some famous personalities, you will find some very disturbing results (Figure 11-1).

Figure 11-1

	Value of Estate	Tax and Probate Cost	Shrinkage
Adlai Stevenson	$1,398,236	$632,895	45%
George M. Cohan	948,945	361,183	38%
Will Rogers	389,371	229,490	59%
Robert Frost	421,678	159,725	39%
Marilyn Monroe	819,176	448,750	55%

Howard Hughes, with his billions, died without a completed estate plan, which led to years of delay and millions of dollars in legal costs. The total amount of taxes that have been claimed against his estate, many different states trying to claim him as a legal resident of their state for estate tax purposes, totals 101%! Lack of estate planning can indeed be an expensive, upsetting experience.

You may assume that since your estate isn't anywhere near as large as those in the table, you shouldn't worry. Wrong. A $400,000 estate (your estate includes your home, personal belongings, life insurance of which you are the owner, gold coins, diamonds, stocks, bonds, real estate, pension or profit-sharing plans, and miscellaneous assets) might incur probate costs of from $30,000 to $60,000. Further, your estate could be held up in probate for months, one or two years, or much longer if your will is unclear or is contested. If for no other reason than to make it easier on those who are grieving for you, put your estate in order now.

Putting Egg on Their Faces

Having dealt for years with thousands of investors in all age brackets and with all degrees of financial sophistication, I am now going to pass along to you a fiendish technique used by many of these persons to revenge themselves on their enemies. Many of the following eleven points will be recognizable to those of you who use them.

1. Determine those persons you really want to get.
2. Name them executors or executrixes.
3. Make sure your will isn't updated according to current laws.
4. If you have moved, be sure your will was written in the state in which you last resided.
5. Check to see that at least some of the wording in your will is ambiguous, or, better, contradictory.
6. Make sure that the beneficiaries can't easily establish the exact proportion they should receive. Chances are at least one of them will contest.
7. Don't leave a special note explaining how to dispose of personal effects.
8. Under no circumstances list your assets or liabilities. This will bring about long, frantic, frustrating searches for relevant documents. Maintain a safe deposit box, but don't say where. Keep these documents in it.
9. Draw up a living trust, making sure it can be easily found, *but don't list assets in it*. It will appear that you intended to consider your beneficiaries but in fact never did. This one will really make them howl.
10. Make it clear that you are opposed to turning off life-support systems under any circumstances.
11. Choose your probate attorney carefully, selecting one who has a history of charging twice the hourly rate while he sips his coffee.

By following only a few of these eleven simple steps, you will guarantee that those unfortunate souls whom you choose to administer your worldly goods will never forget you. They will remember you while the probate courts wrestle over your intentions and the beneficiaries fight it out. They will remember you while cooling their heels in attorneys' offices, while yawning in stifling courtrooms, and while they are rushing about trying to collect the information they are obligated to provide.

On the other hand, if you want your estate to be handled in such a way that it benefits your loved ones, read on.

Proper Planning

Proper estate planning consists of first deciding what you want to have happen to your assets upon your death. Next, through your will or trust, you must clearly state your desires. A living trust is a legal instrument that acts as a "warehouse" for all of your assets. After you die, your assets will be distributed exactly as you decreed in this trust. A will, on the other hand, must be read and interpreted by the probate courts to decide how your estate will be distributed.

The beautiful part of a living trust is that all of the assets which are contained in it will avoid probate. This provides a shield from the public eye. Remember, all wills that go through probate are *public records* and can be scrutinized by anyone who goes down to the courthouse and pulls the files. Crooks often take advantage of grieving spouses by using those public records as leads. In the living trust, your assets are distributed privately and with your wishes, without the expense or delay of probate.

You may ask why your lawyer has never suggested a living trust. The unfortunate reality is that lawyers have a vested interest in remaining silent. The lawyer will receive only $400 to $1000 to set up a living trust, while probating an estate could bring in anywhere from $10,000 to $100,000. According to Norman Dacey, in *How to Avoid Probate!*, fewer than 1% of lawyers issue or even suggest living trusts for their clients. And many lawyers who are willing to write living trusts don't know how, so their clients end up with defective instruments. If you want a living trust, find a lawyer who specializes in estates and trusts or go to a financial institution that has a good trust department. Ask around. Don't just go to any lawyer and ask for a living trust—see an expert. My personal opinion is that it is a shame that the American legal system is so confusing and the tax system so ill-devised that you need to take these measures. But if you tried to leave $800,000 to your children, they might have to pay $100,000 worth of estate taxes and $50,000 worth of probate charges. If you take the time now to develop a proper living trust, not only might you save the $50,000 in probate costs, but you might be able to save a portion of the tax money as well. The last thing you want is for your estate to go to the IRS.

A living trust is not for everyone. The costs and extra work involved must be weighed against the benefits. For my clients, I use a specially designed computer analysis that balances the costs versus the savings. Where there are special needs that justify the added costs, such as avoiding guardianship or taking care of a brain-damaged child, a living trust is the answer.

Setting up a living trust can be a primary step in your estate planning. By breaking your assets down one by one, you get a chance to review how their ownerships and whether these ownerships should be changed to head off estate taxes down the road.

Mr. and Mrs. Smith had a $1 million estate. All their assets were jointly held. Upon the death of Mr. Smith, Mrs. Smith now had $1 million dollars in the estate for herself, which went to her completely tax-free because of the unlimited marital deduction that is now law. However, Mrs. Smith died soon thereafter. Her million-dollar estate was substantially taxed before it was distributed to her children. This resulted in a tax, in 1984, of $249,500: shrinkage was nearly 25%.

Had Mr. and Mrs. Smith each created a living trust and divided their jointly held assets, upon Mr. Smith's death his money, $500,000, would have been in a trust to give his wife a lifetime income. He could even have set her up as trustee so she could manage the money. (However, unless your spouse is very sophisticated in money matters, find an *experienced* trustee.) There could have been provisions in the trust by which she could not touch the principal but just receive the income. This would have enabled Mr. Smith's estate to take advantage of *his* estate-tax credit while giving income to his wife as long as she lived. Under extreme circumstances, she would have been able to utilize a portion of the principal.

By dividing your assets in this manner, you can utilize *two* estate exclusions instead of one. Mr. Smith's estate tax liabilities would have been reduced by *his* legal estate-tax credit. Mrs. Smith's heirs could have used *her* estate credit. If kept as before in a joint name, his credit would have been lost. This would have reduced by $130,500 (in 1984) the taxes on both estates; $119,000 instead of $249,500. This is but one example of how a living trust can benefit you. In 1986 it would have meant zero taxes!

Figure 11-2

INSERT TAX RATE SCHEDULES

Unified Transfer Tax Rate Schedules
for
1984 and 1985 and Thereafter

1984

If the amount is:		Tentative tax[1] is:			
Over	But not over	Tax	+	%	On Excess Over
0	$ 10,000	0		18	0
$ 10,000	20,000	$ 1,800		20	$ 10,000
20,000	40,000	3,800		22	20,000
40,000	60,000	8,200		24	40,000
60,000	80,000	13,000		26	60,000
80,000	100,000	18,200		28	80,000
100,000	150,000	23,800		30	100,000
150,000	250,000	38,800		32	150,000
250,000	500,000	70,800		34	250,000
500,000	750,000	155,800		37	500,000
750,000	1,000,000	248,300		39	750,000
1,000,000	1,250,000	345,800		41	1,000,000
1,250,000	1,500,000	448,300		43	1,250,000
1,500,000	2,000,000	555,800		45	1,500,000
2,000,000	2,500,000	780,800		49	2,000,000
2,500,000	3,000,000	1,025,800		53	2,500,000
3,000,000	....	1,290,800		55	3,000,000

1985 and Thereafter

If the amount is:		Tentative tax[1] is:			
Over	But not over	Tax	+	%	On Excess Over
0	$ 10,000	0		18	0
$ 10,000	20,000	$ 1,800		20	$ 10,000
20,000	40,000	3,800		22	20,000
40,000	60,000	8,200		24	40,000
60,000	80,000	13,000		26	60,000
80,000	100,000	18,200		28	80,000
100,000	150,000	23,800		30	100,000
150,000	250,000	38,800		32	150,000
250,000	500,000	70,800		34	250,000
500,000	750,000	155,800		37	500,000
750,000	1,000,000	248,300		39	750,000
1,000,000	1,250,000	345,800		41	1,000,000
1,250,000	1,500,000	448,300		43	1,250,000
1,500,000	2,000,000	555,800		45	1,500,000
2,000,000	2,500,000	780,800		49	2,000,000
2,500,000	....	1,025,800		50	2,500,000

[1] The cumulated transfers to which the tentative tax applies are the sum of (a) the amount of the taxable estate and (b) the amount of the taxable gifts made by the decedent after 1976 other than gifts includible in the gross estate.

Figure 11-3

ESTATE TAX CREDIT CHART

	Estate Tax Credits	Exemption Equivalent
1982	62,800	225,000
1983	79,300	275,000
1984	96,300	325,000
1985	121,800	400,000
1986	155,800	500,000
1987	192,800	600,000

Note: First take the total value of the estate and what its total estate tax bill would be. Then deduct the estate tax credit.

Estate Reduction

Your life insurance policies are part of your estate when *you* are the owner. When you die, the proceeds of these policies will be included in your estate, and estate taxes will have to be paid on that money. If, on the other hand, you have been giving that money as a gift to your children, and they have paid the premiums or have set up a special trust, they would be the owners of the policy, and they as beneficiaries would collect the proceeds, completely free from your estate and income taxes. It would pass through without probate. The beneficiaries can even be an insurance trust you've set up to take effect at your death so you could continue to "manage" these funds beyond the grave.

Super Trust

The newly revived concept of the irrevocable insurance trust, the super trust, can be used in many excellent ways when combined with the special "Crummey" Powers. (In *Crummey vs. IRS Commissioner*, the court recognized that a provision in the trust giving the beneficiary the power to demand immediate possession and enjoyment of corpus results in a present-interest gift.) Instead of paying your premium for term insurance and adding its proceeds to your estate for estate-tax purposes, the proceeds will avoid this inclusion. By giving money to the trust, with the beneficiaries receiving the gift, they then purchase, through the trust, insurance on your life. As long as the dollar amount is less than $10,000, gift taxes will be avoided (you must live at least three years after this to avoid the possibility of the proceeds of the policy being thrown back into your estate). Upon death, proceeds would pass to the trust for the benefit of your designated parties, thus avoiding income and estate taxes.

Whatever the size of your estate, it is essential to utilize the current laws to preserve its value. You must protect it from the tax collector, from unwanted, possibly dangerous publicity, and from unscrupulous lawyers. You must not allow your estate to cause emotional hardships to your heirs by forcing them to deal with a host of problems while they are mourning your loss. Trusts can also be written to contain provisions for a trustee to manage your financial affairs should you become disabled or incompetent. This can save time, money, and suffering, since you won't be called upon to set up a guardianship when you are in no condition to do so. Be prepared.

Your Will

Your will should be current. Many tax-law changes were enacted in 1982 through 1986 that could change the legal standing or intended objectives of your will. Check with a lawyer to ascertain whether you need any updating. Supplementing living trusts are a number of legal vehicles that can help you reduce your estate-tax liabilities (and often current income-tax liabilities) if done properly. An interesting example is setting up a private annuity. It used to be the case that a father, in order to sell his business and reduce his estate would, on an installment sales basis, sell his company to relatives and the unpaid balance would pass through his estate upon his death, estate-tax-free. Unfortunately, the IRS changed its rules and this can no longer be done. But the same end can now be achieved by taking this asset out of your estate through the use of a private annuity.

Private Annuities

Since the individual can reduce the tax bite on his or her estate and still enjoy the benefits of his property by using the private annuity, members of the family unit will be well served by checking into the applicability of this particular estate-planning device.

This works by giving an appreciated asset a market value to an individual in return for a certain percentage of return each year on an *annuity* basis, to be paid monthly, quarterly, semiannually, or annually. The payments must be based on an actuarial table that reflects your life expectancy. According to this table, issued by the IRS, each payment will be considered a percentage of your principal, plus whatever the agreed-upon interest rate is. You would thereby get back your monies on an annual basis from this relative, or the party you gave the asset to, in exchange for the annuity. As the income is received, a portion will be taxable interest and a portion will be a return of capital based on your original cost. Upon your death, the annuity will cease; the asset will not be included in your estate.

The private annuity has the benefit of avoiding a lump-sum-tax payment which would occur if you sold your appreciated assets, and thus permits you to earn interest on the money that normally would have gone to the IRS. By exchanging these assets or a regular income for life, many benefits accrue. Finally, those receiving your assets, usually your children, can now sell this asset and avoid the capital gains tax. Their cost basis will be determined by the value of the annuity. Since the payments to be made by the children depend upon how long you live, their cost basis is figured to be the present value of the payments to be made to you. This value would be the present market value of the transferred property if the transaction was established so that no gift from the parent to the children was created. Thus, since it is uncertain how long the parent will live, and what the ultimate cost to the children will be, the Internal Revenue Service permits the children to sell the transferred property at once without having to pay an immediate income tax on any part of the cash proceeds.

However, upon the death of the parent, the children's cost basis in the transferred property would then be established to be the amount of payments actually made to the parent. Any difference between the value of the property transferred to the children by the parent and the amount of payments made to the parent would be taxed to the children as ordinary income. Thus, a private annuity can be utilized in order to sell a highly appreciated asset and spread out the capital gain over the parents' lifetime as well as for federal estate-tax savings.

As for the federal estate-tax savings, when the father dies, the obligation of the children to continue the payments comes to an end. Thus, no portion of the assets transferred to the children or any value in respect to such assets will be in the father's estate for federal estate-tax purposes. Also, the assets will have been transferred to the children prior to the father's death, relieving the executor of the father's estate from any problems and delays caused by making a transfer of such property at death. The children, of course, continue to own the property transferred to them by their father.

A private annuity can be used for all or only a portion of an individual's estate, thus allowing for as much flexibility as he or she wishes to exercise over his or her estate. Also, the children can set up a fully revocable living trust to hold some or all of the property that the father transferred to them and obtain all the benefits that a living trust offers. The trustee of the trust can relieve the children of the administrative and investment burdens of such assets while making the annuity payments to the father on the children's behalf.

A flexible plan used to distribute income among family members is to have a parent invest in a tax-deferred annuity for the benefit of his or her children which provides that the annuity income be given to the child or to a separate account set up for the child. The parent then makes a gift to the child's annuity. The annuity invests the loan proceeds in high-yielding investment funds and pays out the income to the child upon entering college. The child is presumably in a much lower tax bracket than his or her parent.

This transaction is a good way to utilize two taxpayers—the parent and the child—to reduce the amount of income tax owed by the total family unit.

The Generation-Skipping Trust

One major estate-planning method used to transfer assets from generation to generation is to give assets away during the lifetime to the desired beneficiaries. Many such gifts are set up so that just the right amount of restrictions are imposed on the property so that it will not be taxed upon the death of the donee. Thus, a generation of estate taxation is "skipped."

Let's illustrate. Mr. Rigly has $200,000, which he places in a living trust. The money is given away by him so that he no longer has interest in it or receives any income from it. Instead, all the income earned on it is paid to his daughter as the income beneficiary of the trust. At the death of his daughter, the trust fund is payable to the grandchildren of Mrs. Rigly. Mr. Rigly may have used some of his unified credit setting up a trust with such a large sum of money, but the amount of $200,000 can bypass the estate of his daughter for federal estate-tax purposes. Thus, it is possible in this procedure to skip or bypass this generation of taxation by establishing the proper type of trust arrangement. This type of trust can work very effectively with much lesser sums of money.

Estate-tax law in 1987 provides that an individual can pass up to $600,000 tax-free in the estate of each child to his or her grandchildren. Thus, a man with four children could pass $2,400,000 to his grandchildren free from federal estate taxes on the estates of the children. (However, under the newly enacted 1986 tax laws, a $2-million maximum limit is set. This limit will expire in 1990.)

The generation-skipping trust also works out very well when it is intended to give a child only a lifetime income interest in property because he or she is perhaps unable to deal with finance, has personality difficulties, or one of many other reasons. The key is to limit the interest of the trust beneficiary to the income from the trust fund, so that the value of the trust fund will not be taxed as an asset within his or her estate at death.

The Charitable Remainder Trust

How would you like to establish a living trust that will give you a lifetime interest of at least 9%, an immediate income-tax deduction, and pass free of state and federal taxes at your death? This type of estate-planning tool is called the charitable remainder trust. It is designed for those who wish to make sizable contributions to a charitable organization and itemize their tax returns. The benefits are attractive, but first there are a few conditions to be met. At the death of the individual beneficiary, the trust fund must be held in further trust for, or distributed to, a charitable organization such as a nonprofit civic group, United Way, a church, or similar organizations. You are permitted to name more than one charity, but no one besides the charities can be the remainder beneficiaries of this type of trust.

A further condition for receiving an income-tax deduction is that the trust must be irrevocable. Once the trust is created, it cannot be amended or modified, except that you are allowed to retain the power to change the charitable beneficiaries. By making the trust irrevocable, the IRS permits the individual to deduct from his or her adjusted gross income the value of the trust that will pass to the charitable organization upon the death of the person creating the trust. The figures for this valuation are arrived at by using Internal Revenue Code tables. For example, if Mrs. Jacobs, age seventy, creates a charitable remainder trust which specifies that she is to receive 8% of the fair market value of the trust fund as valued in the first day of each year, and she places $50,000 into such a trust, the appropriate government tables tell us that the remainder interest for a woman of this age is 41.5% of the value placed within the trust. Thus, $20,750 of $50,000 may be deducted

Figure 11-4

ESTATE TAX

Section 2001. Imposition and Rate of Tax.

(a) Imposition. — A tax is hereby imposed on the transfer of the taxable estate of every decedent who is a citizen or resident of the United States.

(b) Computation of Tax. — The tax imposed by this section shall be the amount equal to the excess (if any) of —

    (1) a tentative tax computed in accordance with the rate schedule set forth in subsection (c) on the sum of —

        (A) the amount of the taxable estate, and

        (B) the amount of the adjusted taxable gifts, over

    (2) the aggregate amount of tax which would have been payable under chapter 12 with respect to gifts made by the decedent after December 31, 1976, if the rate schedule set forth in subsection (c) (as in effect at the decedent's death) had been applicable at the time of such gifts.

For purposes of paragraph (1)(B), the term "adjusted taxable gifts" means the total amount of the taxable gifts (within the meaning of section 2503) made by the decedent after December 31, 1976, other than gifts which are includible in the gross estate of the decedent.

(c) Rate Schedule. —
    (1) In general. —

If the amount with respect to which the tentative tax to be computed is:	The tentative tax is:
Not over $10,000	18 percent of such amount.
Over $10,000 but not over $20,000	$1,800, plus 20 percent of the excess of such amount over $10,000.
Over $20,000 but not over $40,000	$3,800, plus 22 percent of the excess of such amount over $20,000.
Over $40,000 but not over $60,000	$8,200, plus 24 percent of the excess of such amount over $40,000.
Over $60,000 but not over $80,000	$13,000, plus 26 percent of the excess of such amount over $60,000.
Over $80,000 but not over $100,000	$18,200, plus 28 percent of the excess of such amount over $80,000.
Over $100,000 but not over $150,000	$23,800, plus 30 percent of the excess of such amount over $100,000.
Over $150,000 but not over $250,000	$38,800, plus 32 percent of the excess of such amount over $150,000.
Over $250,000 but not over $500,000	$70,800, plus 34 percent of the excess of such amount over $250,000.
Over $500,000 but not over $750,000	$155,800, plus 37 percent of the excess of such amount over $500,000.
Over $750,000 but not over $1,000,000	$248,300, plus 39 percent of the excess of such amount over $750,000.
Over $1,000,000 but not over $1,250,000	$345,800, plus 41 percent of the excess of such amount over $1,000,000.
Over $1,250,000 but not over $1,500,000	$448,300, plus 43 percent of the excess of such amount over $1,250,000.
Over $1,500,000 but not over $2,000,000	$555,800, plus 45 percent of the excess of such amount over $1,500,000.
Over $2,000,000 but not over $2,500,000	$780,800, plus 49 percent of the excess of such amount over $2,000,000.
Over $2,500,000	*$1,025,800, plus 50% of the excess over $2,500,000.*

    (2) Phase-in of 50 percent maximum rate. —

        (A) In general. — In the case of decedents dying, and gifts made, before 1985, there shall be substituted for the last item in the schedule contained in paragraph (1) the items determined under this paragraph.

        (B) For 1982. — In the case of decedents dying, and gifts made, in 1982, the substitution under this paragraph shall be as follows:

Over $2,500,000 but not over $3,000,000 .... *$1,025,800, plus 53% of the excess over $2,500,000.*
Over $3,000,000 but not over $3,500,000 .... *$1,290,800, plus 57% of the excess over $3,000,000.*
Over $3,500,000 but not over $4,000,000 .... *$1,575,800, plus 61% of the excess over $3,500,000.*
Over $4,000,000 .... *$1,880,800, plus 65% of the excess over $4,000,000.*

(C) *For 1983.* — *In the case of decedents dying, and gifts made, in 1983, the substitution under this paragraph shall be as follows:*
Over $2,500,000 but not over $3,000,000 .... *$1,025,800, plus 53% of the excess over $2,500,000.*
Over $3,000,000 but not over $3,500,000 .... *$1,290,800, plus 57% of the excess over $3,000,000.*
Over $3,500,000 .... *$1,575,800, plus 60% of the excess over $3,500,000.*

(D) *For 1984.* — *In the case of decedents dying, and gifts made, in 1984, the substitution under this paragraph shall be as follows:*
Over $2,500,000 but not over $3,000,000 .... *$1,025,800, plus 53% of the excess over $2,500,000.*
Over $3,000,000 .... *$1,290,800, plus 55% of the excess over $3,000,000.*

(d) Adjustment for Gift Tax Paid by Spouse. — For purposes of subsection (b)(2), if —
(1) the decedent was the donor of any gift one-half of which was considered under section 2513 as made by the decedent's spouse, and
(2) the amount of such gift is includible in the gross estate of the decedent,
any tax payable by the spouse under chapter 12 on such gift (as determined under section 2012(d)) shall be treated as a tax payable with respect to a gift made by the decedent.
(e) Coordination of Sections 2513 and 2035. — If —
(1) the decedent's spouse was the donor of any gift one-half of which was considered under section 2513 as made by the decedent, and
(2) the amount of such gift is includible in the gross estate of the decedent's spouse by reason of section 2035,
such gift shall not be included in the adjusted taxable gifts of the decedent for purposes of subsection (b)(1)(B), and the aggregate amount determined under subsection (b)(2) shall be reduced by the amount (if any) determined under subsection (d) which was treated as a tax payable by the decedent's spouse with respect to such gift.

The portions of IRC Sec. 2001 appearing in italics were added or substituted by the Economic Recovery Tax Act of 1981, and are applicable to estates of decedents dying after 1981 and to gifts made after 1981. Act. Sec. 402(d).

Section 2010. Unified Credit Against Estate Tax.

(a) General Rule. — A credit of *$192,800* shall be allowed to the estate of every decedent against the tax imposed by section 2001.
(b) Phase-in of Credit. —

In the case of decedents dying in:	Subsection (a) shall be applied by substituting for "*$192,800*" the following amount:
1982	*$ 62,800*
1983	*79,300*
1984	*96,300*
1985	*121,800*
1986	*155,800*

(c) Adjustment to Credit for Certain Gifts Made Before 1977. — The amount of the credit allowable under subsection (a) shall be reduced by an amount equal to 20 percent of the aggregate amount allowed as a specific exemption under section 2521 (as in effect before its repeal by the Tax Reform Act of 1976) with respect to gifts made by the decedent after September 8, 1976.

against her adjusted gross income as a charitable deduction. If all the remainder interest cannot be deducted in one year because of the annual limits on charitable deductions, the portion not deducted can be carried over a five-year period and used against future taxable income.

At the death of Mrs. Jacobs, the trust fund would then pass to the charities, which would create memorials in her name. None of the money passing to the charities would be subject to state or federal death taxes, since charities are tax-exempt entities.

This type of trust is very desirable when an individual wishes to benefit a charity after his or her death, yet needs to retain the lifetime rights to the income from the property. Once the property is transferred into the trust, many of the benefits of a living trust are available. The trustee may not pay out any money in addition to the interest income to the individual setting up the trust, or the charitable deduction is lost. To ensure that a substantial amount of annual money will be paid to the individual creating the trust for the rest of his or her lifetime, the trust can set forth that 9% to 10% interest income will be paid. One significant tax reason for creating a charitable remainder trust is deferral of capital gains tax when appreciated property is used to establish the trust fund. Since the trust is a tax-exempt entity, the trustee can sell the appreciated property without paying capital gains tax on the profit realized from the sale. For example, if an individual has real estate for which he paid $50,000 and which is worth $200,000 today, he can transfer this real estate to a charitable remainder trust and the trustee can then sell the real estate without having to pay capital gains tax on the $150,000 profit. As the trustee pays out only lifetime income to the individual who set up the trust, the individual may or may not need to pay tax on the capital gain. It would depend on how much regular income, such as dividends and interest, he was paid each year by the trustee from the earnings on the trust fund money. This is an excellent way in which to diversify a highly appreciated asset into an annuity or single-pay life plan while avoiding the taxes on the capital gains.

One final thought on charitable remainders. The tax law permits gifts to charity of a remainder interest in a personal residence or farm without meeting the strict requirements for charitable remainder trusts. This can result in a sizable *current* tax deduction for those willing to donate their residence or farm effective *after* their death.

Many charitable institutions have special funds and advisers to help potential contributors set up a trust. Check first with the charity you're considering, since this could save you legal costs.

Figure 11-5

HOW A CHARITABLE REMAINDER TRUST WORKS

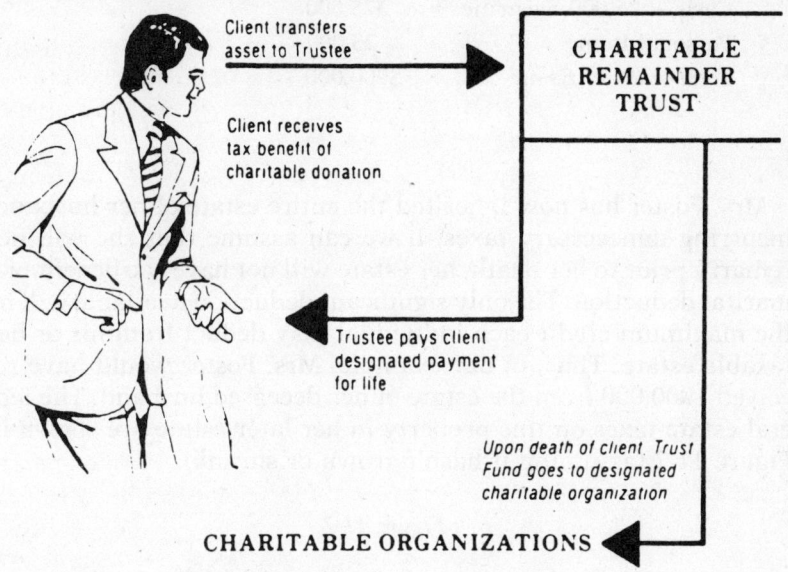

Marital-Deduction Trust

To maximize the federal estate-tax savings on the deaths of husband and wife, it is important that the entire estate not pass directly to the survivor. This would, of course, increase the federal estate-tax liability upon the death of the survivor. This undesirable result often occurs because the husband and wife own all or most of their property in joint tenancy and because the wife (usually the survivor) is named as beneficiary for all the life insurance upon the life of the husband as well as his pension plan or other retirement-plan death benefit. It is better to name a trust as the beneficiary for these death benefits if federal estate-tax savings are desired upon the death of the surviving spouse.

It is common for a husband and wife to have most of their assets jointly owned. Thus, when either dies, all the jointly owned assets pass automatically to the surviving spouse. Let us assume that Mr. and Mrs. Foster have an estate of $900,000, consisting largely of jointly owned assets and life insurance policies which are made payable to Mrs. Foster. Mr. Foster dies, leaving all his property to his wife according to terms of his will. Mr. Foster has given his wife his entire estate. His estate would look like Figure 11-6.

Figure 11-6

Real Estate	$400,000
Life Insurance	100,000 payable to Mrs. Foster
Cash + 25,000 Securities	375,000
Personal Items	25,000
Total Value of Estate	$900,000

Mrs. Foster has now inherited the entire estate of her husband, incurring unnecessary taxes. If we can assume that she will not remarry prior to her death, her estate will not have the benefit of a marital deduction. The only significant deduction available will be the maximum credit each individual may deduct from his or her taxable estate. Thus, in our example, Mrs. Foster would have received $900,000 from the estate of her deceased husband. The federal estate-taxes on this property in her later estate are shown in Figure 11-7 (assuming it hasn't grown or shrunk).

Figure 11-7

Total Estate	$900,000
Tentative Tax	305,800
Amount of Credit—1986	155,800
Federal Estate Tax	150,000

Upon the death of Mrs. Foster, the estate-tax bite certainly is costly! What can be done to ensure that more of the property will pass on to the children and other beneficiaries is to have Mr. and Mrs. Foster establish a marital-deduction trust. We must structure their holdings so that estate taxes will be minimized at the death of both Mr. and Mrs. Foster, in part by avoiding a high proportion of jointly owned property. In our example it would be set forth in Mr. Foster's last will and testament and/or living trust that not more of the value of his estate would pass to his wife than is needed in order to minimize taxes on her estate. A percentage of Mr. Foster's would pass into a trust instead of going outright to Mrs. Foster. This is called a residuary trust. The residuary trust would be set up so that Mrs. Foster could receive certain benefits from the trust property without having its value taxable in her estate at her death. In addition to establishing such a trust, the ownership of the jointly held property and the beneficiary designated on the life insurance policies would be reviewed in order to coordinate such property with the provisions of the trust. The benefits that she may receive from the residuary trust without the value thereof being taxed within her later estate are:

1. *All* of the income earned on the trust principal.
2. Up to $5000 or 5% of the value of the trust principal, whichever is greater, each year, as she may elect to withdraw from the trust.
3. Whatever amounts of the trust principal the trustee deems necessary to provide for the comfort, support, and maintenance of Mrs. Foster.

If needed, substantial amounts of money can be withdrawn each year from the trust for the benefit of Mrs. Foster. At her death, however, only the property she received from Mr. Foster outright or in a marital trust along with any of her own property would be taxable in her estate. The property in the residuary trust will not be taxable. By rearranging the estate planning of Mr. and Mrs. Foster, the federal estate-taxes at *her* death would be somewhat as in Figure 11-8:

Figure 11-8

MRS. FOSTER

Total Estate	$450,000
Tentative Tax	138,800
Amount of Credit	155,800
Federal Income Tax	-0-

MR. FOSTER

Estate (Residuary Trust)	$450,000
Tentative Tax	138,800
Amount of Credit	155,800
Federal Estate Tax	-0-

Figure 11-8 shows how substantial savings can be made in federal estate taxes if Mr. and Mrs. Foster set up the right marital-deduction trust—their money will go to their loved ones instead of to the IRS. Once the estate of a husband and wife exceeds $600,000, tax savings can be had by using the marital-deduction

Figure 11-9

MARITAL DEDUCTION TRUST

HUSBAND

Death

Estate divides into two trusts.

Marital Trust	Residuary Trust
Tax free in husband's estate	Taxable in husband's estate
(a) Wife receives all the income	(a) Wife receives all the income
(b) Wife has control over the principal	(b) Wife can receive restricted rights to the trust principal
Taxable in wife's estate	Not taxable in wife's estate

trust instead of having the estate pass directly to the surviving spouse. Savings increase dramatically with larger estates.

Every married couple should look into the possibilities of this type of trust arrangement to save taxes upon their deaths. These same savings also apply to residents of community-property states (such as Arizona, California, Louisiana, Texas, Utah, New Mexico, and Washington) as well as to all the common-law states.

The soaring divorce rate of the past decades has affected the writing of wills and the administration of estates, for divorced persons often feel responsibilities toward more than one family. If this is your situation, ask about the Q-TIP (Qualified Terminal Interest Provision).

Summary

Using the foregoing legal instruments to shelter your assets from unnecessary taxes and legal costs is a goal worth shooting for. But merely reading about these techniques isn't enough.

Find an experienced certified financial planner who deals with estate planning and can help you determine whether the benefits

Keeping Your Personal and Estate Affairs in Order

outweigh the costs in establishing a trust. Talk with your CPA and get his or her input on trusts. Next, see an attorney who is experienced and specializes in setting up trusts. But don't wait.

The first step is to compile a list of all your assets and how each is currently owned (single name, joint with right of survivorship, joint tenants in common, etc.). Next list your intentions for distribution of your assets and any special contingencies for which you want to prepare. With this outline, you can begin to look at the different types of trusts to determine which meet your needs. Be sure to include your life insurance proceeds with your assets. These proceeds can be made payable to a living trust so you can obtain more flexibility and control over these sums. If your spouse or children are inexperienced in managing large sums of money, this enables you to keep your hands on the wheel as to how the money is invested. Once you've completed the Financial-Planning Summary, go to your tax and legal experts and review the figures with each of them. Then have them design and establish the most suitable investment and legal instruments.

Figure 11-10

FINANCIAL-PLANNING SUMMARY

CONFIDENTIAL

Date _____

Name _____ Age _____

Address _____

Own or rent _____ State _____ Zip _____

Telephone _____

Employer _____ Occupation _____

No. of children and ages _____
_____

Current dependents? _____

Social Security number _____

Approx. net worth _____ Annual income _____

Tax bracket: Last Year _____

                This Year _____

                Next Year _____

Financial Independence
1. What income do you feel would be necessary (in today's dollars, after taxes) for you to become financially independent? _____
2. How would you define your current investment objectives? __
   _____

Present Condition

1. *Income Sources—Annual*

	Combined	His	Hers
Social Security	$_____	_____	_____
Pension	_____	_____	_____
Salary/Work Income	_____	_____	_____
Tax-Free Income	_____	_____	_____
Interest Income	_____	_____	_____
Stock Div. Income	_____	_____	_____
Other Sources	_____	_____	_____
Total Income	$_____	_____	_____

If pensions discontinue or are lowered at death, please note.

2. How are your assets divided currently? (Fill in appropriate amount.)

Portfolio	His	Hers	Joint
Checking/Savings	$_____	_____	_____
Money Market Fund	_____	_____	_____
IRAs	_____	_____	_____
(Spouse)	_____	_____	_____
Pension/Profit Sharing Plan	_____	_____	_____
Tax-Free Bonds 1-5 yr. maturity.	_____	_____	_____
& Bond Funds 5+ yr. maturity	_____	_____	_____
Taxable Bonds 1-5 year	_____	_____	_____
& Bond Funds 5+ year	_____	_____	_____
Annuities	_____	_____	_____
Mutual Funds	_____	_____	_____
Stocks	_____	_____	_____

House/Mortgage _____ _____ _____
Rental Properties _____ _____ _____
Nonincome Real Est.
  (such as Lots) _____ _____ _____
Real Estate
  Partnerships _____ _____ _____
Other Limited
  Partnerships _____ _____ _____
Gold/Silver/
Precious Metals _____ _____ _____
Life Insurance (note
  Owner & Insured) _____ _____ _____
Health Insurance _____ _____ _____
Disability Income
  Insurance _____ _____ _____
Supplemental Medicare _____ _____ _____

3. What large expenditures (capital needs) do you expect during the next one to three years?

   _____ $_____
   _____ $_____
   _____ $_____

4. Are there any special financial events occurring in the next three years (inheritance, mortgage payoff, balloon note due, etc.)?

5. What did you pay in federal income taxes last year?
   $ _____

6. In the event you died today, do you know what your estate-tax liability would be? $ _____

7. Excluding taxes, what is your present outlay for living expenses? $ _____

8. How much money do you feel comfortable having in easily accessible emergency funds? $ _____

9. Do you feel it is important to take into account the effects of inflation on future income? Yes ___ No ___

   If yes, approximately what annual rate of inflation do you expect over the next ten years? _____ %

10. Are you pleased with your present assets in terms of:

Safety	Income	Growth	Hedge Against Inflation
Yes No	Yes No	Yes No	Yes No

11. With regard to your present assets and future investments, which would you prefer? (Check one or more)

	More Income	More Growth	Tax Savings	Preservation	Diversity
On Present Assets	( )	( )	( )	( )	( )
On Future Assets	( )	( )	( )	( )	( )

Investment Philosophy

1. To identify and analyze your investment preferences, please respond to the following items by filling in the blank with:

   > G—Good Experience
   > B—Bad Experience
   > N—No Experience
   > K—Would like more knowledge

		Comments
Stocks	____	_____
Bonds	____	_____
Annuities	____	_____
Mutual Funds	____	_____
Money Market Funds	____	_____

Municipal Bonds   ____ _____
Commercial Paper   ____ _____
Oil & Gas   ____ _____
Real Estate   ____ _____
Insurance   ____ _____
Rare Coins   ____ _____
Options   ____ _____
Precious Stones   ____ _____
T-Bills & Notes   ____ _____
Commodities   ____ _____
Equipment Leasing   ____ _____

Identify the investment area you like the most (whether it is listed) and state why.
_____
_____

Estate Planning

Name of Your Attorney _____
Address of Attorney   _____
                      _____ ZIP _____
Attorney's Telephone: _____

1. *Will Information*   *You*   *Your Spouse*
   Have wills?   Yes   No   Yes   No
   State in which drawn.   _____   _____
   Do you feel changes are needed?   Yes   No   Yes   No

2. Describe briefly what you think your will says: _____
_____
_____

3. What do you think is today's fair market value of your real estate? $ _____

4. Are you aware of the shrinkage of your estate value that could occur due to estate taxes, probate expenses, legal fees,

administrative expensives, and unpaid property and income taxes?

Yes _____ No _____

5. Have you created any trusts in past years? Yes _____ No _____
Have the taxable assets been transferred? Yes _____ No _____
What type? _____
When _____ Trustee(s) _____

6. Are you or your spouse an income beneficiary of any trust?
Yes _____ No _____ If Yes, please explain _____

7. Have you ever filed a gift-tax return? Yes _____ No _____

8. Name and Address of your CPA:
_____
_____
_____

Tax Planning

1. Have you ever had a program for reducing your income taxes?
Yes _____ No _____

2. Check below the tax-planning vehicles you have used.
   - ( ) IRA
   - ( ) Keogh
   - ( ) Pension Plan
   - ( ) Profit-Sharing Plan
   - ( ) Charitable Trust
   - ( ) Retirement Annuity
   - ( ) Irrevocable Trust
   - ( ) Deferred Compensation Plan
   - ( ) Oil & Gas
   - ( ) Real Estate
   - ( ) Cattle
   - ( ) Art
   - ( ) Fixed Annuity
   - ( ) Variable Annuity
   - ( ) Other _____

3. Do you or your spouse anticipate any inheritance funds?
You: $ _____ When _____ From _____
Spouse: $ _____ When _____ From _____

PART II

12. Banks Aren't as Safe as You Think They Are

LAUGHING LENDERS. At the 1985 Federal Home Loan Bank Board Christmas party, staffers wore T-shirts that said FSLIC AID on the front, referring to the cash-strapped thrift insurance fund. On the back the shirts said, WE DO IT WITH MIRRORS, but that message could be read only when held up to a mirror.
—*The Wall Street Journal*

I believe that banking institutions are more dangerous toward liberty than standing armies.
—Thomas Jefferson

Now that your plans are set, you can take a look at the larger world of economics and see how you go about using it to create wealth and security for yourself and your family. Let's begin with banks, since they are the economic institutions we most often encounter.

I clearly remember my first visit to a bank. Grandmother drove me there in her Cadillac to pick up my grandfather. Grandfather was on the board of directors of Royal Trust Banks, of New York, an institution he helped found during the Depression to keep his business alive. (Royal Trust was later purchased by Chase Manhattan.)

I recall walking shyly into a huge open space that gave me the impression of a mausoleum inhabited by living persons. The desks were heavy, somber mahogany, the floor was polished marble, and there was a tangible chill in the air. Looking up at the oil paintings and the dark-suited men and women was an awe-inspiring, intimidating experience for a little boy. I would rather have visited Grandfather's garment-manufacturing firm, where busy workers ran about shouting orders.

My next important experience with a banking institution occurred when, after having saved money from birthdays, allowance, and odd jobs, I went, again with my grandmother, to a large local savings bank near my home in Brooklyn. I remember excitedly entering the bank, for I knew that by opening an account and making a $5 deposit, I would be given my very own Brownie camera. Grandmother had assured me that I was not giving up my five dollars but that it would begin to earn interest for me. She told me that the camera was nothing but an inducement to start a banking relationship. I'll never forget having to turn over my money to a friendly and amused new-accounts officer. I asked to see where the money went to be sure it would be safe. To this day Grandmother doesn't let me forget my concern for the safety of my money. To this day I retain that same concern, except that now I base my anxiety not on lack of understanding, or fear, but on knowledge of the fragile position in which our banking institutions have placed themselves.

What a joy it was as a child to watch my interest credited each quarter without my doing any additional work. As my money slowly increased, I always made sure to get the interest credited in my passbook each quarter so that I could "see" my deposit growing.

Twenty years later I would be traveling throughout south Florida, encouraging people to withdraw their money from banks and savings and loan institutions to open up something that was brand new, called money market fund accounts. It's hard to imagine that in 1978 and 1979 very few people knew what a money market fund account was; yet, with the emergence of Merrill Lynch's cash-management account, the world of banking and finance took a major step forward. The banking-industry deregulation that ensued brought about more changes in three years than had occurred in the last hundred.

Ninety-nine percent of persons I have spoken to about the American banking system have said that although there may have been "problems" during the Depression, there was no longer any need to worry about the safety of our money, thanks to the Federal Deposit Insurance Corporation (FDIC), the Federal Savings and Loan Insurance Corporation (FSLIC), or the State Deposit Insurance Corporation (SDIC). Depositors seem to feel comfortable that should anything go wrong with their bank, the federal or state government would step in and fix things. This complacency is understandable when one looks at the track record from 1929 to 1979. No investor lost deposits in these institutions, and even when the fifth-largest bank in the country, Franklin National, went under with many millions of dollars' worth of losses, investors were given back their money within two years.

Some people felt they were smart to diversify their deposits in different banks and different kinds of accounts to receive the maximum insurance and not to exceed coverage limits. Yet, beginning in 1979, a strange turn of events began to occur in our country, unlike anything seen since the Great Depression.

With inflation battering the values of loan portfolios and interest rates soaring to unprecedented heights, many banks and savings and loans found themselves unable to compete with the newly designed money-market fund accounts that the investment bankers had developed. These accounts, which in 1977 totaled $20 billion, rose rapidly, and over a five-year period received an additional $200 billion. Most of the money came from non-interest-bearing checking accounts, low-interest-bearing savings accounts, and certificates of deposit. This new financial instrument was playing a tune investors wanted to hear—higher interest rates in accordance with the market. Banks and savings and loans that were strapped on the rates of return they could offer under Regulation Q (a regulation they had lobbied for, years earlier, in order to corner the market) found they could no longer compete. They began to fall from grace.

Hundreds of banks across the country entered negative-cash-flow positions, experiencing month after month of net outflows of money. In normal circumstances, banks had been able to depend on a rejuvenating source of new money flowing in after possibly a month or two of high withdrawals. Yet, being able to offer only 5% interest when money market funds were paying 14% and 15%, the "disintermediation," the flight to higher rates, from the financial institutions became unprecedented. One after another, banks and savings and loans began to fail. Lacking cash, within three years more than 1300 institutions went on the in-trouble-of-bankruptcy lists. Bank mergers became the word of the day, and it seemed the only enterprises making money were the sign companies that were constantly changing the names of the banks, sometimes on a monthly basis. Nineteen eighty-two was a glum year as the financial strain began to penetrate the very heart of our economic system, forcing interest rates to go as high as money was scarce, helping bring about one of the deepest recessions we had seen in some time. At the time, I predicted that unless banks and savings and loans were permitted to compete with the money market funds and thereby restore deposits and lower interest rates for homeowners, automobile buyers, and factory builders, there would be another 1929 Depression.

Fortunately the authorities woke up, and on December 12, 1982, Congress finally agreed to permit the lifting of Regulation Q, thereby permitting banks and savings and loans to offer money market funds. Interestingly, at this very point the recession peaked. Unemployment fell, interest rates dropped, and prosperity returned. But the banking industry's lock on depositors' money had been taken off once and for all. Even as $10 to $20 billion a week flowed back into the banking system, there was only temporary relief. Banks, which had not paid interest on checking accounts and only minimum interest on savings, were now forced to pay higher rates than ever to attract depositors' money. The cost of holding deposits skyrocketed, forcing interest rates to stay at levels higher than experienced in some time. With inflation down, real rates of interest (the cost of borrowing money less inflation) stood at historically high levels. Where normally a 2% to 4% spread sufficed, spreads of 6% to 8% were commonplace. And this was just the beginning.

Figure 12-1 illustrates the increasing cost of money. It traces the growth of money market funds in billions of dollars from 1974 through 1982, when Regulation Q was lifted.

Foreign Intrigue

During the '70s, while inflation was bringing the illusion of growth to the US economy, our banks were sitting like fat cats on a heap of garbage. Banks all across America were encouraged by the government to send their depositors' money overseas. Between 1970 and 1980 there was a 500% increase in loans to Third World, "developing," and Communist countries. Some $500 billion was distributed to Mexico and Brazil, to Argentina and Peru, to Poland and the Soviet Union. In their eagerness to earn higher rates of return, US bankers didn't seem to care that the recipients were irresponsible and were wasting most of these dollars on futile projects for the "development" of their countries—meaning the enrichment of politicians.

As interest rates soared and economies worldwide slowed in the late '70s and early '80s, a few skeptics started to wonder how these loans of your money and mine would ever be paid back. The question was answered when defaults began to be announced in the papers, and US banks were left holding the bag. We now hear a great deal about complex "restructuring" arrangements that supposedly will solve the problem by pushing it into the future: URUGUAY, BANKS IN ACCORD TO RESTRUCTURE $1.7 BILLION, according to *The Wall Street Journal* of July 11, 1986. Headlines have also appeared recently on the hundreds of billions due from Mexico, Peru, Argentina, and Poland!

Figure 12-1

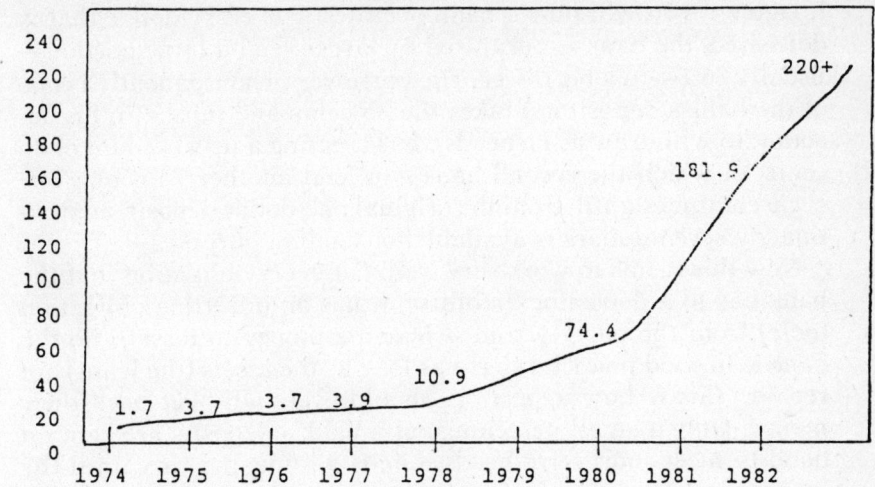

Figure 12-2

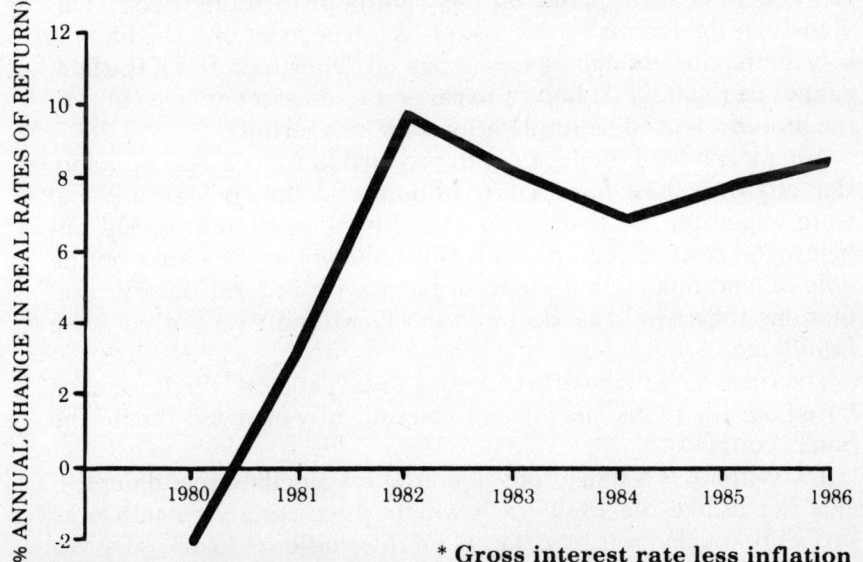

The Greatest Ponzi Scheme Ever

Imagine if you will how a bank operates. For every dollar that is deposited, the bank is permitted by law to lend a large portion—usually 86%—to a borrower. The borrower (who frequently is one of the bank's depositors) takes the 86 cents and puts it in his account, to withdraw as he needs, thus creating a new account of 86 cents, of which the second bank can lend another 74 cents. The cycle continues until, from the original one-dollar deposit, approximately seven dollars is available for lending purposes.

Now this seems to work very well. For every obligation that the bank has to a depositor (liability), it has an offsetting obligation (note) from the party whom it lent the money to (asset). So the bank is in good financial shape as long as the assets (the loans) are repaid. This is how depositors should eventually get back their money. Only a small percentage of a bank's deposits are kept on hand to meet short-term needs. Life is all fine and rosy until the loans (assets) cannot be repaid. All of a sudden we have nonexistent assets and an imbalance between the ability to be paid back from the borrowers and to be able to pay back money to depositors. Following this pattern, about $650 billion of international debt has gone into default and has little or no possibility of ever being repaid. Yet these "deadbeat" loans continue to be carried as assets at full value on the lending institutions' books! Obviously, if the loan is repaid then it is a true asset and the bank is solvent, having enough money to pay off depositors. But if the loan cannot be repaid, is it honest to carry it as an asset at face value of the amount lent? The implications are staggering.

A bank can lend money only in proportion to its assets on hand. If at any time these hundreds of billions of dollars of loans (assets) were wiped off the books, our entire banking system would fall below the reserve requirement. Not only would the banks not be able to lend money, but, in accordance with Federal Reserve regulations they would be declared insolvent and would need to be liquidated.

The rules by which we are playing today, and on which we have based our life plans, may need to be radically changed should the banks collapse.

Today there is a dangerous potential for a deflation and depression not unlike the 1929 crash which, interestingly enough, was probably touched off by defaults on international loans.

If a banking collapse occurs, the enormous amount of money

needed for a bailout would make the dollar virtually worthless overnight.

- Federal Home Loan Bank Chairman Edwin Gray said that the US banking system is fragile. Let's look at some of the mistakes the bankers have made. Perhaps we can avoid making similar ones.
- As mentioned, an astronomical $650 billion in doubtful international debts is currently being carried on the books as assets. And the banks continue to lend money, hoping to at least get their interest back. This is called throwing good money after bad, and in itself could bring the system to its knees.
- There exists a trillion dollars in contingent liabilities from standing letters of credit that may or may not prove to have been prudent investments.
- There has been an appalling increase in bankrupt farms. Many Midwestern banks have gone under, and the Federal Farm Credit System is now insolvent as will as the FSLIC.
- Billions of dollars lent to the international shipbuilding industry will never be repaid. When Japan's major shipbuilder went bankrupt, it owed $2.5 billion. The high-tech industry has been experiencing a shakeout and has lost billions.
- Money market funds have driven up the cost of money. The free lunches that banks once enjoyed on checking and savings accounts exist no longer.
- The banking industry has recognized that many banks have lent over 100% value on many properties.
- Many savings institutions have committed as much as 25% of their assets to dubious junk bonds.
- Tens of billions of dollars lent to oil companies, based on their reserves valued at $28 a barrel, have soured with today's prices less than half their original value. Banks throughout Texas, Oklahoma, and Colorado have closed their doors.
- The beleagured steel industry is the latest major casualty with the bankruptcy of LTV. The mounting losses at US Steel and others now threaten the survival of many Eastern banks (as well as pensioners!).

Do not fail to acknowledge the many problems the banks are having and blindly accept risks or you may, just like a bank, end up holding the bag while saying, "I didn't think it could happen to me." It has become important today to understand the internal workings of your bank and to get statements about its financial health. Reports are available that contain the financial conditions of all banks. They can help you determine the health of your own bank or savings and loan.

Personally, I would like to see much fuller disclosure by banks concerning their assets and loans, their management, and how they are earning their keep. Unfortunately the public is not privy to this information, and the banks oppose "disclosure" on the grounds that it places them in an unfair competitive position.

Investors who have tied up all their money in certificates of deposit and money market funds are paying a high price in terms of taxes, inflation, and potential risk. Bank closures could happen again. Therefore, utilizing a well-diversified portfolio is imperative for investors who intend to survive a banking crisis should one occur. I don't think a nationwide collapse will happen tomorrow, but I do think that there is a high probability of one occurring in the next three to five years.

Hiding your head in the sand by not weighing the risk/reward factors of where you place your money is a sure way to find yourself numbly standing in line if your bank closes. Rethink your investment strategies. Study and apply the Conservative-Investor Portfolios to set up a diversified plan to achieve financial security no matter what happens. Your future depends on it.

An Action Plan

I suggest that you don't leave too much of your investment portfolio in the banking system. For availability of liquid funds, consider a 100% government-backed money market fund consisting of Treasury bills.

However, banks can play a vital role in helping you finance your dreams—as long as you know how to use them instead of being used by them.

"The only time to borrow money from a bank is when you can prove you don't need it." How true. Investors with hardships, unable to show deposits in their accounts or liquid investments, often can't get emergency, investment, or business-oriented loans. *Begin a relationship with a bank when you need it the least.* By borrowing money when you don't need it, and paying it back, you can build a track record with a banking institution to fund your future projects. It is unfortunate that our system is set up this way, for it creates a serious obstacle for most entrepreneurs, who have yet to prove their creditworthiness. Obviously, if you have excellent credit and all the money you need, your need for a loan is minimal. The first step is opening lines of credit. For some, this might be making deposits in a money market fund account or using the bank to deposit your paycheck. Establishing a relationship with a bank officer or two can prove very useful to fledgling businesses. These officers are often able to authorize small loans without committee approval. Being friends with a banker at the civic club or on the tennis court could help make things a lot easier when you need money. Otherwise, unless you are buying an automobile, you must show a long history of employment income. A job history is important when buying a home. Although the house is collateral for your mortgage, you must have a down payment and enough income to demonstrate your ability to pay. Establishing credit can be difficult.

When I first moved to Florida, I had little money and a minimal amount of credit built up in Boston. But in Florida, a transient-filled state, my Boston credit history was worthless. Despite a decent income, as a newcomer I was unable to secure a loan, so I immediately went for the easiest line of credit. I applied for every department store credit card and gasoline card I could find. These were free, with no annual charges, and I needed to show only a short job history. I was accepted for 80% of the cards I applied for. I then used these cards instead of paying cash whenever possible. This (1) helped me establish my ability to take on debt and pay it off and (2) gave me thirty days to pay. (This procedure is not for people who spend beyond their means and then get hit with high credit card charges.) I tried to pay off all my bills each month and not run up excessive interest charges (I was not in a high enough tax bracket to take advantage of these tax deductions).

After about a year of establishing revolving charge accounts, I applied for MasterCard and Visa. These were my entrées to the bank. Promotions were going on, and banks were eager for clients—even with brief credit histories. They were willing to take on a little extra risk since they charged high rates. Within six months I had two MasterCards and two Visa cards, which at that time carried no annual fee. Today, fees have become commonplace, but there are still a number of banks that charge nothing or very little. Get the best deal you can.

I used these cards whenever possible to establish credit and qualify for a bank loan. Finally, with something over a year under my belt in Florida, and having established credit accounts and a small savings account, I went to a local bank for a $1000 personal loan. I didn't need the money. I deposited it at a different bank to begin building credit there. I paid off the loan on time. This thousand dollars, because of the interest I earned versus the interest I paid, ended up costing me about $70 for the year. This sum was tax-deductible and saved me $20 in income taxes. I thought $50 was a reasonable cost to establish credit.

Six months after having paid the loan, it was easy for me to borrow five times that amount from that bank because of my proven credit history.

Many people go to friends or family when needing money and never establish a credit history. Even if you borrow money from relatives, consider depositing it at a bank and then take out a loan based on that deposit. This may cost you a few dollars, but it could save you the humiliation of having to approach a relative again to borrow more money.

Paying Off Loans

As you begin to borrow and make payments, whether they be for a car, housing, credit cards, or installment loans, be sure to pay these bills on time. Going past-due is like receiving a demerit in school that is forever on your record. A payment late by *one day* becomes a mark against you which can be carried forward for years. I've seen loan officers use such "demerits" to deny loans. If you have questions about your credit history, you are permitted to get copies from reporting bureaus to determine exactly what is being said about you. You can correct inaccuracies. On the other hand, don't pay your bills so promptly that you lose the "float" on your account. Often you will find two dates on a monthly statement, whether a mortgage or a credit card. One is the date you are billed, and it says, "Now due" and the other is a different date which says, "Past due on . . ." An example would be the banks with loans or mortgage payments to be paid at the first of the month. Yet the statement says there are no additional charges for payment unless the money is received after the fifteenth of the month. If you send the bank the money on the first, it would lose two weeks' worth of interest. Had you paid it on the twelfth for arrival on the fourteenth or fifteenth, you'd earn extra interest. I recommend that you pay bills a few days before being past-due. But be careful. Supposedly the date you have paid the bill is the date it is postmarked, but you may run into difficulties since for some institutions it is the date they *receive* the money. You do not want to cut it so close that your money was in the mail on time but was received a day late, causing additional charges—which on mortgages and many types of loans can be prohibitive.

Set up your bills to be paid three or four days before past-due and then, if you can, have those checks written on money market funds which are based in another state. This means your bill will be paid on time but it may take five days or more for your check to clear its out-of-state bank. Now you are earning interest on this money during the time while the bill was paid and the money was not yet debited from your interest-bearing account. This is where money market fund accounts such as Merrill Lynch's Cash Management Account (CMA) come in handy. Most brokerage institutions offer these accounts, which combine a money market fund with unlimited checking, a charge card, a securities account, and a margin account. Many brokerage-house customers got tired of receiving a California check for example, when they happened to be in New York, for this often meant an extra two-week hold on their money until they were able to use it—and the issuer of the check was earning interest during that time. (This matter is being addressed by various Congressional finance committees, and you will have to ask your bank how they deal with it.) Be sure your bank doesn't hold your checks before crediting interest or giving you your money. Banks vary in their policies, and sometimes if you are merely in a different *county*, they delay cashing your check for a week or more—out-of-state could be two weeks—even though the funds have cleared the federal system within twenty-four hours.

Credit Insurance

A lucrative source of profit for banks occurs upon the granting of a loan when they charge you a small fee to underwrite enough insurance to pay it off should you die prior to its satisfaction. This coverage is not mandatory, but if taken will be the most expensive life insurance policy you ever will see. I advise that you decline this—and if your personal insurance does not cover the debt as you would like, to take on more term insurance through your agent, which should be far cheaper. If, of course, you are uninsurable and they can give you the credit life without an examination, there could be isolated cases where it could make sense.

Always save your loan documents and give them to your CPA for review at tax time. Different costs may be tax-deductible in addition to interest deductions.

Credit Cards

All credit cards are not created equal. At present there are four basic types: the revolving credit card, the debit card, the equity line card, and the American Express or Diners Club type of card.

(There are "experimental" cards being brought out by companies such as Sears, Mobil, and Shell, but their future is uncertain.)

1. The revolving credit card such as Visa or MasterCard accepts your charges and requires that a minimum portion be paid off each month. They charge high interest, between 16% and 21%. You can charge up to a given limit, and as long as you meet the monthly payment, you are in good standing. An added provision can be (particularly by Citicorp) that each dollar you spend through certain charge cards will create special "credit dollars." You can utilize these to buy products at a discount.
2. Debit cards are specially designed MasterCard, Visa, and American Express cards similar to those used in CMA-type accounts. When the bank receives notice of the charge, it is immediately paid and debited from your checking account, money market fund, or other accounts. This prevents use of the thirty-day-plus float and ensures that you will not be charged any interest. Some debit cards become regular charge cards if you have no cash on hand to cover the purchase, and you make a minimum monthly payment. There are also debit cards that enable a bank's customers to withdraw cash at any time from any of the bank's automatic teller machines and to charge purchases of goods and services directly to funds on deposit in the bank.
3. A hybrid of these accounts is known as an equity line card. These bank cards are used by homeowners who want to utilize their home equity for credit. Many local banks and savings and loans offer these cards, which are like a second mortgage. The cardholder is given an established line of credit based on equity built up in his or her home. He or she may charge against this equity up to that limit at any time. An outstanding balance on these charges is secured by the second mortgage against the home. This can be a good source of emergency funds, especially if you have $30,000, $50,000, or more in home equity. Equity cards can be the least expensive to use—interest rates are around 10% to 14%.
4. The types of cards issued by American Express and Diners Club bill you on a monthly basis and must be paid in full. They have special provisions for travel and other major items that can be paid over an extended period. Some cards, such as the American Express Gold Card, allow you

to write checks against your account, thus providing short-term, high-interest loans.

The charge card business is an enormous one, with participating merchants paying between 1% and 3%. If the company issuing the card can run its business for less than the fee charged, profits are even greater.

Prior to opening my own firm, I secured every charge card possible with the maximum limits. In my initial year, to maintain my standard of living and get myself out of some tight spots, I ran all my cards to the limit before working them down and paying them off in full. This of course can be an expensive way to establish credit. But at a time when bank rates were 14% and 16%, the cards provided an easy method to avoid all the miscellaneous fees involved in borrowing at a bank and still be able to obtain thousands of dollars.

Mortgages

Savings and loans and, more recently, banks are normally one of your first sources for obtaining a home mortgage. Be very careful when doing so, for the differences between institutions can be great. It pays to take a few weeks to check all of the local banking and mortgage institutions. Find out the cost of obtaining a mortgage, the points, legal charges, title searches, etc., as well as prepayment penalties, ability to assume, and how future rates are determined. More than half of all mortgages today are variable mortgages which adjust themselves to assorted indexes or "costs" of money. Even these formulas can vary widely, and sometimes you will find one institution offering you a very low first-year rate and no fees and then indexing itself to a very costly index, which eventually will raise your costs even higher. Whenever possible I would avoid thirty-year mortgages and look at fifteen-year ones. Although this might increase your current carrying costs by 10% to 15%, it will build up equity in your home that much faster. It is amazing how holding a thirty-year mortgage after five years, less than 3% of the loan borrowed has been paid—the rest has been all interest. In a fifteen-year mortgage, equity buildup occurs faster (almost 18% paid off in five years). Investors who have already taken out thirty-year mortgages can determine what the payment would be on a fifteen-year mortgage and can increase their payment each month as if it were a fifteen-year mortgage, paying off their principal on a regular basis (most mortgages permit this).

For example, a fifteen-year mortgage at 12% for $100,000 = $1200.17 per month, or total payments of $216,030.60. A thirty-year mortgage at 12% for $100,000 = $1028.62 per month, or total payments of $370,030. By increasing the frequency of your payments, you can save many thousands of dollars over your lifetime on your mortgages. By paying weekly instead of monthly, you may be able to reduce interest charges an additional 10% to 20%.

Conservative-Investor Portfolios

In my projections for 1987, I do not anticipate that inflationary forces (although building) will emerge at the double-digit level. I rate the potential of a major deflationary depression as 35% to 50% over the next six years. To compensate, for the sake of conservative investors, I have structured the portfolio to have 25% to 50% of its investment with direct and indirect government backing. Obviously, for the aggressive investors, this protection isn't as important. But even for risk-takers it is advisable to maintain some conservative positions in the event of a major economic collapse.

For conservative investors looking for maximum income and liquidity and minimum risk, I make the following recommendations:

- 5% of your portfolio in money market funds for liquid cash and emergency needs.
- 10% in government-backed participating mortgages, to give a balanced income and growth investment with a government guarantee behind it. The expected return of income and growth is 12% to 14%.
- 30% in government securities (for high-tax-bracket investors, municipal bonds with direct government backing) to give maximum credit safety and high current income of 10% to 11% and a tax-free income of 6% to 7%.
- 15% in single-pay plans to give a conservative, insured, tax-exempt 8% income with no market fluctuations and complete liquidity.
- 10% in all-cash real estate to give a 6% to 8% current income as well as 4% to 6% growth. This type of investment is essential to any portfolio, according to Goldman Sachs and Citibank. I concur. (This percentage will change in one to two years when the real estate market settles after the implementation of the new tax laws.)
- 20% in balanced mutual funds to give investors a moderate

Figure 12-3

CONSERVATIVE MODEL PORTFOLIO
(BASED ON A $100,000 ILLUSTRATION AND A 28% TAX BRACKET)

%	Investment	Income Assumption	Earned Income	Tax Benefits	Projected Growth
5%	Money Market Fund	6%	$300	—	—
10%	Gov't-Backed Participating Mortgages	7%	$700	—	5%-$500
30%	Gov't Securities*	10%-11%	$3150	Tax-Deferred	—
25%	Single-Pay Life	8%	$2000	Tax-Exempt	—
10%	All-Cash Real Estate	7%	$700	Tax-Sheltered	7%-$700
20%	Balanced Mutual Funds*	7%	$1400	Tax-Deferred	10%-$2000
	Total income:		$8250	Projected total growth:	$3200
	Taxes Due:		$1162		
	Net Income After Taxes:		$6988		
	Plus Growth Potential:		$3200		
	After-Tax Total* Return:		$10,188†		

*Through variable-life and tax-deferred plans income can be accessed from variable life on a tax-exempt basis. Put one-quarter to one-half of these mutual funds in international funds.
†Less taxes on gains when related.

income of 6% to 8% and a capital gain potential of 10% to 15%. The stock market has tremendous potential for the next two years, with 2500 in the Dow becoming realistic. (N.B. The best way to invest in the stock market is through mutual funds that are within variable-life plans. This permits interest, dividends, and capital gains to compound without current taxes and provides the ability to generate tax-exempt income to the plan holder.)

This portfolio provides immediate liquidity, with 50% directly government backed or insured. Some investors want the liquidity and government safety but don't need the income. They expect to be in a lower tax bracket in the future. The tax-deferred government funds allow them to let their income accumulate from government securities, without any current taxes. In addition, these funds are excellent for those expecting to retire within the next five to ten years, with a much lower tax bracket, or those who are currently retired and want to preserve the safety of these monies in the future for their estate.

Aggressive Model Portfolio

For the younger and more aggressive investor who would, generally speaking, be described as still working and creating a high taxable income, here is a more aggressive approach to minimize taxable income, maximize growth, and provide tax benefits. You would commit:

- 10% of your funds to leveraged real estate trusts and partnerships to maximize growth potential and give moderate, current tax write-offs. Expected holding period eight to twelve years.
- 10% to cable television partnerships to give moderate tax benefits and growth potential in a booming area that is adding 400,000 new subscribers each month. Expected holding period four to ten years.
- 10% to operating business opportunities through trust partnerships and private ventures that become available, to add growth potential by using the American economy.
- Balance these funds with 20% in a government fund to receive tax-free, and/or tax-deferred returns of anywhere between 7% (tax-free) to 10% to 11% (tax-deferred).

Figure 12-4

AGGRESSIVE MODEL PORTFOLIO
(BASED ON A $100,000 ILLUSTRATION AND A 40% TAX BRACKET)

%	Investment	Income Assumption	Earned Income	Tax Benefits	Projected Growth
10%	Leveraged Real Estate	2%	$200	$280	15%
10%	Cable TV	0	0	$280	15%
10%	Operating Business	2%	$200	minimal	15%
20%	Gov't Fund (Deferred)	10.5%	$2100	Tax-Deferred	0
30%	Mutual Funds*	3%	$900	Tax-Deferred	10%
10%	Single-Pay Life	7.5%	$750	Tax-Exempt Income	
10%	Precious Metals, Funds & Mint-State Coins	0	0	0	15%
	Projected Total Return:		$13,710	$4150	$560	$9000

*Put one-third to one-half in international funds.

- 40% in moderate to aggressive growth mutual funds to ride the wave of the bull market, which is expected to last for the next one to two years. Consider placing 5% to 10% of that in gold and precious-metal mutual funds or in gold or rare coins. If in 20% tax bracket or higher, invest through variable-life and variable-annuity plans to avoid current taxes on interest, dividends, and capital gains.
- 10% in single-pay plans to provide a high tax-exempt income and an alternate plan should the investor die before he or she is able to fully realize his or her goals.

Always have set aside enough cash to meet six months' worth of expenditures before determining percentages.

With this plan you provide liquidity with 70% of your funds, but 70% will be aggressively working for you and be creating many tax advantages.

This plan could provide investors in a 28% tax bracket a $4450 net income and $700 because of tax benefits, plus $7000 growth potential. Consider these investments for five- or fifteen-year terms and you should be able to ride any wild economic roller-coaster.

Your IRA money should be considered part of any portfolio, but for IRAs there are specific investments to pursue and others to avoid.

Government-backed and non-government-backed participating mortgages, which give an excellent balance for both inflation or deflation as well as high current rates of return, have been yielding between 10% and 16%. This is the best and most conservative way to put your IRA dollars to work.

More aggressive investors should consider the mutual funds. However, any losses sustained will not be tax-deductible, and any long-term capital gains will be taxed as ordinary income when paid to you in the future. This makes mutual fund investing more appropriate outside an IRA account.

In an IRA leveraged real estate or business funds (for example, cable TV, leasing, research and discovery, or movie partnerships) should be avoided altogether since they may create unnecessary taxes because of special IRS tax penalties due to the debt your investments have undertaken.

Although all-cash real estate and all-cash leasing programs may suit some people, my tendency is to invest IRA monies in very conservative government-backed and non-government-backed participating mortgages. These have been growing in popularity, and there are excellent choices and reputable firms that carry them.

Conclusion

Obviously, the model portfolio that is right for you depends on your objectives and tax bracket as well as current and future needs.

One of these portfolios might be ideal for you, or a combination of the plans could be more appropriate. Each investor must of course look at his or her situation and develop a strategy to meet these needs.

The two model portfolios, figures 12-3 and 12-4, were designed to show you the diversification needed to protect you in this or any other economic environment. Use these guidelines to weigh alternative investments. Then spread your risks so you won't be left in a lurch should one area crumble.

Nest egg investors should remember how fallout from the 1985 collapse of an obscure south Florida securities firm led to a banking crisis that rocked the nation. When banks throughout Ohio, Maryland, and elsewhere were temporarily shut down, shocked depositors suddenly were unable to get at their supposedly safe money. Horror stories abounded. People were reportedly reduced to eating dog food, while others risked losing their homes. This is an example of the risk of putting all your eggs in one basket, even if it's well padded with insurance and other government-backed guarantees.

The Joys of Diversification: A Broad Portfolio Pays Off

Over the past two decades a diversified investment index has outpaced the US stock market and the typical portfolio manager. The index consists of five equally weighted parts: US stocks, foreign stocks, US corporate and government bonds, real estate, and Treasury bills. This index has grown at a 10.2% compound rate since 1965, compared with 9.4% for the S&P 500-stock index and 7.9% for the median US money manager who invested in both stocks and bonds.

Most of the extra gains came from foreign equities and real estate, which raced ahead of US stocks for much of the 1970s and early 1980s. Analysts differ on whether this performance will continue. But they say diversified portfolios can be less volatile than all-equity accounts because swings in different parts of a broad portfolio often offset one another somewhat.

Individual investors could approximately duplicate the diversification index with a combination of Treasury bills, stocks of real estate investment trusts or limited partnerships in income-producing real estate, and mutual funds specializing in blue-chip and overseas stocks and in fixed-income securities.

Figure 12-5

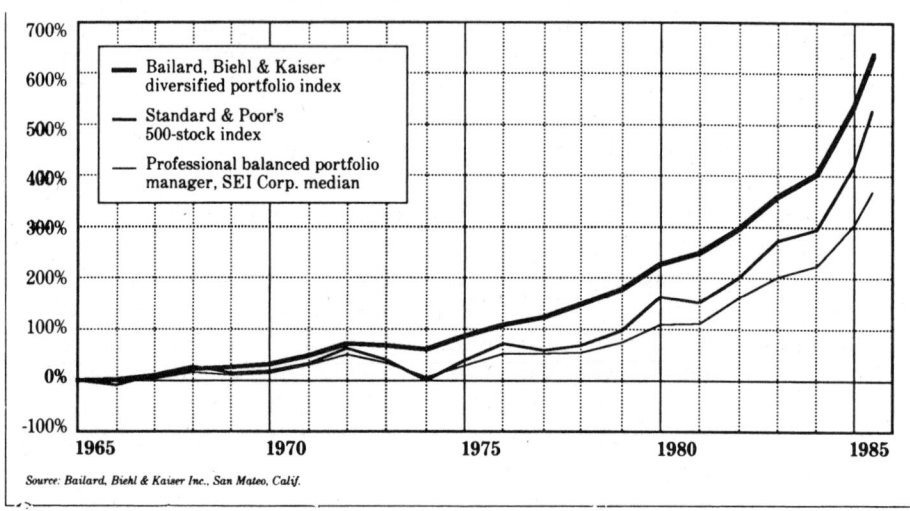

Source: Bailard, Biehl & Kaiser Inc., San Mateo, Calif.

13. Myths About Insurance

To be alive is to expose oneself to risk, whether injury, illness, natural disaster, or death. Today, the trend is to try to take every conceivable precaution: couples often commit 20% or more of their annual income trying to protect themselves from everything imaginable.

Insurance is an attempt to pool risks among a large, diversified group of persons who share the potential costs of something going wrong. Since it is improbable that disaster will strike a million persons simultaneously, "reasonable" premiums can be predicated to indemnify those who do get in trouble.

This concept is used in health and life, homeowners and medical insurance, and has helped spawn one of America's most powerful industries.

In 1984, $154 billion was spent by Americans on life, health, disability, and personal auto coverage, so it's no wonder the insurance industry has well over one trillion dollars in assets and employs more than a million people in the United States. Approximately half are salespersons, who normally make large commissions on premiums.

Time after time, after meeting with couples, I have found very few with a proper balance of insurance protection. Even more amazing to me is how little effort was taken to pay the least for their protection. It is quite normal for 10% to 20% of a person's earned income to go for insurance. Think of the average costs: car insurance, $600; health insurance for your family, $800; life insurance premiums, $1000; homeowner's insurance, $500; disability insurance, $800. This money, if it were to accumulate and compound over a lifetime, could exceed $2 to $3 million: proof enough that in order to build a nest egg, you should understand the uses and abuses of insurance.

America's Biggest Disease

I'll never forget driving along on a beautiful summer day in West Palm Beach and being caught in a traffic jam. There, on the car ahead of me, was a bumper sticker that read, THE TROUBLE WITH AMERICA IS APATHY BUT WHO CARES? I chuckled to myself. How true.... Consider all the people who, burdened with negative mental attitudes, just manage to exist, and never realize their dreams or attain their goals. I meet them all the time. Forty-nine out of fifty of them will never become financially independent. Considering these statistics, what can we do so that they won't become dependent on relatives, friends, or charity for survival?

Life is for living; for taking the risks of reaching for your star. There are a number of insurance myths (including a "next-lifetime" policy to give you a nest egg upon your reincarnation) that you should know about in order to save thousands of wasted dollars for illusory safety.

Only when you marry or assume other financial obligations, when your income becomes imperative to pay debts or finance the baby's future, do you need insurance. Buy term insurance and invest your remaining money in IRAs and other tax-oriented areas.

The A. L. Williams Company has created a multibillion-dollar sales force doing just that—helping people convert their whole-life insurance to term and investing the rest in IRAs. An admirable move, representing quite a victory over the old-line insurance companies that built up their power and wealth through whole-life policies. Unfortunately, despite this step forward, there are still many shortfalls of their company's approach. Buyer, beware.

New competition may come from the banks, for threats to change the insurance laws have begun major breakthroughs in the banking industry.

Myth Number One: Buy whole-life insurance when you are young in order to get lower premiums and a cash-value buildup for your retirement.

Response: I'm amazed when new clients, men and women in their twenties and thirties, tell me that they are paying $500 to $1000 a year for a life insurance policy. As justification they show me a printout demonstrating that the premium, if paid over their lifetime, would produce a large six-figure number.

Since these clients are often single and have no dependents, it is not likely that anyone would be left destitute if they died, so these policies are a waste of money. If the insured had taken those dollars and invested them, his or her overall rate of return would have been two to four times as much. And he or she could have possibly earned ten to twenty times the amount over the same period. *If no one would suffer financial hardship if you died, you don't need life insurance.* (There are two exceptions: insurance for tax reasons and some unusual kinds of investments.) The FTC conducted a major investigation of the industry and established that the insurance companies were paying their whole-life policyholders 3.5% when other markets were offering from 6% to 9%. Do you want to earn the lowest possible rates on your money?

Myth Number Two: All insurance companies charge about the same.

Response: Shop around and reduce your insurance costs. You don't have to pay for the privilege of dealing with a world-renowned company just because you saw its ads on TV and it sponsors the local baseball team. Those advertising and PR costs may be passed on to you. The "name brands" are often no different from the "generic products": similar policies underwritten by more obscure companies but equally rated by independent research companies. Look at the ingredients (this is what a good financial planner will do for you) and get the same insurance benefits at less cost.

One winter, when suffering from a lousy head cold, I went into a pharmacy to pick up a box of Contac, which I knew would clear my head and help me think straight. While standing in line, I happened to look at a similar-looking pill with a brand name I had never heard of, manufactured by a company I *had* heard of, that was selling at half the price. I quickly picked up the cartons to look at their ingredients. Much to my chagrin, they were identical and contained the same number of equal-strength capsules. I put down the well-known brand name, bought the cheaper brand, and enjoyed the same relief for half the price. That was a good return on my money: I saved 50%.

The same applies to insurance. The major insurance companies are often burdened with long-term bonds and mortgages at low rates of return. Their investment returns are substantially depressed because of the nature of their portfolios as compared to firms that have grown recently and placed their investments at times of much higher interest rates. If your financial planner isn't an independent insurance agent as well, have him or her recommend one who can help you shop around among different companies to get the best rates. A few years ago I checked with a few companies when I wanted to get a million dollars' worth of coverage for myself. The best price I could find was $1800. Within a couple of years, new actuarial tables combined with higher interest-rate assumptions being used by the insurance companies made it important for me to continue to shop. In subsequent years I systematically cut premiums to $1400, $1200, and now $850 a year for a million dollars' worth of coverage. And I'm four years older. You should always consider a term-insurance program that allows you to reenter and take another exam to come in at the lower rates. This is a way the healthy are rewarded.

A Trick to Save You Thousands

Insurance companies work funny. If you are thirty and you buy a term policy from a competitive company with good rates, you can expect to pay $800 for a million dollars' worth of coverage. Staying with this company over the next five years, you would, at thirty-five, be paying $1050 and at forty, $1250. Still very competitive rates. But if you are a new customer coming in at thirty-five to buy a million dollars' worth of coverage, that firm would charge you $850 for your first year. And if you come in new at forty, it would charge you $950. It almost makes sense to cancel and get a new policy every year with this company, since it would cut your insurance costs by 30%, 50%, or even 70%!

This is how reenter programs work. Every five years, or maybe every three, or even every year, the insurance company will let you take another exam. As long as the results are good, it will keep you at the lower rates, as if you had just started fresh. If you cannot find companies that do this, you may be forced to switch from company to company (there are more than 1800 insurance companies in America, so you should never run out). Unfortunately, many insurance companies are trying to discourage this stratagem. Many companies may refuse you if it appears you are constantly canceling your insurance or changing it every year. By refusing your business, the companies are probably indulging in unfair trade and antitrust violations. But until challenged and declared in the wrong, they will get away with it, as they did for many years when they put roadblocks in the way of replacing whole-life insurance with term policies. This was once a nightmare of paperwork for the agents.

If you can reduce your insurance outlays by 20%, 30%, or 40%, the money can be saved. Use this method to help build your nest egg.

Self-Insuring

One of the simplest ways to reduce your premiums by 20% or more is to increase the deductible—the amount you pay before the policy pays. Going from $100 to $500 deductible for your car or medical insurance can save you in the neighborhood of $500 every year. You will be insuring only against major risks, not minor ones. To do this, you must minimize risks—practice risk management. For example, to self-insure against minor illnesses that can, when occurring over a period of several years, nonetheless result in high medical bills, eat a balanced diet, exercise daily, quit smoking, and find some think-time for yourself. These actions will cut down the frequency and length of these illnesses. Deductibles can usually be adjusted in homeowner's, automobile, life, and disability insurance. Making yourself more aware of the risks you are accepting and handling them responsibly is not only the way to a greater savings but also to a more successful life.

Myth Number Three: Group insurance is always the cheapest buy.

Response: This is often true in health insurance. But when adding monthly costs deducted for various life insurance programs, I find that unless people are forty or older, they would be better off purchasing term insurance outside of most group plans. For those fifty-five to sixty, group is usually a bargain. But again, shop around and check other plans. Insurance costs have come down drastically. Those of you who are retiring and are having trouble getting on any of the government-sponsored programs or buying separate individual insurance should investigate converting your former group health plan to cover you after you are no longer with the group. You may get special rates.

Myth Number Four: Disability insurance isn't essential.

Response: Disability insurance is frequently ignored—a mistake in my opinion. It's unpleasant to consider, but the chances of being disabled before reaching sixty-five are some twenty times as great as those of dying before that age. How much is disability insurance worth, and how much should you carry? It depends on the size of your nest egg. If you are the head of a large family, with bills to be paid, you could calculate how much your family would need to survive for six months or a year, before insurance would take over. Much depends on your life-style. If you smoke two packs a day, don't exercise, and are fifty pounds overweight, you will need more disability than someone who cares for his or her body. In many ways we create our own risks in life and pay for them accordingly.

Myth Number Five: All insurance promoted through the mail is worthless.

Response: I don't know how often I've been deluged by mass-mailing pieces offering to pay $50 a day for hospital stays, $100 a day if disabled, $100 a day if cancer strikes, or protection against credit-card theft. Millions of people succumb to these pitches, which I think are overpriced and generally worthless. But don't automatically reject life insurance sold this way. Here's why.

The No-Load Industry

No-load mutual funds—funds sold at net-asset value—have constituted one of the greatest growth industries in recent times, one that enabled hundreds of billions of dollars to be raised in a short period. Learning from this success story, some insurance companies now allow you to buy life insurance through the mail instead of from agents. The advantage to you is that a whole-life policy could pay commissions of 240% or more to the agent. And the more that goes to the agent, the less cash-value buildup you will have and the longer it will take to get it. Even term policies can pay out commissions of 40% to 60% of the premium, substantially less than whole-life policies; still, you pay for it. Premiums vary widely; the average commission for a $100,000 term policy could be $100, but for a $100,000 whole-life policy it could be $2000.

Face-to-face confrontations can be valuable, so reducing insurance costs by eliminating the middleman—the sales rep—might not pay over the long run if you anticipate questions or problems concerning your policy. Do what makes you feel the most comfortable, but don't reject the no-loads out of hand.

Innovations:
Whole Life, Term, Universal Life, Variable Life

For hundreds of years, before the first policy was sold over a kitchen table, insurance consisted of pooling the resources of the family or the community in order to share wealth and hardship. Handing over these responsibilities to governments and profit-oriented institutions was a dangerous but ultimately necessary transfer of power—one that lowered the level of individual responsibility. Pooling resources equitably within a large family or a community was profitable when the group consisted of men and women who were responsible, ate properly, exercised, and generally took care of themselves physically and spiritually as prerequisites for belonging to the group, although sharing insurance within a family entailed certain risks because all members had to be included.

Insurance today isn't what it once was. Changing tax laws and investor demands have led to the creation of new types of investments that combine several features. The most popular of these are:

Whole life, which requires that a set amount be paid each year for life or for some agreed-upon period such as twenty, thirty, or forty years. This averages the high cost of coverage when older with the more modest cost when the policyholder is young. The policy pays the beneficiary a death benefit should the worst happen, and also builds a cash value should it not. The rates of return on whole-life policies have been from 3.5% to 5.5%, as commissions for the first few years may run from 100% to 250% of the annual premium. Normally, three or four years pass before a policyholder achieves any significant cash-value buildup. The plans vary greatly and sometimes yield sophisticated opportunities to use tax laws to help you supplement policy costs. Whole life should not be confused with single-pay life, which is mainly an investment product and does not have annual premiums paid by the policyholder. Whole life normally has limited usage and should be purchased only in special circumstances.

Yet, for the income-minded investor, single-premium whole life is a refreshing change from the old whole-life concept. An investor can make a lump-sum payment and have 100% of his money "invested" to earn a high current return (8½% in 1987). The income earned is added to your original principal and may be withdrawn on a no-cost-loan basis each year without creating taxes. This plan provides substantial death benefits (secondary) but is primarily used as an investment vehicle as a municipal bond alternative.

Term insurance, which usually is devoid of the cash-value buildup that whole life has, is in essence a bare-bones policy that charges you for the cost of coverage. These policies normally change the premium requirements every year, whereas a whole-life policy has one set premium for life. Premiums may commence at one-tenth of the whole-life's premium and then end up being three or four times what you would be paying for whole-life insurance. Whereas whole life has you pay the average of these costs over its life, term doesn't. Term premiums can be set for five-year or even ten-year periods, as the features of a whole-life policy are combined with the term policy. *Buying term and investing the rest will produce much better results for your nest egg.*

Universal life combines the features of a term policy with that of an annuity. Developed in the late '70s, its coverage permits large deposits to be made in addition to paying for your term insurance so that these funds can earn interest in either a money market fund or some type of fixed-income side fund. Earnings from that fund are used to pay premiums for your next year's coverage. This permits investors to use pretax dollars rather than more expensive after-tax money to pay for their insurance. Universal life has taken the life insurance field by storm as agents find it harder to sell their high-commission whole-life policies.

Variable life is the next step up. Mutual funds from Scudder, Valueline, American Capital, Merrill Lynch, Prudential and Vanguard (Wellington), and many others can now be bought through this plan. All interest, dividends, and capital gains on these funds (which can be switched among a family of funds) compound tax-free in your account. This combines the features of a term policy with that of a variable annuity. Here an investor can make lump sum or annual payments that (1) pay his or her term-insurance cost and the remainder, (2) can then be invested in mutual funds of stocks, bonds, government securities, zero-coupon bonds, real estate, utilities, precious metals, convertibles, high-yield bonds, international securities, money market funds, or possibly a fixed-rate account. The idea is for the earnings from these investments (1) to be protected from taxes currently, (2) to be used to pay the annual insurance premiums pretax while (3) building up an investment-portfolio nest egg that is free from any current taxation on dividends and capital gains and possibly can be free from future taxation (at death, all proceeds pass to the beneficiary *free* of income tax). Additionally investors can "borrow" their accumulations on a *tax-free* basis at a cost of $0–10 a year per thousand.

I strongly believe *term insurance* is the best when you are young and need maximum coverage at minimum cost. I recommend the *variable-life plan* for superior long-term investment results as you accumulate investment funds. For older people, I suggest using variable and *single-pay life* when needing stable sources of income and alternatives to municipal bonds and taxable mutual funds.

The investment world, like a skillet, is not always level. Portions of your nest egg may burn around the edges from unnecessary taxes. Still, your nest egg as a whole may be nurtured to a healthy chick. Using insurance-policy tax advantages to develop your nest egg is a basic tenet. But remember that improper usage can leave you with egg on your face.

Figure 13-1

Planning for Your Future

CASH NEEDS	Couple #1	Couple #2	Your Data
1. **Immediate money fund:** To pay bills presented after death, such as medical and hospital expenses, funeral expenses, attorney and executor fees, federal estate taxes and probate court costs.	$10,000	$10,000	
2. **Debt liquidation:** Amount needed to pay installment credit, unpaid notes, school and auto loans, and bills.	$ 5000	$10,000	
3. **Emergency fund:** For unexpected bills not readily payable from current income: auto or home repairs, medical bills.	$25,000	$37,500	
4. **Mortgage/rent payment fund (optional):** Some families plan to pay off the mortgage if the insured person dies, so the survivors have a debt-free home.	-0-	$60,000	
5. **Child/home care fund (optional):** To pay for new expenses created as a result of the death of a spouse formerly performing these duties without any cash outlay.	-0-	-0-	

		Couple #1	Couple #2
6.	**Educational fund:** The costs of a 4-year undergraduate education vary, but $20,000/child is usually the minimum that should be provided.	-0-	$40,000
7.	**Subtotal:** Add lines 1 thru 6	$40,000	$157,500
8.	**Available assets:** Such as savings and existing life insurance including amount provided by employer.	$15,000	$50,000
9.	**Cash needs requirement:** Subtract line 8 from line 7. If line 8 exceeds line 7, note negative amount.	$25,000	$107,500

COUPLE PROFILES

Couple #1   30 years old; each spouse earns $25,000; no children; doesn't own a home.

Couple #2   45 years old; one wage earner with income of $75,000; two children in college; house worth $150,000 with a $60,000 mortgage.

DISABILITY INCOME NEEDS	Couple #1	Couple #2	Your Data
1. **Gross income:** Annual wage or salary of the individual to be insured.	$25,000	$75,000	
2. **Income to be replaced:** Multiply line 1 by 60% to 80%, depending on family's needs. Percentages reflect tax savings; benefits from employee-paid disability insurance are	$17,500 ($25,000 × 70%)	$48,750 ($75,000 × 65%)	

tax-free. In general, higher-income families need a smaller percentage of replacement income.		
3. **Annual Social Security disability income:** Benefits depend on age and career earnings. Generally, workers who earn more than $23,000 per year can expect individual benefits of $8000 to $10,500 annually, and 50% more if there are dependent children. Use zero if family doesn't want to depend on Social Security.	-0-	$9000
4. **Required income (subtotal):** Subtract line 3 from line 2.	$17,500	$39,750
5. **Other income sources:** Add all earnings from income-producing assets including interest from bank accounts, money market funds, etc. Don't include the principal, which can erode quickly, or IRA earnings.	$840 (Assumes 7% return on $12,000 portfolio not in IRA)	$2660 (Assumes 7% return on $38,000 portfolio not in IRA)
6. **Disability insurance needs:** Subtract line 5 from line 4. This is the annual gap that could be filled by disability insurance.	$16,660	$37,090

INCOME OBJECTIVE

Based on a study by the Bureau of Labor Statistics, the following are typical income objectives that would permit a family to maintain its standard of living after the death of a wage earner, assuming that the mortgage on the residence is paid or a rent fund has been established, and that educational expenses are provided for separately.

Annual Gross Income	Percentage of Gross Income Required
Up to $35,000	70%
$35,001–$39,000	66%
$39,001–$43,000	63%
$43,001–$48,000	60%
Over $48,000	57%

Note: Use 70% if both spouses work.

SOCIAL SECURITY BENEFITS (Estimated)

Annual benefits to surviving spouse if he or she is unemployed.

Age	Income*	1 Child	2 or More
29 or under	$35,700+	$15,400	$17,900
	30,000	14,300	16,700
	25,000	13,200	15,400
	20,000	12,100	14,100
40	35,700+	13,600	15,800
	30,000	13,100	15,300
	25,000	12,900	15,100
	20,000	12,000	14,000
50	35,700+	12,800	14,800
	30,000	12,500	14,600
	25,000	12,400	14,500
	20,000	11,800	13,800
54 or over	35,700+	12,600	14,700
	30,000	12,400	14,400
	25,000	12,300	14,300
	20,000	11,600	13,600

Annual benefits to surviving spouse if he or she is employed.

Age	Income*	1 Child	2 Children	3 or More
29 or under	$35,700+	$7700	$15,400	$17,900
	30,000	7200	14,300	16,700
	25,000	6600	13,200	15,400
	20,000	6100	12,100	14,100
40	35,700+	6800	13,600	15,800
	30,000	6600	13,100	15,300
	25,000	6500	12,900	15,100
	20,000	6000	12,000	14,000
50	35,700+	6400	12,800	14,800
	30,000	6300	12,500	14,600
	25,000	6200	12,400	14,500
	20,000	5900	11,800	13,800
54 or over	35,700+	6300	12,600	14,700
	30,000	6200	12,400	14,400
	25,000	6100	12,300	14,300
	20,000	5800	11,700	13,600

INCOME NEEDS	Couple #1	Couple #2	Your Data
1. **Income:** Combined income of wage earners.	$50,000	$75,000	
2. **Income objective:** Annual income needed after death of wage earner. See "Income Objective" table.	$35,000 (70% × $50,000)	$42,750 (57% × $75,000)	
3. **Survivor's Social Security benefits:** See "Benefits" table. If no minor children, use zero.	-0-	-0-	

*Use latest annual income of deceased. Actual benefits determined by wage history of deceased. Benefits to spouse are payable until the youngest child reaches age sixteen. Spouses receive no benefits until they reach age sixty or if there are no minor children at home.

4. **Income shortage subtotal:** Subtract line 3 from line 2.	$35,000	$42,750
5. **Other income:** This includes income from the other spouse when both work, trust income, and income from producing property not included in line 8 of "cash needs" worksheet.	$25,000	-0-
6. **Total annual income shortage:** This is the amount of annual income to be replaced. Subtract line 5 from line 4.	$10,000	$42,750
7. **Endowment required:** Amount of life insurance needed to provide this income; derived by dividing income shortage (line 6) by a projected interest rate. Use a 7% rate as a conservative estimate but raise the rate if you expect survivors to use some of the principal.	$142,857 ($10,000 ÷ 7%)	$427,500 ($42,750 ÷ 10%)
8. **Cash requirement:** Amount from line 9 of cash needs worksheet. Note if negative amount.	$25,000	$107,500
9. **Life insurance required:** Add lines 7 and 8.	$167,857	$535,000

14. Why Mutual Funds Never Perform the Way You'd Expect

Mutual funds have been the fastest-growing investment area in America during the past decade. Billions of dollars have poured into these funds from investors seeking the expertise of professional management while choosing from a wide range of investment objectives. The most popular of these funds, of course, have been money market mutual funds through the sophisticated linkup between brokerages and banks. Money market fund accounts with checks, credit cards, flexibility to buy stocks and bonds, and go on margin have overtaken the financial services field. More than $200 billion has been invested here. Investors seeking professional market guidance for stocks, bonds, government securities, municipal bonds, junk bonds, and combinations of the above have invested in tens of billions more. A new awareness has evolved in the marketplace. Mutual funds have become buzz words used by publications to promote an entirely new range of financial services to the public. *Money* magazine has been a leader in bringing the complicated world of Wall Street into the home by combining the *People* and *Look* magazine concept with financial reports. Using colorful illustrations, graphs, and other devices, *Money* has helped reeducate the American public in financial management. More newsletters advising how to switch among mutual funds, or when to buy and sell stocks in different mutual funds, have come to the market in the last ten years than in the entire history of man.

Given the thousands of funds to choose from and the tremendous amount of information available to help evaluate these funds, why is it that controversies still rage on mutual funds and their benefits? I will give two sides of the story to help you distinguish among the risks and rewards, pitfalls and benefits.

The advent of the Individual Retirement Account (IRA), which permits investors to earmark $2000 a year in earned income for building a retirement nest egg, has probably more than anything else opened up opportunities for the mutual fund market. IRAs represent billions of dollars every year, and even today only a small segment of workers, about 10%, are exercising their option to use self-directed investments in the mutual fund area. This opens up a marketplace that has touched only one in ten people, leaving tremendous growth potential. I would not be surprised if the number of mutual funds once again doubled in the next ten to fifteen years, as more and more workers look toward mutual funds for their IRAs, pension plans, and other investment vehicles.

Question: What is a mutual fund?

Answer: A mutual fund is an offering by a professional management company. It involves the pooling of monies from a great number of investors—hence "mutual"—to invest in a diverse selection of stocks and/or bonds, depending on which fund you join.

Q: How exactly does it work?

A: Once you have placed your money with a fund, the company will use those dollars to invest in stocks, Treasury bills, and other instruments. You have the option of receiving monthly dividends, withdrawing funds (which involves selling a part of your principal investment), reinvesting dividends in the plan, or choosing from among various options offered by that particular company.

Q: Why should I consider a mutual fund and not individual stock market trading?

A: In a mutual fund, the buying and selling of the securities is controlled by a *professional* team of managers. If you were to thoroughly research your own securities, you would have little time to spend on your own career, let alone to enjoy life. A mutual fund manager's full-time job is to buy and sell each security. He or she visits companies, speaks with top management, and has vast amounts of information flowing through his or her office. He receives daily reports on various companies, the industry, the economy, the impact of new tax laws, and much more. His objective is to make well-timed decisions in managing your investment dollars. His ultimate goal is to earn the highest possible profit for the investors.

Q: What types of mutual funds are available?

A: A great number. Stock funds emphasize anything from growth to income and safety. Specialty funds invest in specialized areas, which include utilities, gold and other precious metals, municipal bonds or government securities. There are also "contrarian funds" specializing in stocks that are out-of-favor at the present time, but that are expected to soon rise again. Balanced funds may combine bonds for good income and stocks to achieve growth.

Q: How do I know if a mutual fund is for me?

A: This depends largely on your investment temperament. If you are comfortable with the day-to-day market vacillations, a mutual fund could be for you. You must also consider your investment goals. Figure out exactly what you are looking for, discuss it with your investment planner, and decide together whether a mutual fund is for you. Consider the fund as an intermediate-term investment and expect to stay in it for at least three to five years, preferably eight to ten. As investment markets go in cycles, it is important that this money not be required for short-term needs like a vacation or a new car.

Q: How diverse is this investment?

A: Mutual funds are prohibited by law (Investment Companies Act of 1940) from investing more than 5% of their assets in any one company, and they can't own more than 10% of the outstanding shares of any company. Still, we always recommend that you place *no more* than 20% to 25% of your money in any one investment area. So, while the investment itself may be diverse within the stock market, if you have much more than 25% of your money in mutual funds, I do not consider your portfolio properly diversified.

Q: Is this a taxable investment?

A: Yes, unless it is sheltered by a deferred annuity, variable-life, or retirement plan.

Q: What should I look for in a mutual fund?

A: Management! A mutual fund is only as good as its managers. Many companies can say, "I led the country last year." Great, but how did they do five or ten years ago? Are they going to manage this fund in the future or turn it over to someone else? You should also look for a family of funds (a group of many funds managed by the same people). This allows for greater choice, and, in many cases, telephone "switchability." In other words, within some groups of funds, you can switch from one to another several times per year at no cost via a simple toll-free phone call.

Q: How can I invest in a mutual fund?

A: Portions of a mutual fund, called shares, must be purchased through qualified financial service institutions such as financial planners, banks, and broker-dealer firms. A minimum initial investment of anywhere from $250 to $500 is usually required, and about $50 is necessary for subsequent investments. You can make a lump-sum investment, have money debited directly from your checking account, or make periodic payments.

Q: What kind of performance can I expect?

A: This depends largely on the managers of the fund, and not necessarily on the market itself. Even if the market is on a downswing, your managers could have sold at the apex and may be preparing to buy at rock-bottom to await a jump in price. Any growth funds that I normally recommend have a minimum average performance of at least 20% per year for a period of five or more years. (This is no guarantee of future performance.)

Most magazines or newsletters that track mutual funds normally use the results of the past three-, five-, and ten-year periods, cumulatively, to compare funds. This is like trying to build a baseball team based on performance from the past five or ten years and not looking to see what might be going on *this season*. One of your first moves when evaluating a consistently winning team is to see if the personnel who helped that happen are still on board. As in sports, there are retirements, transfers, and burnouts. You could base your decision on past performance and get a team of rookies who need five years to get their act together, but in the meantime are taking credit for the achievements of their predecessors. Know whose talents you are buying.

Remember that rules can change; you could find yourself locked into a position longer than prudent. You could misinterpret economic signals. Specialty funds are a good example of the need to check out the management of your mutual fund or funds. Gold funds had a good track record for a decade or so, but people who bought them in 1983 lost money through 1986. Utility stocks did well from 1983 through 1986, but were weak from 1980 to 1983. Bonds, which were stellar performers from 1984 through 1986, nonetheless haven't made up for all the losses they inflicted on portfolios in the late '70s and early '80s.

A Checklist for Mutual Fund Purchases

Be sure that:

- You have maximized your flexibility by considering a "family" of funds in which you can move around at no extra charge. ($5 standard charge)
- Your fund has a good performance record.
- Management experts responsible for that record are still on board.
- Your money won't be needed for short-term purposes or emergencies.
- The fund is compatible with your goals for growth or return.

- Dollar-cost-averaging is considered to help build your nest egg.
- You are willing to monitor your fund's performances or have a financial planner do it for you.

Load Versus No-Load

It is vital to monitor the performance of the fund managers both in good times and in bad. The funds that were able to stay positive when the market dropped 15% to 20%, and those that substantially outperformed in an up-market are the ones that should be top candidates on your list. The managers should feel confident of their abilities and have similar, quality personnel involved. Too often decisions are made on which funds to buy based on whether the fund is load or no-load. It might be best to pay an up-front load and have a professional adviser suggest a fund. The adviser will help monitor your investment and move you to different funds at pivotal times. Investors should understand their own sentiments and abilities as well as their weaknesses when making investment decisions.

Investors constantly seem to look for a free lunch: they tend to think that an investment with no commission presents a better, safer opportunity.

Let's look at the $1 trillion banking system, which charges no commissions to put your money in their CDs or money market funds. Banks offer by far the most common of all no-load investments. Yet, isn't there a load when you get 6% interest while they lend your money at 11% to 12%? They are charging you 50% per year of income earned! Banks must find some way to pay for their overhead, fancy offices, and gift-giving programs.

No-load investments, whether in banks, money market funds, mutual funds, or limited partnerships, must be viewed within their proper perspective. Nobody goes into business intending to give away services without making a profit.

The question is this: Is it better to disclose up front the profit you're making by helping investors place their monies in various areas? Or should profit be hidden behind an array of elaborate prospectuses and accounting methods? Is there such a thing as a free lunch? Definitely not.

That is the first thing you must learn before basing your investment decisions strictly on load or no-load.

A "no-load" investment avoids paying up-front commissions to the person placing you in that investment. Because these investments do not pay investment bankers for their services, they are, quite logically, unwilling to deal in this area unless they charge annual fees. Even though the fund is no-load, you are charged annual fees to pay for management, staff, and advertising. This means you must look deep into a prospectus to assess the expenses involved in any fund, whether it is a mutual fund or a limited partnership. (This now creates "phantom income"—in the 1986 Tax Law change, advisory and investment charges must exceed 2% of your adjusted gross income before any can be tax-deductible. Before 1987 these fees were debited by the fund before distributing interest, dividends, or gains. There were no tax consequences. Now these fees will become taxable to a certain degree for investors, even though they don't receive the money. In some funds the taxes due will exceed distributions made. Hence "phantom income" variable annuities and variable life can solve this problem.) In some mutual funds, the annual fee can run up to 3% a year, and in limited partnerships from 3% to 10% of the income generated.

True, in a no-load fund, more of your money is available for investing. But the question remains: Who is giving you free advice—and is this advice worth the paper it's written on? What motivation is there to be accountable to you when your investment planner has no vested interest or responsibility in whether he or she is right or wrong?

Timing, which is so important, tax considerations, estate considerations, and better alternatives are part of the expertise you buy when going into a load fund.

For no-load investors, it is common to pay an annual fee for review and management of assets. And this fee can exceed the cost of working with a financial planner who earns his or her fees by placing the money up front. Remember—your financial planner does not usually charge annual fees, but nonetheless maintains a vested interest in order to keep your business. If something goes wrong, you can meet with him and work it out. In a no-load fund it can be very frustrating working with an array of poorly trained service reps at the end of an 800 phone line.

Even insurance companies are adopting the no-load concept. As I mentioned, many are selling products by mail without using agents. Single-pay life plans now enable investors to have 100% of their money as cash value immediately.

You would be foolish to attempt piloting a jumbo jet if you had not first trained to fly a smaller aircraft. Are you qualified to pilot your financial future?

An excellent compromise has emerged in the last few years that appears to encompass the best of both worlds. Many funds have now come out with "vanishing-load" investments. This permits 100% of your funds to go directly into the investment without any sales commission. As long as an investor stays with the fund for the required time (usually five years), a sales charge will never be deducted. (Normally the sales charge diminishes by 1% each year, so that in the fourth investment year there would be only a 1% charge.) As most of these funds are part of a family of funds, you can switch around within the group without incurring any deferred sales charges. These are most attractive in variable-life plans.

The financial adviser you are dealing with is paid a commission directly from the company, not from your funds. This gives him or her motivation, and you the greater amount of money actually invested. However, these funds often do have expenses that are slightly higher than "no-load" funds in order to reimburse the syndicator for the sales costs involved. Just as no-load funds must foot the bill for massive advertising, vanishing-load funds must pay for their promotion by the financial planner. There are many excellent "compromise" funds of this nature. But, since the commissions are often half of what a load fund pays, sales representatives often play them down.

No-load and vanishing-load investments are an excellent way to put more of your money to work—but only if you are certain that they are the right investment vehicles to meet your objectives and tax situation.

When Peter Lynch, of Fidelity's popular Magellan Fund, which has grown from a few hundred million dollars to nearly two billion, was asked for his opinion on this subject, his response was candid. He pointed out that, despite his fund's great performance, when a fund grows to an enormous size, it may no longer be able to maintain previous dynamic growth patterns, even with the same first-rate management. When a few stocks soar, the gains are diluted when there are billions of dollars in the fund. The same gains can make an impact when the fund is a small one. Lynch said he would look for a smaller fund moving ahead with good, proven management. He felt this would be a way to outperform by two or three times the achievements of the larger funds. His concern is shared by many professionals, and underscores the need to seek out opportunities. Despite his fund's large size, it still manages to be one of the industry's stellar performers. *Don't expect large funds to always be the best place for your money.* Stock and bond mutual funds are aggressive investments and must be considered as such. Over the long term, study upon study has shown that the stock market has returned a 9% to 9.5% annual return. A good mutual fund can more than double that. Advocates and detractors lock horns over these figures as one camp criticizes the "timing" factor which investors add to the mutual funds. Many mutual fund buyers buy at the top of the markets and sell at the bottom. This is why dollar-cost-averaging is an excellent way to deal with nest egg mutual funds over a long term. The minimum term to be considered in placing money in mutual funds should be four to ten years.

When you dollar-cost-average, you invest the same amount of money in the same security at the same interval over an extended period of time, with the assumption that the stock market will fluctuate but eventually go up.

Assume you can discipline yourself to save $100 a month or at some other interval, and that you have the earning capacity and self-discipline to continue this for a long period. It makes little difference in your final results whether the market goes up, down, or sideways when you start: the key is to get started!

If you are paralyzed into a state of indecision on what to buy, when to buy, and when to sell, which has caused you to fall into the delay-linger-wait syndrome, skip buying a particular stock and instead choose a *family of mutual funds* with good management and a commendable performance record during good and poor markets. Pick a family with a conservative and an aggressive growth fund, government funds, and a money market fund. A fund is especially adaptable to dollar-cost-averaging because under an accumulation plan you can buy fractional shares. And don't overlook mutual funds investing in overseas markets: they were the top performers for 1985.

At least one study has shown that US stock prices have not advanced to any appreciable extent during the past nineteen years. When inflation is taken into account, stock market participants have suffered severe losses in purchasing power. On an inflation-adjusted basis, the Dow Jones Industrial Average would need to double today to reflect real price changes. Gasoline costs four times what it did in 1966. A German car is priced four to five times as high, and residential real estate today is out of nearly everyone's financial reach. Unless you've traded the market especially well, a buy-and-hold strategy has not been a great success.

The cumulative return of US stocks from 1970 to 1980 was a mere 16%. At the same time, other major international stock markets soared or, at a minimum, kept pace with inflation. Hong Kong, the world's third-largest financial center, saw its stock market advance by nearly 600%. Singapore advanced by 300%. Markets in Japan and Australia doubled. American investors enjoyed a compounded rate of return of slightly more than 1% per year—hardly the stuff to write home about. (However, 1985 was great and may be the beginning for a major move to 3000 on the Dow.)

Today, the financial press proclaims that the US market is at an all-time high, in value as well as volume. Unfortunately, many foreign markets continue to outstrip us. In 1984 our domestic market placed ninth in performance compared with eighteen major international markets. Even Italy did five times as well, despite the all-powerful dollar. Even worse was 1983. US stocks ranked eleventh out of eighteen during that year.

Foreign markets, in my view, represent an excellent opportunity to score startling profits. The performance of these markets historically has been substantially better than that found in the United States. Today, fund managers domiciled in North America manage hundreds of billions of dollars in investment funds, and less than 4% of these funds held by institutions is diversified outside the United States. Fund managers are only now discovering the international share market. Massive amounts of cash rushing into growth markets such as Japan, Australia, and Hong Kong will have a significant result. The past strong performance of these markets may even be surpassed. Profits may await the investor who gets in early.

Overview

As you can see, mutual funds are not the place for the uninformed or those unable to tolerate a certain degree of risk; 20% to 30% of your money in stock mutual funds and possibly up to 40% in government bond or income mutual funds would be a maximum that I would ever accept for any portfolio. The need for direct-participation programs with direct ownership through partnerships is also important.

For investors who are interested in more information, I suggest the following newsletters: Donoghue's *Moneyletter* Guide on Mutual Funds, PO Box 540, Holliston, MA 01746; *Fundline,* David H. Menashe & Company, PO Box 663, Woodland Hills, CA 91365; *Mutual Funds Forum,* Investment Company Institute, 1775 K Street NW, Washington, DC 20006; *The No-Load Investor,* PO Box 283, Hastings-on-Hudson, NY 10706; *Switch Fund Advisory,* Schabacker Investment Management, 8943 Shady Grove Court, Gaithersburg, MD 20877; or *United Mutual Fund Selector,* United Business Services, 210 Newbury Street, Boston, MA 02116.

Other annual publications on your list of reading materials should include Donoghue's *Mutual Funds Almanac;* Johnson's Company Charts; Weisenberger Investment Companies Service; Mutual Funds Directory and the No-Load Mutual Fund Directory.

Figure 14-1
FORBES 1986 HONOR ROLE

Fund/distributor	Performance UP	Performance DOWN	Manager (consecutive years as manager)	Net assets 6/30/86 (millions)	Maximum load	Annual expenses per $100 assets
Acorn Fund/Acorn	B	A	Ralph Wanger (16)	$ 425	none	$0.78
Amcap Fund/American Funds	B	A	Michael Shanahan (1)	1,506	8.50%	0.54
American Capital Pace Fund/American Cap	B	A+	John Roche (1)	2,229	8.50	0.60
American Capital Venture Fund/American Cap	B	A	Robert Meyer (1)	415	8.50	0.68
Claremont Capital Corp/closed end	B	A+	Erik Bergstrom (10)	61	NA	1.06
Evergreen Fund/Lieber	A+	B	Stephen Lieber (15)	714	none	1.08
Fidelity Destiny Portfolio I/Fidelity	B	A	George Vanderheiden (6)	1,166	NA[5]	0.60
Fidelity Magellan Fund/Fidelity	A+	A	Peter Lynch (9)	7,412	3.00	1.08
Growth Fund of America/American Funds	A	A	William Newton (1)	829	8.50	0.69
Janus Fund/Janus	B	A	Thomas Bailey (17)	542	none	1.01‡
Mass Capital Development Fund/Mass Financial	A	B	William Harris (16)	1,035	7.25	0.71
NEL Growth Fund/NEL	A	B	Kenneth Heebner (10)	313	8.00	0.83
Nicholas Fund/Nicholas	B	A+	Albert Nicholas (17)	1,084	none	0.86
Over-the-Counter Securities Fund/Review	B	A	Binkley Shorts (5)	263	8.00	1.25
Partners Fund/Neuberger	B	A	Philip Steckler (11)[6]	431	none	0.93‡
Scudder Development Fund/Scudder	B	B	Edmund Swanberg (15)	359	none	1.30
Shearson Appreciation/Shearson	B	B	Harold Williamson (5)	279	5.00	1.10
Sigma Capital Shares/Sigma	B	B	Richard King (19)	102	8.50	1.01‡
Sigma Venture Shares/Sigma	A	B	Richard King (16)	93	8.50	0.95‡
Tudor Fund/Weiss, Peck	A	B	Melville Strauss (13)	191	none	0.95
Twentieth Century Select Investors/Twentieth Century	A+	B	James E. Stowers (15)	1,987	none	1.01
United Vanguard Fund/Waddell & Reed	B	B	Henry Herrmann (10)	525	8.50	1.05‡
Value Line Leveraged Growth Investors/Value Line	B	A	Mark Tavel (14)	306	none	0.80

[1] Most plans have lower minimum investment requirements for IRAs. [2] Average of price-to-earnings ratios for stocks in portfolio, weighted by size of holding as of 3/31/86. [3] Greater of security sales or purchases, divided by average net assets. A measure of trading activity. [4] Value on 6/30/86 of $10,000 invested 9/30/76, after taxes, for hypothetical upper-income investor (see text for details). [5] Monthly contractual plans only. [6] Second manager, Dietrich Weisman, has two years' tenure. [7] Fund has 12b-1 plan (hidden load) pending or in force. NA: Not available or not applicable.

Minimum investment[1]	Weighted average P/E[2]	% of assets in cash	Portfolio turnover[3]	Average annual total return	Hypothetical investment results[4]	Fund (consecutive years on honor roll)
$1,000	28.3	10.0%	low	21.8%	$55,990	Acorn Fund (3)
1,000	24.7	17.1	low	22.3	54,889	Amcap Fund (8)
500	24.6	19.1	average	27.1	78,222	American Capital Pace Fund (5)
500	28.1	2.4	high	24.2	59,307	American Capital Venture Fund (4)
none	20.9	24.7	very low	25.0	75,735	Claremont Capital Corp (3)
2,000	17.9	10.0	average	27.9	92,297	Evergreen Fund (2)
NA[5]	16.3	1.2	average	24.1	50,420	Fidelity Destiny Portfolio I (4)
1,000	18.8	1.0	average	35.1	151,684	Fidelity Magellan Fund (5)
1,000	35.8	11.7	low	23.4	62,987	Growth Fund of America (4)
1,000	31.1	28.9	very high	21.9	50,934	Janus Fund (5)
250	23.1	1.5	high	24.1	61,688	Mass Capital Development Fund (2)
250	33.4	0.5	very high	23.8	61,248	NEL Growth Fund (2)
500	19.6	37.7	very low	25.1	75,700	Nicholas Fund (5)
500	20.6	7.0	low	24.5	62,745	Over-the-Counter Securities Fund (5)
500	15.1	15.2	very high	21.8	50,716	Partners Fund
1,000	25.8	2.8	low	21.7	61,805	Scudder Development Fund (2)
500	21.1	15.4	average	20.7	54,754	Shearson Appreciation
none	21.3	26.6	very low	20.9	52,544	Sigma Capital Shares
none	26.2	10.0	very low	23.7	66,823	Sigma Venture Shares (2)
1,000	29.0	1.5	high	23.1	72,130	Tudor Fund (2)
none	22.2	1.0	high	29.6	108,588	Twentieth Century Select Investors (8)
500	26.6	15.3	very high	22.1	52,104	United Vanguard Fund (2)
1,000	22.7	5.5	high	24.3	61,769	Value Line Leveraged Growth Investors

Mutual funds rarely perform the way you expect, because you don't see the many intricacies involved in their management. With proper planning and utilization of a professional who continually analyzes these to make you aware of opportunities, investment in mutual funds can be a profitable and rewarding adventure. Trading them on a short-term basis or expecting miracles overnight, failing to manage and switch funds when they are not meeting your performance criteria, and not properly diversifying among different areas and segments of the industry can create problems instead of pleasures. Mutual funds are an excellent way to get a good understanding of our capitalist system and may be one of the most lucrative places to invest your money between now and 1988, particularly since the last bull market wave could ride the market past 3000. Because of their liquidity (i.e., the ability to sell your shares quickly and return your money) and the many different objectives they can fulfill, mutual funds are a vital part of any portfolio when carefully chosen and put in proper proportion. Mutual funds in the variable-life plans may be the best investment of the century.

15. Why Trading Stocks Will Lose You Money—But Make Your Broker Rich

While leafing through a newspaper one Sunday, I was struck by the number of brokerage houses advertising for sales help. Big display ads listing the brokerage houses in prominent letters announced in the fine print that "if you have a good sales background and would like to get into the securities business as a stockbroker, please come see us as we are hiring."

Nowhere was it mentioned that you needed to be a business school graduate, have an understanding of the securities industry, or have any experience managing money. The ads made it clear that these firms were merely seeking sales reps.

Upon your hiring by a major brokerage house, after having gotten through tests to determine that you can assimilate a lot of information and have the ability to sell yourself well to the public, you then go through a training program to become licensed. Training can be anywhere from one to two weeks of intensive studies of the 1934 Securities Act and of how stocks, bonds, and margin accounts work. Then you must pass a long exam administered by the New York Stock Exchange, in which nothing whatsoever is mentioned about financial planning, risk-reward analysis, tax analysis, estate planning, or other important areas. Next, you get some training on how to sell your company's products. This may take anywhere from one to four weeks. Then you are seated at a desk with a telephone and put to work. Hopefully, you know a lot of people around town, or you'll be forced to open a phone book and start dialing for dollars. That's the basic training of a stockbroker.

Sometimes, of course, the one or two weeks of intensive training is altered to a leisurely two to three months. But in all cases emphasis is on (1) passing the exam and getting your license, (2) learning what products your company offers, (3) learning selling techniques, and (4) using the phone to prospect and open accounts.

If you were to believe the ads, you'd think that by just going to the brokerage house and meeting with an account executive, you would receive "complete financial planning." Unfortunately for investors, the ad agencies representing these firms are a lot more creative than most freshly trained brokers.

One firm wants you merely to "listen" when it talks, even though it might not have much to say that is right for you. Other firms suggest that bulls can stroll harmlessly through china shops or that you can build houses of cards. Because of a firm's size (or is it the size of its advertising budget?), you are led to believe that any investment you place with them will make you money. Then, after seeing slick brochures, fancy offices, and electronic equipment everywhere, you're hooked. Everyone seems to be wearing Brooks Brothers suits as they put on a Broadway-quality song-and-dance routine of which Bob Fosse would be proud.

Unfortunately, as tens of thousands of investors across the country have learned, very often you are dancing to tunes you didn't want played. You soon find yourself in over your head or getting nowhere as your broker moves you from one position to another. *Stockbrokers get paid whether you make or lose money.* This is especially important during a broker's first few years. The only way he or she learns about the business and the market is by practicing with your money!

I'm astounded by how often knowledgeable people with a lot of common sense are willing to entrust their portfolios to inexperienced and virtually untrained salespeople. These portfolios often represent a good portion of their life's savings. Most often their stockbroker has never had that kind of money of his or her own. So, thanks to sales patter and slick advertising, you trust a novice with your hard-earned funds. This is like heading for the sticks and offering a million-dollar contract to some unproven youngster to play ball for the New York Yankees. Sure, the kid was able to pick up and swing a bat, hitting a few winners. But with no experience, without a fielding or batting average to show his consistency, who knows what you've got? George Steinbrenner would be laughed out of town for doing anything so absurd. But isn't it just as outrageous to turn over a portion of your nest egg to someone without a batting or fielding average?

I started out as one of these untrained kids without a track record myself. To this day I am dumbfounded at the confidence that was shown in me just because of my good presentations.

I'm sure people at first selected me because of the prestigious firm I worked for. They assumed my supervisors would be hanging over my shoulder, helping ensure that I made the best decisions for my clients. But the sad fact is that there was and is very little proper financial planning, not much training, and hardly any monitoring to back up the investment suggestions that stockbrokers make to their clients.

The Proper Profile

What profile should you look for before turning over all or any of your money to a person designated to help you earn a good return?

First, you want someone with a minimum of five, perhaps even ten, years of trading experience. Then find out how he or she analyzes companies, industries, and the marketplace. How does he stay on top of all this data? Does he visit the companies that he takes major positions in or confer with the CEO, controller, or other important managerial people? Does he read industry publications to get an understanding of market trends for the products and services of companies he is recommending? Does he or she analyze the financial statements to ensure that nothing is being covered up with accounting magic? If he has a number of different stock positions, does he have an organization that helps him monitor these areas and at the same time give good service to his clients? Does he have any vested interest in recommending or sticking with a particular company which might prevent him from making the most profitable moves for you? What motivates his or her selling of one stock and buying another? Is it to generate more commissions for himself (called churning and it's illegal) or to generate more profit for you?

This is not to say that there are not some excellent stockbrokers with long track records who have developed specialties and have served their clients very well. I would not be surprised if as many as 5% of the profession falls into that category. I hope one of them works for you.

Find a properly trained, properly motivated, and fully experienced manager to manage hard-earned nest egg dollars.

Discount Versus Major Brokerage Houses

About ten years ago the future of the brokerage industry changed drastically. Whereas commission rates were once fixed by the New York Stock Exchange, the rules were finally relaxed and brokerage houses gained the right to set their own fees. An onslaught of entrepreneurs jumped to compete with the large houses, realizing that they must maintain high fixed-rate commissions to offset overhead from top-heavy management, research, and maintenance of hundreds of offices nationwide giving high commissions to their stockbrokers.

Discounters like Charles Schwab, Alan R. Bush, Quick & Reilly and a slew of others began opening branches throughout the country, manned by salaried stockbroker-clerks who would simply accept an offer and place it for clients. The cost of paying high commissions or hiring expensive analysts was bypassed. In return, the client received from 50% to 80% discounts on transaction costs. This makes an awful lot of sense.

At the moment you purchase any stock, you are an immediate loser because of (a) transaction costs and (b) the spread between the bid and the ask. Reducing the purchase cost by over 50%, and then again saving on selling, allowed many traders to increase their returns by 1% or 2% a year. On a large portfolio that can be substantial. For smaller investors, discount brokerages now enabled them to be more agile, to get in and out of a particular security without high transaction costs. Those costs can run anywhere from .75% to 1.50% for each buy and again for each sell. (Smaller amounts of odd lots, that is, less than a hundred shares, and low-priced stocks can increase the percentages—some are as high as 10% to 20%. I have seen stocks that cost more to sell than they yielded. Nevertheless the transactions were made for tax purposes.)

At first the major houses pooh-poohed the discounters. The public was slow to catch on, as public relations campaigns claimed major houses were "full service" and thus better able to help clients by providing market analyses and more of this and that (a lot more BS). Then, little by little, the discounters fought back, expanding their services so that the only major difference might be that the old-line firms provided institutional research and had high-priced analysts on staff.

Discounters have eaten into the major houses' profits considerably and, in fact, have become such a profitable outlet that one of the country's largest firms, Charles Schwab, was bought out by a major banking institution.

A few years back the banks and savings and loans also tried to expand their services and compete for the money which was being drained from their reserves, CDs, and savings accounts into brokerage money market funds. They began offering discount brokerage services to help keep their client base from eroding any further and to prevent large cash balances from idling at the brokerage houses instead of at banks. This has been very unprofitable for many banks and savings and loans. Although there are many

Figure 15-1

No. of shares @ price	200 @$28	300 @$38	500 @$66	1000 @$42	1500 @$33	2000 @$23
The Discounters' Discounter	$30	$36	$60	$80	$120	$120
Major Brokerage House Avg.	$122	$202	$435	$530	$660	$620
Major National Discounter	$70	$91	$156	$183	$206	$195

still getting involved in the field, just as many are pulling out because of high costs.

The winner among all this turmoil has been you, the investor. Instead of having a fixed place to do business, the marketplace is now able to provide competitive alternatives. As you can see from Figure 15-1, transaction-cost differences can be significant. Unless you like supporting companies that air clever commercials, I see no reason to deal with an old-line brokerage house. Unless their costs can be reduced to compete with the discounters, I recommend that you use discount brokers offering the best price and service. (Discount brokerage firms are usually manned by salaried brokers who execute stock trades at one-half to one-quarter of what the commission brokers such as Merrill Lynch and Hutton charge.) Obviously it is not only price that matters—you also need to be concerned with service; for example, promptly receiving the proceeds from stock sales, having intelligent, well-mannered people to deal with, and enjoying open, two-way communication.

Aggressive Investment

According to the New World Dictionary, "aggressive" means "taking the first step in an attack. . . . *Informal:* very active, energetic." The aggressive investor exchanges current income for larger future profits. I would be aiming for 15% to 20% annual return to justify the risk involved in growth investments.

I consider the stock market to be an aggressive growth investment. It is, in my opinion, a sophisticated numbers game, like blackjack. If your numbers add up right, better than the house, you win. If they don't, you lose. This might sound oversimplified, but if you think that the stock market is not a risky investment, just look at its fluctuations over the past decade. The Dow Jones Average has gone from 1000 to 750; back to 1000 and back to 750 again; up to 1300 and back to 1000; then to 2200. And who knows what is next?

Stock represents partial ownership of a corporation. The definition of ownership means you have control over that which you own, so if you don't like the way things are going, you can change them. That which you do not entirely own, you do not entirely control. Thus there are relative degrees of ownership: unless an individual invests a sizable amount of money in a corporation, it is unlikely he or she will be able to exercise any significant control over it. The major corporations are controlled by (1) the group or groups that own a large percentage of it and (2) the institutions that do 80% of all trading in stocks.

A person who buys a stock is counting on management to earn regular profits. But even if management succeeds in doing this, there is no reason to assume that the stock will gain in value. Nor does a loss on the balance sheet mean the stock price will decline. *The most misunderstood concept in dealing with the stock market is believing that how a company is run or the general state of the economy has a direct bearing on the price of its stock.*

Types of Stock Analysis

Fundamental analysis informs us that a stock's price is predicated on basic earnings, dividends, backlog of orders, capability of management, the outlook for the product or products, and the outlook for the particular industry. It therefore embraces masses of statistics that determine whether the company's stock will rise. Unfortunately, these factors have very little relevance. Yet, if you read *The Wall Street Journal* and turn to the next to the last page, you find quotations from assorted analysts using "fundamental" approaches to tell us why the stock market in general or a particular stock is going up or down and what they foresee happening next. *Business Week, Forbes, Time*—all carry various "expert opinions" explaining how the market is moving in accordance with these numerous economic indicators. They quote bank trust officers, money managers, large brokerage houses, vice presidents, and, without fail, they have their own personal views and interpretation of the vast array of fundamental data. For every person reading these indicators as positive (bullish), there is someone else who interprets them as negative (bearish). Remember that statistics can be misleading and can be used to prove almost anything. The key must be your own intuitive weighing of the factors of supply and demand.

One factor in buying stocks is pivotal: timing to buy low and sell high. When was the last time your broker recommended you sell all your stocks and wait in the money funds until time to buy again? When was the last time he or she suggested you short stocks because the market was going down and there seemed to be a good profit potential? Shorting stocks is a bit complicated, but basically it's selling your stock at a high price and borrowing it to deliver to another person in the hope of watching the price decline, then buying back the stock at a lower price and delivering it to the person from whom you borrowed it. In other words, selling stock at $100 a share with an agreement that you will borrow it from someone to deliver within six months. In six months you buy the stock in the open market for $50 a share and deliver it to the person you borrowed it from, usually the brokerage house. This would mean that you sold it for $100 a share and bought it for $50 a share—or made a $50-per-share profit. The same profit as buying at $50 and selling at $100. *To be conservative—buy low, sell high, wait in the money funds in between.*

When the market rises, often 80% to 90% of all stocks go up. When it declines, 80% to 90% of all stocks go down. There is no need to try to pick out one of the more than 20,000 stocks that are going to beat the market trend, unless you want to outperform it (suggested) and can afford the additional risk. The key here is finding an analyst who helps you read the trends of supply and demand, of buying low and selling high. Such a person is called a technical analyst. He is more interested in the charts of what the buying and selling *patterns* have been for a particular stock than what the earnings or growth outlook of the company or the industry are.

Technical analysis involves evaluating various supply and demand factors as shown on a graph that illustrates the point of accumulation and distribution of the stock (or the stock market) over an extended period. It relies on the interpretation of these graphic indicators of supply and demand. Normally one would want not only to track stock-price patterns on a graph, but also graph the volume that accompanies the pattern. Then the technical analyst, through use of broad indexes concerning the industry and the market as a whole, evaluates whether there is a bullish trend or a bearish movement expected for that particular stock.

Unfortunately, technical analysis is left open to a lot of interpretation, so your technicians will probably disagree widely on what different graph patterns mean.

Utilities—the Illusion

Many investors have been turning to utility common stocks, since they normally pay a good dividend and are sold as safe investments. If you think that a utility is a safe investment, examine comparable stocks. Be warned: investments in utilities, despite what most brokerage houses say, are not always reliable ones that you can depend on for guaranteed income. (Investors needing regular income and minimal market fluctuation might consider *preferred* stocks of utilities as a more conservative approach than common stocks.) Most people would agree that if we owned stock XYZ, which was currently priced at $100 and had a track record over the last couple of years of fluctuating between 40 and 100, we would call it a volatile stock. Yet, if we had a *utility* stock, ABC, which fluctuated between 20 and 10 over the last few years, wouldn't the utility stock have exactly the same percentage of fluctuation as the "volatile" stock? The illusion with utilities is that because they are so low-priced, the point movements are small. But each point movement represents a large percentage movement. If you bought the utility at 15 and it drops to 10, it has lost one-third of its value. Don't forget the commission it cost you to buy and the commission it will cost you to sell (usually about .5% to 1% each way). And the spread between the price at which you bought (the ask) and the price at which you sell (the bid) may be another half a point or more. Utility dividends *can* be cut and utilities *do* involve a lot of risk, but you are usually not told this when you buy. Your broker will point out that electricity is a necessity and that the company has been paying dividends for so many years, and so on.

But General Public Utilities, prior to the Three Mile Island fiasco, was stable. Yet, owing to a small problem in the nuclear reactor, the company not only had to shut down, but its stock dropped 75% and its dividend was completely omitted. A nuclear power plant could have a minor glitch that could devastate a utility's stock price and eliminate dividends. Regulatory commissions might not grant the rate increases the company desires to keep operating costs in pace with inflation.

Recently rated as high-performing companies, Long Island Lighting, Public Service of New Hampshire, and Public Service of Indiana were all considering bankruptcy. Georgia Power was suing for the right to issue $750 million in securities to help complete three plants. Disasters were created by the new power plants in the Washington Public Power System, too.

Utilities with oil as their means of generating power can run into oil scarcity. We've seen oil embargoes before, and it could happen again. Such embargoes have occurred twice in the last ten years. What would happen if we had a severe oil shortage and utilities needing oil had to cut back, perhaps close down altogether? There would be losses and dividends cut. These are real considerations. The same thing can happen to coal-powered utilities. A few years back there was a coal strike; there could be another. Even if no fuel or major problems arise, you can be adversely affected by high interest rates, since utility stocks are bought like bonds, by investors looking for high dividend-returns. If the stock market drops, utilities are further hurt because they are just another stock in the stock market. Fluctuations in the Dow Jones Utilities Average often move in the same direction as those of the DJIA, and have similar percentage moves.

My disillusionment with utilities stems entirely from what I consider an improper balance between risk and reward. To receive a 7% to 8% dividend and have my principal fluctuating 20% to 40% with no guarantee on my dividend in my opinion is foolish. Particularly when at the same time, an 8% to 10% insured and guaranteed return exists within single-pay plans with *no* market fluctuations or 10% to 11% in government funds with less volatility. Weigh your alternatives before investing.

Utility Funds

Growing in popularity during the last five years have been the specially managed utility trusts. These are mutual funds consisting mainly of utility stocks, but which as trusts do not distribute dividends. To get income the trust shares are sold, so your dividends, which are compounding within the trust, are paid to you as long-term capital gains (60% tax-free). Some of these funds even write covered options on their utility stocks to generate more income. These trusts could add 3% to 6% to your yield while you enjoy professional management and diversification. The funds are less aggressive than owning individual utilities and should represent only a small portion of any income-oriented portfolio. Unfortunately the new tax law eradicates these benefits.

Figure 15-2

Top Performers in Each Fund Category

Fund	% Change in Net Asset Value 2 Mos. 1986	1 Mo. 2/86	12 Mos.	Assets # 12/31/85	% Yield°
Aggressive Growth Average	**+ 9.7**	**+ 7.4**	**+37.3**	**239.7**	**1.4**
Pacific Horizon Aggr. Gro.†	+16.8	+ 8.7	+38.9	22.3	0.3
Constellation Growth Fund†	+15.7	+ 9.6	+25.9	102.5	0.0
Investors Research Fund	+15.7	+ 9.0	+25.0	44.1	1.7
Quasar Associates†	+15.0	+ 8.4	+40.7	115.3	0.1
Hartwell Leverage Fund†	+14.8	+ 9.4	+23.2	33.6	0.0
Balanced Fund Average	**+ 7.4**	**+ 6.2**	**+29.3**	**195.4**	**5.3**
United Continental Income	+11.6	+ 8.0	+36.9	118.5	3.6
Loomis-Sayles Mutual†	+11.4	+ 7.2	+42.3	120.9	4.2
Axe-Houghton Fund B	+10.3	+ 8.3	+38.8	168.0	4.9
Strong Investment	+ 9.6	+ 8.0	+26.3	220.6	5.8
Kemper Total Return	+ 9.3	+ 7.1	+26.3	388.9	4.4
Equity Income Fund Average	**+ 8.0**	**+ 6.0**	**+28.7**	**379.0**	**5.7**
United Income	+15.6	+11.0	+41.4	675.6	3.0
Eaton Vance Utility Trust	+10.9	+ 6.7	+50.9	604.1	3.8
Vanguard Qual. Div. Port II†	+10.8	+ 6.7	+33.6	93.4	9.8
Financial Programs Indus. Inc.†	+ 9.5	+ 7.1	+29.8	272.1	4.7
★Fidelity Equity-Income†	+ 8.7	+ 6.4	+24.6	2,238.6	5.6
Fixed Inc. Fund Average	**+ 4.0**	**+ 3.4**	**+21.4**	**684.9**	**10.2**
Hutton E.F. Invt. Ser. Bond†	+11.1	+ 9.1	+26.2	233.8	2.2
AIM Convertible Yield Secs.	+ 8.7	+ 6.1	+19.3	21.6	5.1
Security Bond	+ 7.6	+ 3.1	+22.2	38.2	10.4
IDS Bond	+ 7.3	+ 6.4	+27.6	1,503.2	10.3
National Securities Preferred	+ 6.7	+ 4.7	+27.0	4.4	8.3
Income Fund Average	**+ 5.5**	**+ 4.7**	**+23.0**	**98.2**	**7.8**
Lexington Corp. Lds. Trust	+ 9.6	+ 9.9	+35.5	12.9	14.9
Mass Financial MTR	+ 9.0	+ 7.2	+29.7	241.5	5.4
Criterion Commerce Income	+ 8.7	+ 7.9	+22.7	60.7	3.4
Dreyfus Special Income†	+ 8.0	+ 4.1	+26.7	118.0	6.7
Franklin Income	+ 7.9	+ 5.4	+21.8	126.5	9.1
International Fund Average	**+ 9.1**	**+ 7.4**	**+47.8**	**133.7**	**1.0**
Fidelity Overseas	+18.2	+14.7	+69.7	174.2	0.0
Merrill Lynch Pacific	+15.0	+10.9	+51.7	151.4	0.5
Alliance International	+12.8	+ 8.6	+81.4	103.2	0.2
Scudder International†	+11.5	+ 8.5	+61.7	427.4	1.2
Price International†	+10.2	+ 9.3	+60.8	376.8	1.1
Municipal Bond Fund Average	**+ 7.8**	**+ 3.6**	**+23.3**	**611.5**	**7.2**
SteinRoe Tax Exempt Bond	+12.6	+ 5.0	+31.7	356.7	6.8
Lutheran Bro. Muni. Bond	+11.4	+ 5.4	+27.8	154.8	7.0
Federated Tax-Free Income Fd.	+11.0	+ 5.1	+26.8	162.0	7.6
American Capital Muni. Bond	+10.6	+ 4.3	+30.7	120.0	6.9
Van Kampen Merritt Insd. Tax-Free	+10.5	+ 4.8	+29.7	216.1	7.1
Natural Resources Average	**− 3.5**	**− 0.6**	**+ 1.4**	**127.8**	**3.2**
Price New Era†	+ 7.5	+ 5.2	+22.9	529.2	2.7
Neuberger & Berman Energy†	+ 0.9	+ 3.3	+12.5	395.3	4.8
Dean Witter Nat. Resource Dev.†	+ 0.8	+ 4.1	+ 0.3	21.9	0.0
First Investors Nat. Resources	− 4.6	− 6.4	−14.0	9.5	1.1
Vanguard Spec. Port-Energy†	− 6.7	− 1.6	− 2.5	2.2	6.3

Global Fund Average	**+ 9.4**	**+ 7.4**	**+40.3**	**496.2**	**1.8**
Oppenheimer A.I.M.	+15.4	+11.1	+62.4	280.6	0.4
★Putnam International Equities	+13.5	+ 9.6	+69.1	90.4	1.5
Mass Financial MFI-B	+12.2	+ 9.3	+50.5	61.2	5.7
Paine Webber Atlas	+ 9.5	+ 8.6	+72.3	118.9	0.7
Templeton Global II	+ 9.4	+ 8.1	+24.9	355.7	1.7
Gold Fund Average	**+21.5**	**+ 0.6**	**+13.1**	**140.9**	**2.8**
United Services Gold Shares†	+35.6	+ 3.6	+ 5.5	238.0	5.5
Strategic Investments	+31.7	+ 3.4	+ 0.2	79.0	2.8
Fidelity Select Precious Metals	+22.7	+ 1.3	+13.4	123.6	3.7
Franklin Gold Fund	+22.6	+ 0.8	+10.6	99.1	3.2
Vanguard Spec. Port-Gold†	+21.6	+ 1.5	+22.2	20.7	3.6
Growth Fund Average	**+ 9.0**	**+ 7.3**	**+25.5**	**252.7**	**2.1**
Bruce Fund†	+16.6	+14.7	+45.2	1.4	10.3
Loomis-Sayles Cap. Dev.†	+16.5	+11.8	+49.2	170.4	0.7
Wood Struthers Neuwirth†	+15.5	+13.1	+36.4	21.6	0.3
National Securities Growth	+15.2	+10.1	+30.2	69.6	1.3
Steadman Ocean, Tech & Gro.†	+14.3	+11.2	−11.6	4.9	0.0
Growth & Income Average	**+ 8.0**	**+ 6.7**	**+26.0**	**456.6**	**3.5**
Delaware Fund	+13.1	+ 9.5	+34.7	365.5	2.7
AMEV Capital	+12.4	+ 8.7	+34.8	80.6	1.2
Mass Financial MFD	+12.4	+10.0	+28.4	236.3	2.1
Value Line Fund†	+12.3	+ 9.2	+31.6	206.1	1.3
Stratton Growth†	+12.0	+ 8.8	+26.6	15.9	0.9
Option Growth/Income Avg.	**+ 4.1**	**+ 3.7**	**+14.2**	**401.7**	**3.5**
Colonial Cap. Appreciation	+ 8.6	+ 8.0	+23.9	8.9	1.8
Pru-Bache Option Gro.†	+ 6.4	+ 5.2	+25.8	53.8	2.1
First Investors Option Fund	+ 5.6	+ 5.4	+11.1	195.2	2.4
Franklin Option	+ 4.9	+ 4.9	+18.6	11.3	2.5
Putnam Option Income	+ 4.8	+ 4.2	+16.8	1,190.8	2.8
Small Co. Growth Fund Avg.	**+ 9.2**	**+ 6.7**	**+20.3**	**207.5**	**0.6**
Fidelity Over-The-Counter	+14.9	+ 7.1	+71.0	162.6	0.1
GIT Special Growth†	+14.0	+ 7.2	+38.7	6.8	0.6
Van. Naess & Thomas Special†	+12.8	+ 8.2	+17.2	35.8	0.0
Mass Financial MEG	+12.0	+ 8.2	+19.7	204.1	0.0
United New Concepts	+12.0	+ 8.7	+32.0	34.4	2.6
Specialty Fund Average	**+ 9.9**	**+ 7.0**	**+29.7**	**88.1**	**1.9**
Fidelity Select Financial	+17.0	+10.4	+50.3	143.2	0.9
Century Shares Trust†	+15.4	+10.1	+41.9	122.9	2.7
Fidelity Select Leisure	+14.2	+10.4	+46.9	84.2	0.1
ABT Utility Income	+13.7	+ 5.1	+34.0	85.8	7.9
Financial Portfolio-Leisure†	+13.4	+12.3	+30.6	1.3	0.3
Market Indicators:					
Open End Fund Average☐	+ 8.6	+ 6.5	+25.2	—	2.8
S&P 500 Stocks	+ 8.0	+ 7.5	+29.6	—	3.5
Dow Jones Industrials	+11.2	+ 9.2	+37.9	—	3.6
NASDAQ-OTC Composite	+10.7	+ 7.1	+26.5	—	0.0
Consumer Price Index	NA	+ 0.3	+ 7.6		

■ Including all dividends & capital gains. ☐ Excluding fixed income funds. † No Load ‡ Low Load ★ Supervised List. ° Based on latest 12 months' dividends.

The Stock Market

In the last few years, since the publication of my book *Your Money or Your Life*, I have conducted seminars for over one hundred thousand people in South Florida. It's always fascinating to see how my audiences relate to my comments on how investors react to buying high when the news is good and the media proclaim, "Buy, buy, buy!" When your newspaper carrier is giving you hot tips, and when the market already has made a major move, *watch out*. It seems as soon as *you* buy, the market begins to drift sideways and then slowly downward. And you never get that phone call from your stockbroker to sell. I have listened to countless stories about how true this is. It's tough for a stockbroker to call with news that you've lost money and things aren't going as expected. Not only that, but those mighty analysts in the ivory towers of Wall Street who alerted your broker to a buy signal on the stock never seem to change the recommendation and tell you to sell, except when there is very bad news and the market already has discounted and made its move downward.

Why do you virtually never receive that phone call to sell? Simple. Analysts who recommend buying the stock of Company A rarely advise selling that stock because if, in the future, Company A wants an underwriter for a new stock issue, it wouldn't choose the analyst who told his or her clients to get rid of its stock! The brokerage house is protecting its relationship with companies that offer stock, not with you. (Brokers also fail to recommend sells because of (a) laziness and (b) hopeless optimism.)

When the market goes up, there will be certain leaders. Some of your stocks might be leaders, and some might be part of the secondary movement that bull markets usually have. Within these time frames, different groups of stocks will take the lead, each reaching a certain peak. You should sell at the peak. A good money manager buys into an industry while it is out of favor and its stock prices are low. When it is at the height of its fashionability and its stock prices are high, he or she sells and moves the money into a depressed industry.

The majority of investors, however, lump most of their stocks together and don't diversify. They stick with one stock, don't sell when it goes up, and then panic and sell when it sinks, thinking they're going to lose their money. Too many people with limited knowledge try to outguess the market. The market fluctuates between 20% and 30% every few years. Unless you can expect a reward of 20% or more when you are evaluating your risk/reward, playing the stock market is not for you.

A look at the average performances of the top eighty mutual funds shows that these are over 30%. Remember, there are hundreds of mutual funds. The key is to find investment managers who have a good sense of market timing and have consistently, year after year, made high returns on their money.

Utilizing Other People's Talent and Experience

Mutual funds became very popular in the '60s and '70s, and even more so in the '80s, as investors realized that there are certain prerequisites for making money in the stock market.

1. Holdings must be evaluated on a daily basis, the prevailing economic moods must be gauged, and technical factors and market responses must be assessed. It is necessary to recognize downturns and upturns before others do.

2. It is necessary to look for the lowest commissions. Institutional commissions cost, at a few pennies a share, much less than the major discount houses.

3. A good money manager must be found. The best ones visit the companies they invest in, speaking with the president, and perhaps the heads of marketing and quality control, and get a feel for the company. When preparing to commit millions of dollars of other people's money to these companies, they look for the best inside view possible.

4. Money managers might have three computer terminals linked to the other major institutional analysts and money managers for an up-to-the-second alert on new information pertaining to the companies they are dealing with, and any information about the major industries in which they are involved.

Professional money managers have their fingers on the market's pulse. They follow your stocks, pay institutional commissions (one-third or one-fifth that of the best discount house), *create* the trends, and, for the most part, do a lot better than the individual investor. A major advantage to letting someone else manage your money is that the hard work, constant checking, aggravations, frustrations, and assorted upsets can be kept away from you, the individual investor. You can enjoy your life while hardworking professionals keep an eye on your money. A money manager's purpose is to make you profits. How nice to be able to carry on with your life as someone else uses his or her energies to work for *you*.

How do you decide which money manager to choose? Look at his or her track record, discover his perspective on future events, and make sure his outlook and yours are compatible.

There is another possibility for those who have $100,000 or more that they want in the stock market but don't want to place in mutual funds or with stockbrokers. Groups of professional money managers throughout the country accept sums of money, normally $100,000 and up, to manage for clients. After establishing your objectives, needs, and tax bracket, a professional money manager will design a portfolio for you and will monitor it, giving you monthly and quarterly reports and trying to produce good profits in the market or markets you have selected. Use the same criteria you went by to assess a mutual fund manager as you examine his or her expertise and track record in various markets. These special programs can cost more than some mutual funds or other forms of investment, but profits can also be greater.

Portfolio managers/investment advisers must by law show you how they run their business and should provide you with a past-performance record. Analyze it in regard to the type of account you want.

For example, a money manager who shows you that she has made 40% a year for aggressive portfolios while you are a conservative investor looking for moderate growth and good current income will be on a different wavelength. She may have done well for certain types of accounts and poorly for others. Get a good grasp of a prospective money manager's specialty to see if and how it could work for you.

There are usually annual fees for managing a portfolio. But since portfolio managers usually trade in large blocks, the commissions for trading will very likely be below those of discount brokers. Portfolio managers work at the institutional rate, probably one-fifth that charged by a discount broker.

Professional management of your portfolio would be an excellent compromise if you don't like mutual funds but want personal attention and supervision.

16. Why Bonds Can Be Charity

Consider the following two investment strategies. Which would you choose?

Investment number 1. Put $10,000 in an investment that will guarantee you $1000 a year. After twenty years you will be guaranteed and insured to have your full $10,000 returned. Unfortunately, because of inflation, the $10,000 returned to you purchases only $3000 worth of goods and services. The $1000 a year you are receiving as income from this investment will in its tenth year purchase only $500 worth of goods and services. The last check you receive, although still a thousand dollars, purchases only $300 worth.

Investment number 2. This consists of a similar arrangement. This time the amount is only $2000. You have agreed to forego any income so it will compound. After twenty years that $2000 becomes $10,000. Of course, along the way you pay taxes on the assumed increasing value of the investment, which is compounding without income, from which to pay the taxes. Each year, for the next twenty, there will be negative cash flow, possibly a hundred dollars or more per year in taxes: you pay hundreds of dollars a year in taxes without ever having received any money. Of course, at the end of twenty years when you receive the $10,000 for your original $2000, you will be able to purchase $4000 worth of goods and services. The only problem is that over those sixteen years, having to pay taxes has eaten into another of your investments. So even though these funds doubled in purchasing power, your other funds were cut in half. After sixteen years, you have the same purchasing power with these funds that you had when you started!

The first example that I used is a twenty-year, high-rated municipal bond. Whereas you, the investor, received an income each year that bought less and less goods and services, you were paid back with less than one-third of the purchasing power you had lent.

The second example is of a zero-coupon corporate bond, a relatively new type of bond developed by J. C. Penney. Now there are government, corporate, and municipal zero-coupon bonds. A zero-coupon bond is basically a $5000 bond which is bought for a large discount depending on its stated interest rate. You might pay $2000 for a ten-year, 10% bond. Then, in the ten years, upon maturity the bond would pay off the $5000. No interest is paid during the ten years, and this is why it's called zero coupon. It must be held for a long period. The bond issuer has an advantage because it does not pay interest to the bond holders until later. But the issuer can write off the cost of the bond's average yearly appreciation and reduce taxes on it. These bonds are designed to allow investors with long-term objectives to invest their money for appreciation and to lock in the interest rate on reinvestment. The problem here is, not only do people lose the current value of their dividend interest, but the amount of purchasing power upon maturity may be only fifty cents on the dollar. And they also have great market fluctuations.

The Ideal Solution: Participatory Lending

Liquidity and predictability of an "income stream" are among the biggest advantages of bonds. If you can afford to tie up money for extended periods, and aren't overly concerned about risk, invest in the highest-quality insured or government-guaranteed instrument to get the best credit risk. If you want to hedge the inflation risk (loss of purchasing power on maturity) and the rate risk (locking in a rate now when rates may go higher later), you can strike an excellent compromise.

Participating mortgages and participating bonds are popular in Europe and are used extensively by insurance companies there. When lending the money, you accept a slightly lower rate of interest on your bond in return for a percentage of any future profits that the project or building might make. It is easy to see the concept working locally at a shopping center. A company lends money to build a shopping center and receives a 10% payment from the developer. In return, it works a clause into the agreement whereby once the tenants' business exceeds a certain gross amount, the insurance company gets a percentage of that increase. In ten to twenty years, depending on the maturity of the mortgage, or when the property is sold, the insurance company shares 25% to 50% of any increase in value, thus hedging its bets against inflation in more than one way.

First, as inflation increases the cash flow of the businesses in addition to getting a portion of the rent increases on the underlying leases, the participating mortgage also receives a percentage of the increasing business volume. When the property is sold, it receives a percentage of the appreciation. Thus, if inflation is high, it will be offset by rent increases and business volume to increase the cash flow to the lender. Property values normally would increase substantially; the principal invested would be protected from inflation by having a percentage of the inflating value of the property to offset the decreasing purchasing power of the original principal invested.

These types of investments are excellent for fence sitters who aren't sure if the economy will go into a deflationary period or into an inflationary boom first, last, or whenever. Investors with only $2000 or so can invest in government-guaranteed participating mortgages, non-government-guaranteed participating mortgages, and participating corporate bonds.

About Bonds

Here are the basics of different types, along with some of their salient features.

Intermediate- and *long-term bonds*, which normally pay the highest rates of return, have been volatile during the last decade. There are also *bond funds*, set up to grow minimally each year. I counsel caution before placing large sums of money in any sort of non-governmental bond or bond fund. You can check credit ratings all you like; your bond may have a top rating; but it won't make any difference if interest rates go up. The market value of your bonds will decline if the economy suffers. If another depression comes, there could be defaults on a wide variety of corporate bonds.

Call bonds give the issuer the option to call in your bond for repurchase before the maturity date. Example: XYZ's 15%, twenty-year bond stipulates that any time after the first five years, the corporation reserves the right to repurchase it at a price of 103. (You are usually paid a small profit.) It may be called in five years, ten years, or never. Nonetheless, the issuer reserves that right. If, in six years, interest rates are 9%, it would be of great advantage to the company to call in its 15% bonds and reissue new ones at 9%. Because of this, a twenty-year callable bond will not increase in value as much as a twenty-year noncallable bond would as interest rates decline. The callable bond always carries this termination risk.

Be cautious when buying any bonds for more than eight or ten years. One possible exception is *floating bonds* from a very highly rated company with good earnings reports. Make sure the company will survive any general economic upheaval. For investors who want to commit their funds for longer periods, the alternative is *participating-bond instruments*, which are slowly starting to develop a niche.

Why not enjoy a government guarantee instead of a corporate guarantee for your money? You get a portion of your principal back each month to hedge your position instead of waiting until maturity to receive any of it. You can have an inflation hedge to receive a portion of property-value increases as well. Consider long-term investments issued by the government through the Government National Mortgage Association (also known as Ginnie Mae).

Tax-Frees

Municipal bonds are a well-known type of debt obligation. Instead of a public corporation raising money to finance its growth, municipalities, states, cities, and towns borrow money from the public to build schools, water and sewer systems, highways, and other projects. These have the same types of ratings as corporate bonds and in general behave the same way as a corporate bond does relative to market risk, paying every six months and having different types of revenue and collateral behind the bonds. *General-obligation bonds* depend on the taxing authority of a particular government to pay them off. *Revenue bonds* are debt issues that have a specific revenue set aside to pay off the interest and principal.

Although municipal bonds are also known as "tax-free" bonds, this is a misnomer. They contain a hidden tax—a lower interest rate. For example, when thirty-year AAA-rated taxable bonds were paying 13%, thirty-year AAA-rated municipal bonds were paying 10%. So "tax-frees" can pay considerably *less* than taxable bonds: that lowered rate is the tax bite. Most investors should not consider tax-free bonds until they reach the 25% to 30% tax bracket. Differences between taxable and tax-free vary greatly, so compare your net yields from each before deciding. In early 1986 the tides were reversed, with rate differences so narrow as to allow low-tax-bracket investors higher rates by going tax-free.

Municipal bonds have maintained their tax-free status because the government agrees not to levy any federal income taxes on any bond issued by municipalities. This has been under attack by Congress, yet so far has been left alone. The exception is when municipal-bond income is added to adjusted gross income and one-half of Social Security benefits to determine if those benefits will be taxed. This amounts to indirectly taxing municipal bonds.

Under the 1986 tax revisions three major categories of municipal bonds have been created.

The first consists of "public-purpose" bonds, a group that includes securities issued directly by state or local governments or their agencies to meet essential government functions such as highway construction and school financing.

The second category consists of bonds issued for "nongovernmental purposes." These include bonds that finance housing and student loans. States will have a limit on the amount they can issue. Purchasing these after August 7, 1986, will treat interest earned as a "preference item" that must be added to taxable income if the taxpayer has to calculate the alternative minimum tax (this occurs when a taxpayer has an undo amount of tax deductions from various investments).

The third category is *taxable* municipals. Viewed as issued for nonessential purposes, these include upgrading pollution-control facilities, building stadiums, or financing loans to farmers. These still may be exempt from state and local taxes in the states in which they are issued.

The values of municipal bonds have eroded over the 70s because of inflation, yet have done well in the inflationary 80s. A fixed-income vehicle for any extended period of time is a poor investment in an inflationary environment. During inflationary times we must look to variable-rate and participating-bond investments, which have a chance to outpace inflation or at least keep up with it. Encouraging news in the municipal bond market has been the recent introduction of tax-free participating-bond funds that give the investor a percentage of the increasing value of the project that the bond finances.

Tax-Free Housing Bonds

Tax-free housing bonds are a popular instrument developed in the late '70s to create funds for the sagging housing market. Many states offered, to the public, bond issues earmarked to supply funds for mortgages in their jurisdiction for certain segments of the housing market. (Under the 1986 tax revisions, each state is limited in the amount of the bonds it can issue. Anything in excess of this limit is taxable.) Alaska has been the most prominent issuer, and many millions of dollars have been channeled into the mortgage market from these. The advantage to the buyer of these bonds is the ability to get long-term rates (thirty years) coupled with the ability to get back portions of the principal before the thirty-year maturity. As the original mortgagors pay off their mortgages or sell their homes, these funds will be funneled back to bond holders on an indiscriminate lottery basis as the principal is paid back to the issuer. Usually there is a special reserve fund and insurance clause to protect bond holders against defaults.

Before purchasing a high-yield, tax-free housing bond (or any bond for that matter) and paying a premium (more than face value at maturity), make sure there isn't any hidden provision, as New York recently found, to redeem the bonds at par value before the expected maturity date. Surprised investors who purchased 12.5% New York State Tax-Free Housing Bonds for 127 ($12,700 per $10,000 bond) in March 1986 were aghast when these bonds were redeemed at par ($10,000) eight years earlier than expected, reducing their return to a loss.

Look for professionally managed mutual funds for these bonds to ensure profitable investment.

Bonds can be charity! This, of course, does not mean that they don't have a place in your portfolio. It does mean their place should be understood and limited.

When inflation is low and interest rates high, as we have recently seen, bonds are an excellent investment. They have been paying the highest ever in real rates of return. Many investors complain loudly today, wishing they could continue to get the 14% to 15% on their bonds in a marketplace that has brought the rate down to 10%. They apparently feel they were making more money at 15% than they are today at 10%. Not true.

When interest rates on tax-free municipal bonds went to 14% to 15%, there was a 13% inflation rate, thereby giving only a 1% to 2% *real* rate of return after inflation. Today, you can receive 7% to 8% on long-term municipal bonds, and with an inflation rate of 1% to 3% you receive a 6% real rate of return. This is over a 300% increase in real rates of return today compared to when interest rates were higher.

Bonds are an interesting investment, particularly for the aggressive investor who follows interest-rate trends. Buy them when rates are high and sell when they are low. Then wait for interest rates to jump and buy again. By continuing this strategy, the *total rates* of return can be improved by two or three times while the after-inflation rate of return increases some tenfold.

This strategy demands timing expertise, and finding that might be difficult. Yet, just as there are stock and mutual fund timing services, there are also bond advisory services that take you in and out of the market when appropriate.

Using government mutual funds for these purposes can be profitable if bought and sold right. For more aggressive investors, buying and selling zero-coupon bonds has even more profit potential. Not only is the interest rate on your bonds fixed, but so is its reinvestment rate. These bonds fluctuate more than regular bonds when interest rates rise or fall.

Government-Backed Municipals

Probably the best bet in our current low-inflationary, but financially dangerous, period is those tax-free municipal bonds and funds that escrow their money to retire their bonds in the form of government securities. Upon the maturity date of the municipal bond, a Treasury bond matures simultaneously to pay off bond holders by the trustee who has been holding the bonds.

Nonrated Bonds

There are many small bond offerings, from one to ten million dollars, that carry no Standard & Poor's or other rating-service evaluation. Health-care facilities such as nursing homes and life-care centers are popular examples. Often there is no rating because of the high cost of obtaining one, but sometimes it is, logically, because of the weakness of the bond. These bonds must be considered speculative, as the buyer has no way to determine the credit standing and payback ability of the issuer. Also, the resale market is often difficult, with large spreads between bid and ask. These bonds are suitable only for high-risk investors who determine no future need for their principal.

Nursing-home projects and *nonrated bonds* abound. But unless you have the full inside track and are a speculative investor, avoid them.

Short-Term Bonds—Government Agencies

There are many governmental agencies that provide some indirect security for those purchasing their obligations. These obligations are rated secure by the marketplace, and since they are not directly government-backed, they usually pay up to .5% higher rates of return than a government-backed issue. *Fannie Maes* are in many respects similar to Ginnie Maes, and are often found to be paying .5% or more higher rates of return. Shorter-term paper such as Federal Home Loan Notes, Farm Credit Bureau Notes, and other agencies' issues often pay higher rates of return than the same maturity in a direct-obligation Treasury bill or bond.

When investing in any of these areas, be careful to commit no more than 15% to 20% of your portfolio. The next three to four years will probably be extraordinarily volatile, with major deflationary and inflationary swings. Consider variable-rate investments and be ready to move.

Understanding Market Risk

If you are considering any of the investments discussed in this chapter, please remember that when your money is committed for any length of time, it cannot adjust to prevailing market conditions. Therefore, should you need this money prior to maturity date, you are incurring market risk. Bonds are, generally speaking, stable and safe: you will very likely get your money on maturity. But no one has found a way to predict interest rates one hundred percent (if you have one, please let me know). So, if you need your money before maturity, you might receive only 75 cents or so on the dollar if interest rates happen at that moment to be unfavorable for bonds. This could be a rude surprise. Diversity between short-, intermediate-, and long-term bonds, with single-pay plans to hedge your position.

Yields

In bond purchasing, confusion may occur when one broker quotes you a price and yield for a bond while another quotes you the same price with a different yield. That's because there are two types—a current yield (or current return) and a yield to maturity. Assume you are purchasing $10,000 worth of ten-year government bonds for $8000, paying 8% on the face value of $10,000, or $800 per year. This works out to a 10% *current* return. Another broker told you the yield on this investment would be 12.5% after adjusting for capital gains. He was talking about yield to maturity. In addition to $800 a year interest income, you also receive a $2000 capital gain over the next decade until the bond matures. He divided the $2000 capital gain you would receive by ten years, which would give an additional $200 of appreciation per year, received only if you hold the bond to maturity. Adding the $800-per-year income to the $200 average annual capital gain, he came up with $1000-a-year return on your $8000 investment, or a 12.5% yield.

Bonds are usually issued in $5000 units. Always purchase the type of bond that best suits your income objectives. If you want high current income and aren't so concerned about appreciation or capital gains, don't buy any type of discounted bond. For maximizing income, buy premium bonds and pay more than the face amount to receive a higher current interest rate. Discount bonds are attractive if you want low current income and more principal growth.

In the last decade, brokerage houses have put together municipal and corporate investment trusts that represent a diversified portfolio of twenty to thirty different bonds with similar ratings and maturities. Longer-term issues such as Treasury bonds and Treasury notes should be avoided because of the danger in fixing a rate for more than one year. Utilize the managed bond funds instead.

New Treasury issues that are basically zero-coupon bonds (they pay no interest until maturity) try to do away with downward fluctuations by locking in a compound rate of return over an extended period. In my opinion, the only place for these zero-coupon bonds might be to help fund a future balloon note or other fixed obligation coming due. A major drawback is that even though you don't receive the income now, you'll be paying taxes each year as the bond value increases, unless it is a municipal bond.

Profiting at Death

Flower bonds are a government security worth considering—but because of their low rate of return not until your death appears imminent. These sell at large discounts and have the extraordinary feature of allowing your estate to apply their full face amount to pay estate taxes, even though you may have purchased them at 30% to 40% discount only two months before. Assume you'll have a $300,000 estate-tax liability. After purchasing $300,000 *face value* of these bonds for $200,000 or maybe less, your estate will be able to submit the bonds to the government for $300,000 worth of estate taxes, a $100,000 immediate appreciation. Of course, the yield-to-death rate can't be computed exactly until you die. When terminal illness strikes and you know insurance can't be purchased to fund your estate-tax liability, flower bonds are excellent, despite their low current return. Even though you can't take it with you, flower funds ensure that you needn't leave it to Uncle Sam.

Highest-Yielding Government Securities

For high yield, investors often look to Ginnie Maes—long-term investments issued by the government through the Government National Mortgage Association to enhance mortgage-market liquidity. They package FHA and VA mortgage loans in multi-million-dollar pools sold to investors in minimums of $25,000. On average, these pools have a twelve-year life. As monthly payments are received from different loans, they are passed on to investors, with both principal and interest. It becomes crucial for you to set up a systematic reinvestment plan on your return of principal to be sure you don't spend your originally invested principal. With varying types of Ginnie Maes, you face the problem of not knowing the exact maturity date. Some investment houses try to sell Ginnie Maes with the yield figured to twelve years. Others, when selling an older Ginnie Mae, try to quote yields on the remaining five or six years of average life. Each could prove true, but you'll never know until the years pass. For particulars on various types of Ginnie Maes and a greater understanding on how to read their sometimes confusing monthly statements, consult your certified financial planner. For cautious investors who want the highest possible yield with the least amount of credit risk, Ginnie Maes can be very attractive. There are also specially designed mutual funds that own Ginnie Maes and Treasury bonds that utilize special management techniques to increase current income by 20% or more.

The key to bonds is making sure they meet your quality standards and that you can afford the degree of market risk until maturity.

Bonds are safety-rated, principally by Standard & Poor's and Moody's, through a rating system. AAA-rated bonds have the highest rating assigned by Standard & Poor's. Moving down the ladder from AA and A, we see BBB, BB, B, along with CCC and CC. The Bs and Cs are regarded as predominantly speculative. BBB indicates the lowest risk and CC the highest.

While the Bs and Cs will likely have some good features and protective characteristics, these are outweighed by the uncertainties or major risk exposures to adverse conditions. Single C is reserved for income bonds on which no interest is being paid, and a D rating indicates the bond is in default of interest and/or payment of principal is in arrears. Plus and minus signs may be added to the letter designation, showing relative standing within the major rated categories. Nonrated (NR) indicates that no rating has been requested, that there is insufficient information on which to base a rating, or that Standard & Poor's does not rate that particular type of bond as a matter of policy.

For more information, I suggest you examine a Standard & Poor's Bond Guide, which you can order directly from Standard & Poor's, 25 Broadway, New York, NY 10004. Cost is $12.95 a copy.

The rating of a bond directly affects the cost which the corporation will incur in raising capital through the bond markets. The higher the rating, the lower interest it will need to pay. You might see a ten-year AAA-rated bond paying 10%, a ten-year AA-rated bond paying 10.5%, an A-rated bond paying 11%, a BBB-rated bond paying 12%, and a CC-rated one paying 13%. Each has the same ten-year maturity, but the riskier the bond, the higher the percentage rate. Sometimes a specific bond of a corporation's bond issue changes rates. Thus, in addition to the risk of the market price going up and down, you have that of the bond lowering its rating. This usually depresses the bond price because it would now need to yield a higher rate of return in accordance with its lower rating. A better rating can work in reverse.

Floaters

For those in low tax brackets wanting to emphasize income with low market and rate risk, *floating-rate* corporate bonds offer a good opportunity. Often these bonds index their rates to the prime rate, to a government bond, or to the London Interbank offering rate. These bonds change their interest rates weekly, quarterly, or semiannually, and may offer a special premium over their chosen index. Citicorp, Manufacturers Hanover, and Phillips Petroleum all offer different types of floating-rate notes.

17. Why Direct-Placement Investment Trusts and Limited Partnerships May Be Your Best Bet

When investing, you have seven primary areas to choose from: (1) a bank (CDs and money market funds), (2) an insurance company (annuities, single pay, universal life), (3) real estate, (4) tangible assets such as gold, silver or gems, (5) operating businesses, (6) debt instruments (bonds), and (7) equity instruments (stocks).

Among your best bets are direct-placement investment trusts and limited partnerships, which allow income to be fully passed through to you before taxation. This income then can be sheltered, since all depreciation, interest costs, and operating expense deductions (as well as income) are passed through to you. Direct-placement investments give investors a *limited time period* to be in an investment. Normally, upon sale of the specified property, your share of the proceeds is completely refunded to you. Also, your liability will not exceed your original investment.

I consider these direct-placement investments as the most exciting, valuable major investment vehicle of the '80s. The programs can offer a much larger return on an investment than CDs or bonds. Unfortunately, confrontation with the huge legal document called a prospectus becomes a major stumbling block for some investors, causing anxiety and undue confusion. Prospectuses are designed to inform you about risks, costs, and conflicts of interest; the track record of the general partner putting the deal together; the partnership objectives and who is qualified to invest; as well as relevant tax and legal opinions.

These documents are written by CPAs and tax attorneys, who are better with numbers than at writing elegant prose. Hence, many headaches and yawns for investors.

Nevertheless, you must either study the prospectus yourself or turn it over to your certified financial planner for scrutiny. Using direct-placement investments as a vehicle without looking them over thoroughly would be like driving a Porsche toward a destination with your eyes closed.

As tax laws limit the deductibility of losses from these "passive" investments (you do not actively manage the assets), it becomes vital to have a sound economic structure. All-cash and low-leverage-deals become more attractive as the income from these investments can be fully tax-sheltered from the tax write-offs generated by these and other similar direct-placement investments.

Esoteric Partnerships

In the partnership realm of direct investing, you can get involved with everything from pay telephones, orbiting satellites, thoroughbreds, and wind and solar generators to specially designed computer programs. These partnerships—mainly private deals for big-time investors—put you into a wide array of investments to experience direct benefits as well as risks. Cattle-breeding and cattle-feeding programs often have produced excellent ways to defer taxes, but I've yet to see one make impressive profits. Alternative-energy partnerships may in certain states produce excellent tax credits (which make them nearly irresistible); still, the economics of the situation must be examined. Be careful of projections that promise high rate increases or value increases because of inflation. Satellite- or aircraft-leasing programs could be an excellent opportunity for multiple write-offs, but their equipment and maintenance costs are unfortunately sky-high. In most communities, just by checking the newspapers, you can find private venture-capital deals. Buyer beware! Many I've looked at weren't worth the paper on which they were advertised. I've seen countless schemes over the years by which apparently sophisticated investors were lassoed into questionable partnerships. Don't get burned. Get solid reviews from competent advisers with expertise in finance and taxation.

Investment success can be found in almost any endeavor when properly planned, operated, marketed, and financed. Over 90% of all businesses fail within the first ten years. Half of those that survive three years won't exist within seven. This gives you an indication of the risks. Look for proven track records when determining whether to get involved in a limited partnership. Evaluation of economic trends and government policies as well as tax-code implications relative to your financial situation is imperative.

Don't become too enamored of early high cash-flows. This may be a return of principal or a very expensive way to give you a false sense of security.

I once helped a conservative investor reposition $300,000 from a taxable CD into an insured and tax-free investment (which doubled his rate of return) after overcoming strong objections stemming from his fear of doing anything different or what he defined as risky (even though insured). You can imagine my amazement when this same investor committed a large sum of money (against my advice) to an oil-and-gas-drilling partnership with a high initial cash flow. Too often, investors make the mistake of judging investments by immediate cash flow and not by long-term, overall return (income plus capital gains plus tax benefits).

Direct-placement investments are excellent for getting high rates of return for your nest egg and should be fully examined.

Direct-Placement Mutual Funds

It wasn't until the late '60s that mutual funds took their next step. Because of tax changes, public partnerships began to spring up, growing during the last sixteen years to $4 billion.

Why have investors been pouring billions of dollars into public partnerships and trusts? A limited partnership, or a finite investment trust, is a mutual fund of various properties put together with a specified goal in mind by a general partner (the money manager), who takes on the responsibility for buying, managing, and selling the properties in the partnership for the benefit of the limited partners (the investors). For a minimum investment of $5000 (many partnerships today have $2000 minimums for IRA plans), each group of investors pools a few million dollars toward a special business objective. The partners do not actively manage anything, but share in the income and gains of the general partner's endeavors. Each partner has limited liability and can lose no more than his or her initial investment. The general partner might personally assume certain liabilities for the venture, signing notes, mortgages, or personal assurances. Because of the tax laws, the partnership is set up so that usually 99% of depreciation, interest costs, depletion, expenses, and losses will be passed through to the partners to reduce their taxes, and 85% to 95% of the income also will pass through to them in the form of capital gains, rental income, or income from other sources. (Stocks do not pass any of the tax benefits through to the investor and are taxed at the corporate level *before* paying you a dividend—which is then taxed again!)

Investment trusts and limited partnerships, like mutual funds, have different degrees of conservatism or aggressiveness and have

Direct-Placement Investment Trusts & Limited Partnerships

similar objectives. There are income limited-partnerships, growth-and-income limited partnerships, and pure-growth limited partnerships. There are partnerships set up for pension plans, IRAs, and Keoghs, while others are created especially for high-tax-bracket investors.

WHO CAN INVEST?

Most conservative partnerships require $25,000 to $30,000 total income and at least that amount in assets. I feel this is discriminatory and improper. It penalizes young couples who have not yet reached the required net worth level and want to invest in some hard assets with their $2000 IRAs. As long as the proper risks are disclosed, I believe any investment should be open to an investor as a constitutional right.

Like mutual funds, investment trusts and limited partnerships follow the entire risk spectrum. Because one limited partnership is speculative and goes bankrupt does not affect other limited partnerships except for those that are managed similarly and are in the same field. To lump all investment trusts and limited partnerships together is naive. I have seen this happen in sensational articles in a number of major magazines and even more newspapers. Citing a very speculative limited partnership that was oriented to tax shelters for high-tax-bracket individuals, *Forbes* and then other respected US magazines and newspapers made some wild and unfair accusations about the industry as a whole.

For growth and income, look for *conservative* investment trusts and limited partnerships with low amounts of leverage and small tax deductions that are just enough to tax-shelter your income. Avoid the risk of foreclosure through the lack of leverage, and by purchasing apartment complexes, office buildings, and shopping centers that are *already* leased out in fast-growing areas where rents are lower than they should be. Rent can rise, increasing the cash flow and value of the property. Buy properties that already have a positive cash flow, not ones that "we *hope* to build, *hope* to lease out, and on which we *hope* to get a positive cash flow." This is the difference between conservative and aggressive objectives.

Your financial planner earns his or her pay by informing you of the different tax-advantaged investments that you can get into to avoid paying taxes on earned income, Social Security, and on interest and dividends. Also, he or she can sift through and properly evaluate piles of information on the many different products to ascertain truth versus pipe dreams, fantasy versus reality.

OFFERING AND ORGANIZATION

A 2% charge is incurred to organize and offer interests in the partnership. Fees to cover legal costs in preparing the prospectus, accounting, escrow, printing, and bureaucratic filing are included under this heading. These charges aren't any different from those incurred in offering any new security. Without them, no new security could ever reach the marketplace to raise new capital for business.

If we were to eliminate this charge, diversification within our portfolio would ultimately be narrowed to a choice between Treasury bills and certificates of deposit!

SELLING COMMISSIONS

Admittedly, an 8.2% commission rate is much higher than would be incurred if a stock or bond were being purchased. But it is no higher than the charge for purchasing mutual fund shares. Remember that much more time is spent by the broker in investigating and then selling limited-partnership interests than is required to sell stocks or bonds. You might purchase stocks recommended by your broker during a two-minute telephone conversation. Much more analysis is required of your broker when considering a shelter. Today there are no-load partnerships for investors to choose from as well.

ACQUISITION FEES

An 11% fee is payable to the general partner for finding, structuring, analyzing, and evaluating property acquisitions and for negotiating and acquiring the properties, including fees and commissions. The best way to evaluate this fee is to compare it to the real estate commission you probably would pay if you acquired property individually—about 6% of the purchase price.

If the acquisition fee were expressed as a percentage of the purchase price of properties in a partnership, it would be about 3.6%. Therefore, for less than you would pay a real estate broker interested in selling you a property, you have the services of an experienced partner who has a *vested interest* in the ultimate income and appreciation from the property.

If the general partner did not perform this service on the investor's behalf, someone else would have to be hired or you would have to do it yourself. Consider the expense involved in traveling around the country to look at fifty properties in order to find just a handful.

Direct-Placement Investment Trusts & Limited Partnerships 203

PROPERTY-PURCHASE COSTS
This charge is for legal fees and expenses, filing fees, travel, engineering, consulting, and appraisals incurred in connection with property acquisitions. You might also pay interest expense on loans or other costs incurred in guaranteeing loans by the general partner. If you think you can have these services performed at a cheaper rate, pull out the settlement sheet for the purchase of your house. I looked at mine, and would have been thrilled to have gotten by with 1%.

WORKING-CAPITAL RESERVE
Commentators often erroneously lump in the working-capital reserve with other front-end charges. But this isn't a fee. It is money set aside for future operating needs. It doesn't line anyone's pocket except perhaps the plumber's if the pipes leak.

As most limited partnerships have limited liquidity, an investment trust that provides quick marketability by trading on a stock exchange is very attractive. Be certain, however, that it is a finite investment trust (one with a set term of existence—eight or twelve years, for example), rather than one that perpetuates itself forever as a stock.

CONCLUSION
We live in a world in which people expect to be reasonably paid for the services they render. Competition forces the sponsors to keep their fees in line; reputable brokers won't handle outlandish investments if they want to stay in business. *You need a professionally trained eye to see an investment's fine points with clarity. Don't pay needless attention to red herrings tossed about to create conflicts.*

Would you feel confident grading a diamond? Would you be able to put on a loupe and detect any possible flaw or determine the true quality and value of the color or configuration of the stone? Would your spouse be able to? Would you invest $50,000 in a diamond, relying solely on your mother's advice?

Can you open up an engine, look at it, know the names and functions of each part, and diagnose major problems?

Or what about trying to determine if a painting is an original valued at $1 million or a copy worth $10,000? Would you get an expert opinion and pay someone trained to authenticate the painting, even though you might have surface knowledge of the fine arts yourself?

The ability to recognize the fine points, the details, to grade differences in the shades of gray to ensure that it is casting its proper shadow and color represents the value of your financial planner. A CFP separates facts from myths, potential return versus sales hype. Without thorough and continued study of each new investment concept and tax change, you will likely go nowhere. You will probably be paralyzed; afraid to make moves because of media sensationalism and lies. You will make illogical decisions or sit on the fence because of baffling economic fluctuations. (When have economic conditions not been in a state of flux?)

In the income and growth area for limited partnerships, look for those real estate, oil and gas, and equipment-leasing partnerships that have minimal leverage (no more than 30% leverage and 70% cash) and that have a respectable tax-sheltered cash flow, with potential growth in an inflationary environment. They should also have the ability to generate a good cash flow and remain sound in a deflationary environment.

Real Estate

I believe the best opportunity for the late '80s in real estate investments will be in rental apartment complexes. During the past five years, vacancy rates have declined by 50% as the number of families in the formation years has risen from 5.1 to 9.4 million in the past ten years. Middle-income housing costs and interest rates remain high; upward of 40% to 50% of the annual budget of married couples is usually needed to buy housing, making it impossible for many people, particularly young couples, to own real estate. Currently, the average-priced house with available interest rates would mean a monthly mortgage payment of approximately $620 plus an additional $150 for taxes and insurance. That is $770 per month to buy an average house, putting down 10% and paying 11% interest. A family would need $28,000 to $34,000 income to consider buying this house. The average family earns $18,000 to $22,000. The housing crisis therefore presents us with an excellent investment opportunity.

Here are some major conclusions about public real estate limited partnerships and finite investment trusts.

THEIR PERFORMANCE EXHIBITS THREE DISTINCT
PHASES OF DEVELOPMENT

In the *start-up phase* (years 1–4), front-end fees are paid from money raised to offset normal costs of the offering, property acquisitions, and securities commissions. The remaining funds are used to purchase properties. So the starting net equity in the property portfolio is less than the amount raised from investors. During this stage, benefits are generated from tax savings and, to a lesser extent, from cash flow from operations. Any appreciation of property values during this period typically offsets these front-end fees.

In the *operational phase* (years 4–9), properties begin making money. Although a small percentage of benefits results from the profitable sale of a few properties, the majority is the result of income from property operations.

In the *liquidation phase* (years 9–15), the remaining properties are sold. In this stage, appreciation provides the major part of the benefits.

PUBLICLY OFFERED REAL ESTATE LIMITED PARTNERSHIPS AND FINITE INVESTMENT TRUSTS HAVE BEEN SUPERIOR INVESTMENT VEHICLES DURING THE PAST DECADE

The life cycle plays a large role in the timing of that return. Figure 17-1 shows the dramatic jump in average returns through the life of a partnership. It also demonstrates that in order to make the most money, investors should hold for the long term.

Figure 17-1

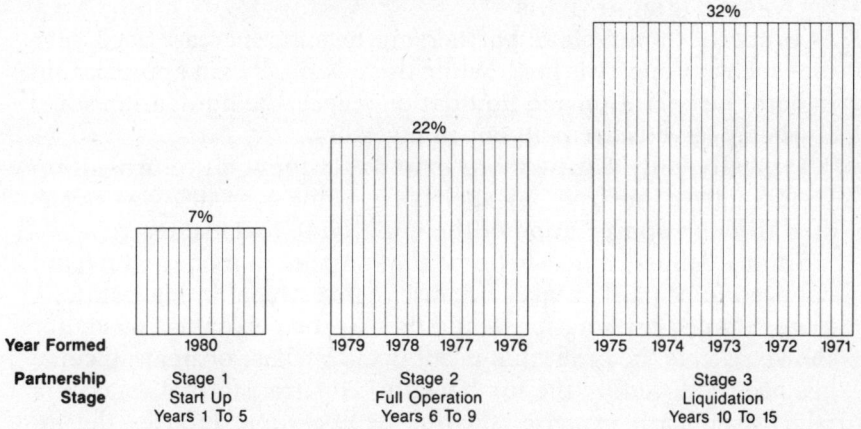

The Average Before-Tax Returns For Publicly Offered Real Estate Limited Partnerships Formed 1971-80 For The Period 1971-84 *

* Returns, as presented in FIGURE 4, are imputed from after-tax for 38% tax bracket investors and include Liquidity Fund's estimate of the equity appreciation which has not been returned in dollars, but are still retained in the properties or notes received for the prior sales.

HIGH INVESTMENT YIELDS

Real estate limited partnerships have produced high returns, substantially outperforming other investments as well as beating inflation. The average one produced benefits equivalent to a 21.3% before-tax rate of return—the only nonexotic investment instrument to substantially outpace inflation during the last fifteen years.

From 1971 through 1984, the average RELP (Real Estate Limited Partnership) gave investors in the 38% tax bracket a 13.2% after-tax rate of return. To match this performance, an investor would have had to find, for example, a money market fund with a 21.3% before-tax interest rate.

RELPs have two to six times higher compounded returns than other popular investments. In comparison with RELPs, the most common public investment vehicles, such as stocks, bonds, and T-bills, were poor performers from 1971 to 1984 on a nominal, non-inflation-adjusted basis.

While other investments were failing to keep pace with inflation (7.3% from 1971 to 1984), RELPs provided a good return. Even after adjusting for inflation, the average publicly offered RELP paid a 5.9% after-tax real return during that period.

THE PROPERTY-HOLDING PERIOD IS IMPORTANT IN
DELIVERING HIGH RETURNS

As properties appreciate, partnership benefits increase each year that such a property is held. While there is significant appreciation in both the operation and liquidation stages, the liquidation stage is when proceeds are paid out to investors.

Typically, only a little more than 8% of the total returns to investors have come from tax-sheltering, while over 40% was generated through appreciation of the underlying real estate.

Simply defined, a tax shelter is that amount of money which did not need to be paid in taxes because of investment in real estate. A more detailed explanation would be that the percentage of shelter shown reflects the profit that is not taxed because ordinary income has been reduced by the tax benefits. This transformation occurs when a noncash expense, such as depreciation, reduces the investor's current taxable ordinary income and therefore his or her tax basis (even though the property may be increasing in value).

CONCLUSION

For the most part, performance of publicly offered RELPs and investment trusts met or exceeded expectations; probably why they continue to keep attracting investment dollars. According to Robert A. Stanger & Company, a New Jersey–based expert in real estate syndications, RELPs raised $4.47 billion from investors in 1983, with an increase of 23% in 1984 to $5.5 billion.

Liquidity Fund data indicates that the investors have typically been in the 38% tax bracket and are investing less than $10,000 each. Combined with investors from prior years, these figures suggest that as many as 1.5 million small investors have embraced the partnership concept of investing in real estate.

A good portfolio mix today consists of 50% to 90% apartment complexes in diversified locations that are in the emerging growth areas across the country. There are also excellent buys in areas depressed by the switch from an industrial-base economy to one of service and information. Many suburbs of major cities have undergone a demographic transformation in the past six years, bringing renewed strength to their areas. Depressed prices can be found in high-unemployment areas into which the government is pumping money. Injections of federal funds can substantially lower the unemployment rate, revitalize the area, and send real estate prices skyrocketing.

Energizing Your Egg

Another dynamic income and growth area for more aggressive investors is oil and gas master limited partnerships. A master limited partnership is a *tradable* unit of a limited partnership arrangement that can pass tax benefits (depreciation, depletion, etc.) through to the owners to shelter all or part of the income from taxes. Stocks cannot pass through these benefits, and regular limited partnerships are relatively illiquid, with no regular market. Master limited partnerships are available in real estate.

We all know that oil and gas prices have been declining for quite a while. Over the next ten years we may see $5-a-barrel oil before prices start to rise again. But in the long term I expect inflationary spending and the subsequent budget and trade deficits in both the United States and the Arab countries to push oil prices up substantially.

Because publicly traded master limited partnerships are liquid, you can act quickly, unlike with regular limited partnerships. Investors who think that now is the time can earn from 9% to 12%, mostly tax-sheltered, while looking for potential major appreciation. Do be sure that the partnership is well financed and has little or no debt.

BENEFITS AVAILABLE

Relatively conservative oil and gas income master limited partnerships could pay a return of between 10.5% and 15% once the shakeout is over. Already proven and producing oil and gas reserves are bought and sold at current market prices as they are pumped out. The general partner will use the newest, economical methods to extract the most oil and gas possible. Because of oil-industry fallout from 1981 to 1986, because of high interest rates and overproduction, many independent oil and gas producers that were highly leveraged were forced to liquidate at very low prices. This has produced a great opportunity to buy properties with cash at heavy discounts and is one of the major reasons for the merger mania in oil going on today. It is cheaper to buy existing reserves (and companies) than to look for reserves. As inflation and sanity return to the marketplace, the trick is to accumulate oil and gas reserves before prices rise again.

PETROLEUM ROYALTY TRUSTS—MORE LIQUIDITY

Royalty trusts, while relatively new investment vehicles (North European Oil Royalty, first traded in 1975, being one of the oldest), appear to be sound investments for a stable and improving income. The better-situated RTs should also show appreciation in time and appear undervalued at current market levels. Significant interest in RTs was generated in 1979 with creation of the first trust by Mesa Petroleum. Currently, ten major ones are trading on the New York Stock Exchange.

Investors in RTs own units of beneficial interest, i.e., direct-ownership interests in productive acreage, reserves, and wells. Such interests are carved from assets of petroleum-operating companies, and in all but one major case have been spun off to stockholders, based on share ownership in the operating company. Ownership of units in an RT makes it possible for the investor to receive income derived from all or most of the oil and gas production from properties owned by the trust. This occurs without this income flowing through a petroleum company, where it is taxed, and then taxed again, when received as dividends by stockholders. Owners of such units regularly have been permitted to deduct from income distribution charges for depletion of reserves of fields held by the trust as well as abandonment losses and termination of royalties.

In many cases production dedicated to royalty trusts is from relatively long-life, mature fields. In addition, certain of the trusts also hold royalty interests in undeveloped properties which, if productive, eventually will provide additional income to the owners.

Certain producing properties are also susceptible to infill (development) drilling to bolster reserves and production. In RTs, sponsoring companies maintain varying interests in properties after distribution, running between 1% and 25%. The trustee of the RT collects income from the producing properties, pays all operating expenses, and then distributes virtually all available income to the unit holders on a monthly basis.

Tax-Deferred Real Estate Appreciation and Mortgage Interest

For some investors, participating mortgages are attractive, but, until they retire, the adverse tax consequences prevent them from considering them. An investment combining the advantages of a tax-deferred annuity with those of participating mortgages has evolved. By using special laws that insurance companies enjoy, these two popular concepts have been merged to permit investors to put money into high-yielding participating mortgages while compounding on a tax-deferred basis. Later, when you retire and enter a lower tax bracket, you can begin to take withdrawals— taxable *only* on the amount you withdraw. Your beneficiaries are always guaranteed to receive 100% of your purchase payments, less any withdrawals, or the contract value, whichever is greater. Since it is a no-load investment, 100% of your money goes to work for you. Since it is an annuity, it will avoid probate. There is a 1% to 2% charge deducted each year to insure your account, but the expected yield is 11% to 13% plus chances for appreciation.

Cable TV

The purpose of these limited partnership programs is to acquire systems with growth potential and to develop that potential, thereby increasing the value of the system to the owners and to the communities it serves. A cable system's value is increased in four ways: (1) saturation—enlisting new subscribers within the franchised area, (2) extension of the system into new areas not previously served, (3) rate increases for the program services, and (4) expanding on existing services. Investors will receive their share of tax deductions from equipment depreciation, interest expenses, and investment tax credits. Equity buildup through debt reduction and capital appreciation are the benefits. Programs have averaged five to seven years, and the maximum life can be seventeen years. Some properties are paid for in cash, others leveraged.

The real attraction of this investment centers on use of these lines for two-way information exchange in shopping, banking, and general business, all of which is now becoming available. Premium channels like HBO, Showtime, and Disney are moneymakers used by more than 50% of subscribers, and home-shopping channels also add more revenue to be received by the partner. Investors expect to receive moderate tax benefits in the initial year and then income and capital gains beginning in year three until final sale. Each partnership will invest its funds to buy the best cable properties available. If you are an income-orientated investor, you now can purchase mature systems for cash and generate an attractive current income while having an opportunity for future gains in revenues and system growth.

Leasing

Leasing is a form of investing that can help return a high-cash-flow initial income with moderate tax benefits. It also is an excellent vehicle to use in conjunction with moderately leveraged real estate partnerships that provide low income in the first years. Leasing is a growing industry. It has become an attractive vehicle for American industry to finance its acquisition of capital equipment. Leasing is utilized more than bank loans, corporate stocks or bonds, or any other means of financing equipment acquisitions. Equipment leased in the United States has grown from $43 billion in 1980 to approximately $75 billion in 1984. The fastest-growing area of equipment leasing today is predominantly office-related: data- and word-processing. By purchasing these types of equipment and leasing them to Fortune 500 corporations such as major telephone companies, automobile companies, and aerospace manufacturers, you can get a high-credit lease with a determinable cash flow that pays handsome returns. Experienced management is important. By properly setting up and handling a program, an investor could enjoy a 13% to 15% cash flow, 50% of which is tax-sheltered for the first five years.

This means your money would be quickly returned to you and could act as an excellent balance to other investments that are more growth-oriented and less income-oriented. Putting $20,000 into a moderate leveraged real estate program or aggressive mutual fund, balanced with $10,000 in an equipment partnership that is buying on a cash basis could create excellent benefits. By pooling investors' capital, a partnership can buy many types of equipment on lease to a wide variety of companies in assorted industries. These programs normally run between eight and

Direct-Placement Investment Trusts & Limited Partnerships 211

twelve years and may in the initial years require a portion of the cash flow to reinvest in new equipment to help return to the investor a minimum of the original investment. Leasing has many applications for portfolios and should be considered for high-income investors in a 28% or higher tax bracket.

Summary

Because of their high returns, direct-placement limited partnerships and finite investment trusts are two of the most exciting of the various investment opportunities for the coming years. While so-called esoteric partnerships are primarily for high rollers, there are attractive direct-placement mutual funds for people with modest portfolios. For growth and income, look for conservative limited partnerships with low leverage and small tax deductions that are just enough to provide shelter. Major opportunities exist in real estate partnerships, particularly in rental complexes. More aggressive investors should examine growth areas in oil and gas master limited partnerships. Always seek management with a proven track record. Generally, partnership performance exhibits three phases: *start-up* (when front-end fees are paid), *operational* (when benefits begin coming in), and *liquidation* (when appreciation is the major benefit).

Whether in the esoteric areas or in the more prosaic investments such as real estate, gas and oil, cable TV, or leasing, understand the risks and expenses involved.

Review the Following Considerations

1. Do you feel the investment area has a positive outlook over the next five to twelve years?
2. Are you able to commit your funds for the life of the partnership? There will be a large discount if you need to sell early.
3. Are you able to make use of any of the tax advantages involved? To what degree?
4. Are the general partners experienced, with a proven track record? Are they well financed?
5. Is the fee structure in line with the industry norms? Check the Stanger Register, the guide to limited partnerships.
6. Does it fit in with your overall nest egg strategies?
7. Have you *and* your CFP reviewed the prospectus? Do you both feel comfortable with its structure?

18. Government Subsidies Can Make You Rich

Although the Constitution clearly states that all *men* are created equal, all *investments* are not. Our tax system is designed to promote incentives in areas that have been most heavily lobbied by interest groups.

Through its tax laws, the government subsidizes one type of investing at the expense of another. Consider the penalties of inflation and taxes for a saver who goes into a money market fund at a bank or savings and loan. If he were earning 8% while in a 33% tax bracket, he would first have to give back one-third of his earnings to the government, leaving him only 5.4%. Additionally, with a 5% inflation rate, his net return after taxes and inflation turn out to be a mere .4%! On the other hand, there is the individual to whom the bank lent money to purchase real estate, which is what most savings and loans do. If you borrow the money to buy a property, you are permitted to reduce your taxes by one-third of the interest you pay if you are in a 33% tax bracket. Thus, an 11% mortgage costs you only 7.3% and the government subsidizes the other third by giving you tax benefits. Lower taxes combined with a 5% inflation rate lower the value of the money that you pay back.

After taxes and inflation, your net cost to borrow the money is 2.3%. Since you used the bank's money to buy property, the 5% appreciation achieved on the property (which because you leveraged the purchase using 20% of your money and 80% of the bank's) ends up with a real rate of return of more than 13%. A $100,000 property with 80% borrowed and $20,000 down with a 5% increase in price (or $5000) based on a $20,000 investment is a 25% return minus the net cost of borrowing the money after inflation and taxes. Thus, a $2700 net return on a $20,000 investment assuming the interest expenses were covered by rental income. The government goes one step further and says that the income you receive to pay off your loan will not be fully taxable to you. Since the building has increased in value, the tax authorities will let you pretend that for tax purposes its value went down (depreciation) and let you shelter a portion of the income you receive, while being able to write off the interest expense of buying the property. This is government subsidy at its finest.

Whether real estate, insurance, research and development companies, oil and gas, or manufacturing, the government subsidizes owners and penalizes lenders (savers). Being a lender, not an owner, is not a productive way to *build* a nest egg, although it may be necessary when preserving for maximizing income at a later date. Consider that when a lender watches his or her money market rates drop from 12% to 5%, he *loses* the additional interest he or she was making before, and there are no tax benefits. Yet, should someone who owns property lose income or capital in an investment, the loss may *increase* his or her tax benefits. When you suffer loss, it can be partially subsidized through lower taxes on other sources of income. Your losses can reduce your taxable income by up to $3000.

Probably the biggest area of government subsidies was discussed in our chapter on retirement plans. Whether they be an IRA or Keogh, profit-sharing or pension plans, the government uses a new set of rules to protect investors' money from taxes to build future nest eggs. The diversity and sophistication of many of these retirement plans are astounding, permitting individuals and corporations to cut tax liabilities while opening up a new realm of investment opportunities. There is no current taxation on their income or capital gains. Considering the role taxes play in your present and future, it becomes crucial to understand the tax codes and how they affect you.

Protecting Your Nest Egg From the Wolves (the IRS)

In today's topsy-turvy world of economic change, it is more important than ever that every American draw up a battle plan for this war against new, even more complex tax laws. You must shield yourself against the high-handed and underhanded manipulation of the economy by politicians, along with their policies of on-again, off-again inflation.

The Last Great Tax Shelter

Although most of the tax-saving strategies of the past have been made obsolete by the 1986 tax revisions, one of the major tax benefits of home ownership, although reduced, still remains intact and attractive. Homeowners may still write off the interest on the mortgages for their first and second homes up to an amount that equals the cost basis of their property plus any improvements. This means if you purchased a house for $100,000 that has a remaining mortgage of $60,000, even though the house may be worth $200,000, you may not take on more than an additional $40,000 of mortgage and deduct that interest *unless* that mortgage loan in excess of $100,000 is for purposes of medical education expenses, a trade or business, or investments such as securities or real estate partnerships.

However, interest on mortgage loans to finance investments falls under other rules as well, and the investment-interest deduction would be restricted to the amount of net investment income received. As an example, on the $100,000 house, if you had put $20,000 into improvements and your house is now worth $200,000, with an existing $60,000 mortgage you would be able to increase your loan by $60,000 without showing any further justifications. If, however, you took out a mortgage for $100,000 and invested this money in a stock or real-estate transaction, you would be able to write off only that portion of interest on the mortgage on the $40,000 above your initial cost basis to the degree that you received either dividends, interest, or rental income from those investments.

If you paid an additional $4000 in interest on that mortgage and received only $3000 of income from that investment, you would be able to write off only three of the additional four thousand dollars of interest. If, however, you use that additional $40,000 to finance a trade or business, you should still be able to write off the full extent of the interest paid. It becomes vital, therefore, to keep good records so you can readily prove that the mortgage interest expense was incurred for investment, business or trade, medical or educational expenses. Under the tax plan, 35% of the excess amount over the purchase price plus improvements will be disallowed in 1987, 60% in 1988, 80% in 1989, 90% in 1990, and 100% in 1991. Therefore, even if you have excess interest paid you will not be fully penalized until 1991. Yet, if your loans were completed by August 15, 1986, the full deductibility of the interest regardless of the cost basis of your house will remain intact.

Finding Your Tax Bracket

In 1987, for a married couple filing jointly, on the first $3000 earned (from working, interest, dividends, or capital gains), you

Government Subsidies Can Make You Rich

Figure 18-1

1987 TAX CHART

Taxable Income	Base Tax Due on this amount	plus	This % of taxable Income Above This Amount
0	0		11%
$3000	$330		15%
$28,000	$4080		28%
$45,000	$8840		35%
$90,000	$24,590		38.5%

pay zero federal income taxes. On the next $25,000 (anything over $3000 up to $28,000) you pay 15%. From $28,000 to $45,000 you pay 28%.

As you can see, we still, in spite of tax "reform," pay progressively higher and higher income taxes. In effect, we have a "progressive penalty system"—the more productive you are, the more prudent a saver, or the better the investor, the more you pay. This is a good way to demotivate people and reduce initiative, especially when you can get handouts from the government to replace, or nearly replace, the amount of lost income.

Why is it that if you are smarter and harder-working than your neighbor, and make twice as much money as he does, that you pay four times as much in income taxes? In addition, you will pay more to support a gigantic "negative" industry spawned by the maze of almost incomprehensible tax laws that grows even more complex in spite of so-called reforms. CPAs, tax lawyers, tax specialists, investment specialists, probate lawyers, estate lawyers, estate planners, and trust officers all owe their jobs to the government-created industry based on confusion over taxation.

In this country we have *triple taxation:* you are taxed when you *earn it*, taxed when you earn *on it*, and taxed when you *leave it* or *give it* (commonly known as transfer taxes).

One of the first considerations in financial planning is to determine your tax liabilities, current and future. Any way you can reduce your taxes immediately puts money into your pocket instead of the IRS coffers. Think of having an invisible pickpocket walking around with you named Uncle Sam. It would behoove you to keep your money out of his reach. If you feel guilty about this

Figure 18-2

ESTATE AND GIFT TAXES

[¶ 43]

Table of Unified Estate and Gift Tax Rates for U. S. Residents and Citizens

Unified credit.—The unified credit for estates of decedents dying during 1985 is $121,800. For decedents dying in 1986, the credit is $155,800. Any part of the credit used to offset gift taxes is not available to offset estate taxes.

Estate taxes.—Estate taxes are computed by applying the unified rate schedule to the cumulated at death and lifetime transfers and subtracting the gift taxes payable. The unified rate schedule is effective for gifts made after December 31, 1976 and to estates of decedents dying after that date.

Gift taxes.—Gift taxes are computed by applying the unified rate schedule to cumulative lifetime taxable transfers and subtracting the taxes payable for prior taxable periods. There is an annual $10,000 exclusion for gifts, with an annual maximum of $20,000 for spouses for gift-splitting. Additionally, there is an unlimited exclusion for payments of tuition and medical expenses.

Generation-skipping transfer tax.—The determination of the tax on generation-skipping transfers is computed using this schedule.

Unified Transfer Tax Rate Schedule *

If the amount is:		Tentative tax [1] is:		
Over	But not over	Tax +	%	On excess over
0	$ 10,000	0	18	0
$ 10,000	20,000	$ 1,800	20	$ 10,000
20,000	40,000	3,800	22	20,000
40,000	60,000	8,200	24	40,000
60,000	80,000	13,000	26	60,000
80,000	100,000	18,200	28	80,000
100,000	150,000	23,800	30	100,000
150,000	250,000	38,800	32	150,000
250,000	500,000	70,800	34	250,000
500,000	750,000	155,800	37	500,000
750,000	1,000,000	248,300	39	750,000
1,000,000	1,250,000	345,800	41	1,000,000
1,250,000	1,500,000	448,300	43	1,250,000
1,500,000	2,000,000	555,800	45	1,500,000
2,000,000	2,500,000	780,800	49	2,000,000
2,500,000	3,000,000	1,025,800	53	2,500,000
3,000,000	....	1,290,800	55	3,000,000

* This rate schedule applies to estates of decedents dying, and gifts made, in 1984, 1985, 1986 and 1987. After 1987, the top tax rate will fall to 50%, to be applied to amounts in excess of $2,500,000.

[1] The cumulative transfers to which the tentative tax applies are the sum of (a) the amount of the taxable estate and (b) the amount of the taxable gifts made by the decedent after 1976 other than gifts includible in the gross estate.

Unified Credit

The unified credit is subtracted from the taxpayer's estate or gift tax liability. However, the amount of the unified credit available at death will be reduced to the extent that any portion of the credit is used to offset gift taxes on lifetime transfers. In addition, the amount of the unified credit will be reduced by 20% of any portion of the $30,000 specific gift tax exemption allowable under pre-1977 law that was used with respect to gifts made after September 8, 1976 but before January 1, 1977. Thus, under this rule, the maximum reduction of the unified credit will be $6,000 (20% of $30,000).[1]

For estates of decedents dying in 1981 and thereafter, the credit is phased in as follows:

Year	Amount of Credit	Amount of Exemption Equivalent
1981	$47,000	$175,625
1982	62,800	225,000
1983	79,300	275,000
1984	96,300	325,000
1985	121,800	400,000
1986	155,800	500,000
1987 and thereafter	192,800	600,000

State Death Tax Credit for Estate Tax [2, 3]

Estates of decedents dying after 1976

Adjusted Taxable Estate [4]		Credit =	+ %	Of Excess Over
At least	But less than			
$ 0	$ 40,000	$ 0	0	$ 0
40,000	90,000	0	.8	40,000
90,000	140,000	400	1.6	90,000
140,000	240,000	1,200	2.4	140,000
240,000	440,000	3,600	3.2	240,000
440,000	640,000	10,000	4	440,000
640,000	840,000	18,000	4.8	640,000
840,000	1,040,000	27,600	5.6	840,000
1,040,000	1,540,000	38,800	6.4	1,040,000
1,540,000	2,040,000	70,800	7.2	1,540,000
2,040,000	2,540,000	106,300	8	2,040,000
2,540,000	3,040,000	146,800	8.8	2,540,000
3,040,000	3,540,000	190,800	9.6	3,040,000
3,540,000	4,040,000	238,800	10.4	3,540,000
4,040,000	5,040,000	290,800	11.2	4,040,000
5,040,000	6,040,000	402,800	12	5,040,000
6,040,000	7,040,000	522,800	12.8	6,040,000
7,040,000	8,040,000	650,800	13.6	7,040,000
8,040,000	9,040,000	786,800	14.4	8,040,000
9,040,000	10,040,000	930,800	15.2	9,040,000
10,040,000	....	1,082,800	16	10,040,000

Estates of Nonresident Aliens Dying After 1976

A separate estate tax rate schedule applies to nonresidents not citizens dying after 1976. The amount of estate tax is determined by applying the rate schedule to the cumulative lifetime and deathtime transfers subject to

---
[1] Generally, the unified credit amount is the same throughout an entire year; however, as a transitional rule, only $6,000 of the unified credit could be applied against gifts made after December 31, 1976 but prior to July 1, 1977.
[2] There is a limitation on the credit in estates of nonresident aliens dying after November 13, 1966. See Code Sec. 2102.
[3] The above table may not be used in computing taxes on estates of certain members of the Armed Forces.
[4] The adjusted taxable estate is the taxable estate reduced by $60,000.

attitude, remember that the Supreme Court has ruled that every American has the legal right to avoid as many taxes as he or she legally can and to pay only his obligations under the law.

Many investors make the mistake of creating high tax brackets for themselves because of their ignorance of the numerous alternative investment vehicles. I'm stunned by how many people come to see me wanting to reduce their income taxes while enjoying income and safety. Their investments might be: a $600,000 portfolio with $200,000 in bank certificates of deposit, $200,000 in a money market fund, and $200,000 in government bonds. This $600,000 is all in taxable investments. Averaging 10%, there would be $60,000-a-year *taxable* income, placing them in a 28% tax bracket. A good portion of this money goes for taxes each year. After taxes are paid, the 10% return is reduced to approximately 7.2%. When inflation is running at 7%, after one year these investors have gained only .2% in purchasing power. It would almost have paid to buy $100,000 worth of goods and services today, since they would only be able to afford those same goods and services a year later thanks to inflation and taxes.

These people should transfer large portions of their funds from taxable ventures into tax-deferred or tax-exempt ones, which we have already discussed at length.

Write down the highest level of taxes you are currently paying according to the appropriate table. (See tax shelters in this chapter.) This is your marginal tax bracket, the highest level at which your income is taxed.

Tax Subsidies

Tax shelters are investment instruments, frequently aggressive ones, made for the purpose of obtaining substantial tax benefits. The tax benefits usually vary according to the degree of risk and the return on your money. Write-offs can be 50% to 100%.

Why You Should Reach for the Stars

As we have discussed throughout this book, you should reach for a star and try to put it in your pocket. With our current tax system and possible amendments over the next few years, the government subsidizes the occasions when you reach for a star and fall flat on your face. As long as you can pick yourself up each time, you need not be alarmed. Future wealth in your nest egg will be determined by the number of times you get back up on your feet and keep going. Consider the difference between playing it "safe" and using to your advantage the plans and tax laws discussed in this book.

If you had $100,000, would you prefer to invest it at a guaranteed rate of 10% for twenty-five years to ensure that it would grow into a million dollars? Or would you rather invest that $100,000 in ten different areas, even though you knew that over 50% of the investments you chose would turn sour and only a few would perform as you expected with a 20% + return? Most people feel more comfortable in accepting the guaranteed million than taking the risk of investing their money in many different areas and losing in a number of them.

Consider, however, that for the five $10,000 investments that went sour, you might have received tax relief up to $14,000, which immediately cut those losses by almost 30%. Should half of the other investments perform at the 20% to 25% rate that was your objective, at the end of the twenty-five years you would have more than $12.5 million, compared to the guaranteed one million. Even if 90%—nine out of ten investments—went bad, you would have $2.5 million accumulated at the end of that same twenty-five-year period if only one investment produced at the 25% rate. Plus you would have had tax savings of up to $26,000, which would have then given you that money to invest again (instead of its going to the IRS) and possibly permitting one other good investment to accumulate to another $2.5 million.

Either way, by using our system and becoming an owner to obtain the tax benefits, the growth benefits, and the other advantages that one enjoys through owning versus lending, you can see how government subsidies for your investments can make you rich.

19. The World Before You

Today we stand on the threshold of a dream, as technology continues to revolutionize our society. How prepared will you be to accept the challenges thus presented and to move positively so that the waves of high-tech change will carry you toward your goals? How durable and flexible are your career plans and your nest egg design? The possibility of extended periods of inflation or painful periods of deflation must be factored in to your plan. I can't overemphasize the need to diversify your portfolio as well as your career and business options. If you are flexible, you will be able to move swiftly if something unexpected happens that upsets your overall plan.

The Challenges We Face

Will the politicians ever get their free-spending habits under control?

Will taxes go up or down?

What impact will the $5.5 trillion annual budget and the $1.5 trillion interest cost on the US debt (if Peter Grace's estimates are correct) have in the year 2000?

Will Washington continue to indefinitely subsidize farmers, causing artificially high food prices and forcing taxpayers to support an inefficient system?

Will the attempt to solve unemployment by creating jobs in the "defense" industries burden us with intolerable expenses?

What will be the effects of the increasingly sophisticated and centralized systems for accumulating data, financial and other, about us?

How will Washington react to default by countries that can't pay their share of the $650 billion owed in international debts?

Will the disturbing insolvencies of the FSLIC and the Federal Farm Credit Bureau as well as of hundreds of banks affect you?

Never before in history has such an array of new financial products combined with deregulation created such dynamic and exciting times for investors. Dozens of prime opportunities exist today for investors to leverage even modest funds in national money pools and build nest eggs. Nest egg investing is a program that will help prepare you emotionally and financially to meet tomorrow's challenges with a strong, determined, and positive attitude. Nest egg investing will allow you to cross new frontiers of excellence in every facet of your life.

Glossary

above par
  A price above the face value (par value) of a security.
alternative minimum tax (AMT)
  A formula used as an alternative to the federal tax tables for investors with large capital gains or write-offs. Each tax is computed separately and then the *highest* one paid.
amortization
  Reducing, extinguishing, wiping out; to charge off gradually.
analyst
  A trained person who investigates the facts concerning a security or industry.
arbitrage
  The purchase of a security or commodity in one market and the almost simultaneous sale of the same security or commodity in another market at a different price.
at a discount
  A below face value (par value) security.
at par
  The price that equals the face value (par value) of a security.
blue chip
  The stock of a leading company that is known for excellent management and a conservative financial structure.
boiler room
  Space in a bucket shop allocated to high-pressure securities sales representatives.
bucket shop
  An illegal establishment run by irresponsible brokers who are not members of the exchange. The term originated in London around 1825 and stemmed from the beer swillers' practice of going from street to street and draining every keg they found.

Glossary

call
: A stock option contract which obligates the writer or the seller thereof to deliver upon demand 100 shares of a particular stock at a set price within a specified time limit. The opposite of a put.

commodity
: A transportable article of commerce or trade such as corn, wheat, cotton, sugar, coffee, or oats.

convertible bond
: A bond that carries with it the privilege of conversion or exchange for common stock of the same company at a fixed price for the common whenever the investor feels this would be to his or her advantage.

corporate bond
: An instrument written under seal whereby a corporation acknowledges a stated sum is owed, which it will repay at a specified date.

debenture
: An unsecured, long-term certificate of debt; a corporate IOU.

default
: Failure to perform a contract obligation.

discount
: The amount by which a security sells below its face value.

equity
: The value of a property in excess of all liens and claims against it.

FIFO
: First in, first out. A method of calculating inventory values.

goodwill
: An intangible asset.

hedge
: An operation intended to protect against loss in another operation.

hypothecate
: To pledge negotiable securities or other property as collateral for a loan while still retaining title to them.

LIFO
: Last in, first out. A method for calculating inventory values.

limited partnership
: A partnership consisting of general and special partners with at least one member being fully responsible for all debts.

liquidity
: Readily convertible into cash with little loss in value.

municipal bond
: A bond issued by a town, city, county, or state.

no-load fund
　A mutual fund that charges little or no commissions to the buyer of its shares.

options
　An agreement that conveys the right to buy or sell a specific security at a stipulated price and within a stated period of time. If not exercised during that time, the money paid for the option is forfeited.

par value
　The face value of a security regardless of its denomination.

preferred stock
　A portion of the capital stock of a corporation that ranks after all bonds or other debt but has certain preferences over the common stock.

put
　A stock option contract that obligates the writer, or seller, to accept delivery of 100 shares of a particular stock at a set price within a set period of time.

speculation
　A calculated risk taken to gain a quick profit.

spread
　The difference between the bid price and the ask price.

straddle
　A double stock option contract with identical striking prices, which entitles the holder to deliver (put) or demand (call) the stock named by the contract on or before a fixed date.

strap
　A combination of stock option contracts consisting of two calls and one put.

strip
　A combination of stock option contracts consisting of two puts and one call.

tax-preference items
　Accelerated depreciation on real and leased property, depletion, intangible drilling costs, accelerated cost-recovery deductions, stock options, adjusted itemized deductions, and capital gains deductions.

technician
　A chartist whose market forecasts are based mostly upon changes taking place in various stocks he or she studies closely.

write-off
　An accounting procedure that cancels a debt or a claim.